CONTENTS

FOREWORD

Forty years have elapsed since the event of August 23, 1944. It has ushered in a new epoch in the history of the Romanian people, an epoch of deep restructuring and transformations within the framework of a revolutionary process, the main stages of which were the anti-fascist and anti-imperialist revolution for social and national liberation—triggered off by the armed insurrection—the democratic revolution, the socialist revolution and the building up—under way—of the multilaterally developed socialist society.

August 23, 1944 was not only the beginning of a new era in Romania's history but, through its strategic-political consequences, it was "one of the decisive events of World War II;" this fully justified assertion belongs to one of the most reputed specialists in the history of Eastern Europe, the English historian Hugh Seton-Watson.[1] The rapid sequence of military-political developments during the great world conflagration of 1939-1945, often attributed a spectacular halo with powerful emotional connotations by the public opinion, has not always allowed a correct assessment of their true share of the issue of World War II. To take one well-known example, let us remember that the precipitated evacuation of the British Expeditionary Force from Dunkirk—called even to the present the "miracle" of Dunkirk—was initially considered a "triumph of improvisation amidst chaos" only to appear, as soon as facts could be reconstituted on the basis of an attentive study of the sources, as the "success of discipline and good organization;"[2] on the other hand, what was temporarily seen as a German victory proved to be—when, after the war, the circumstances in which the famous "Halt-Befehl" of May 24, 1940 was given were made known—"Hitler's first great strategic error."[3]

The strategic-political significance of the event of August 23, 1944, or, to be more precise, its role in speeding up the collapse of the Nazi Reich has not yet been adequately reflected in the foreign historiography, while opinions as justified and authorized as the one quoted belonging to Hugh Seton-Watson have remained, unfortunately, only sporadic. Many of the works published abroad—extensive syntheses on the history of World War II, chronologies, and the like—show not only a lack of knowledge of the strategic-political importance of Romania's actions in August 1944, but also of the very events which developed then in the Carpathian-Danubian area: thus, one speaks of "Romania's capitulation," while her contribution to the defeat of Hitler's Germany, both through the change she effected on August 23, 1944, and the subsequent participation of the Romanian army in the anti-Hitler war within the military operations carried on in Hungary, Czechoslovakia and Austria, is underestimated or utterly neglected.

The causes of this underrating—whether involuntary or deliberate—should be traced back to August 1944. While the Romanian insurrection was under way, the news about the successes of the Red Army and the liberation of Paris was the main stories on the front pages of the dailies appearing in the allied or neutral countries. The news about the overthrow of Antonescu's regime and Romania's turning weapons on Nazi Germany also appeared on the front pages of the respective newspapers, it is true, but the space reserved to it was smaller, and most of the time it showed only briefly or incompletely—sometimes even inaccurately—the scope of of consequences by Romania's new stand. Becuase of a mental attitude deeply rooted in the collective consciousness of foreign countries in general, and of West-European countries in particular, Paris was much more appealing than Bucharest. However, as we shall have the opportunity to show in this book, the events taking place in Romania were by far more important for the speeding up of the end of the war than those in France. Of course, there had been some keen observers and commentators who grasped the significance and scope of the impact the events of August 23, 1944 were to have on the course of World War II, from the very first moment, but their opinions—included in the pages of this book—did not enjoy the deserved reverberation at a time when, as we have said before, everybody's eyes were turned to the City of Light and to the actions of the protagonists of the anti-Hitler coalition.

Romania's being denied the co-beligerent status—a profound and serious injustice as compared to her sacrifices and military contribution to the crushing of the Third Reich—led to blurring the correct assessments made under the immediate impression of her courageous action. In this way, a true stereotyped image was reached, a sort of historiographic cliche, in which August 23, 1944 appears as the action of a minor sattelite of Nazi Germany, which, faced with a military catastrophe, eventually managed to save itself from the sinking ship onto that of the winners. From this light one acknowledges, in the best of cases, Romania's political ability, but ignores or even contests the value of the Romanian military contribution to the victory over Hitler's Germany.

It is the purpose of this book to provide the reader with a true image of the strategic-political consequences of the event of August 23, 1944, and even try to assess the time by which Romania's action shortened the war, thereby putting an earlier end to the massacres and devastations on the European continent and saving so many lives and assets from destruction. Anticipating our conclusions—the readers will be left to appreciate the arguments underlying them—let us say from the very beginning that, in the light of the historical sources, viewing August 23, 1944, as one of the decisively important events of World War II is beyond any doubt whatsoever. Since such an assertion might be suspected of subjectivism and national pride, we have repeatedly resorted to foreign sources and opinions with a view to substantiating our demonstration.

The endeavours of the Romanian historiography have provided us with a solid documentary basis through the publication of the four volumes dedicated to the August 23, 1944 interval from the wide corpus of *Documente din istoria militară a poporului român* (Documents on the Military History of the Romanian People) and of many reminiscences published either in the collection *Memorii de război* (War Memoirs) or in separate volumes. To all this one should add the rich documentary sources in Romanian and foreign archives revealing the serious consequences of Romania's actions upon the strategy, politics and economy of the Nazi Reich, the worsening and acceleration of the crisis which led to the latter's downfall.

The documentary sources, German in particular, have allowed not only the exact assessment of the impact the events in Romania had upon the development of World War II, but also—and this should be insistently pointed out—the individualization of the Romanian factor within the military developments in the Carpathian-Danubian area. It is common knowledge that the event of August 23, 1944 took place concommitantly with the Jassy (Iași)—Kishinev Operation mounted by the 2nd and 3rd Ukrainian Fronts of the Soviet Army. Highly reputed specialists, for example, Basil H. Liddell-Hart, who, in their writings, have made pertinent remarks on the Wehrmacht's catastrophe in Romania, have not always managed to dissociate the results of the Romanian actions from those of the Soviet offensive. The sources at hand—first and foremost the file of orders of the German "South Ukraine" Army Group in the territory of Romania—enable one to make such a distinction. Our approach to this matter has been exclusively guided by the wish to make a rigorous reconstitution of the historical facts and of their consequences. It is beyond dispute that the German-Soviet front was the decisive front of World War II, that Germany lost the war as a result of the defeats sustained in Moscow, Stalingrad and Kursk, and that the Soviet Union bore the brunt of the anti-Hitler war and sustained the most numerous human losses. While acknowledging these truths, which are axiomatic, we nevertheless want to reveal the exceptional value of Romania's contribution to the anti-Hitler war and, first of all, of the event of all, of the event of August 23, 1944 as a duty of honour to those who fought and died on the battlefield for the crushing of fascism. *Suum cuique tribuere* (to each his own) is not only a law principle but also a historiographic one, an elementary duty of intellectual and professional probity.

In one of his works, entitled *La place des Roumains dans l'histoire universelle* (The Place of the Romanians in World History), the great Romanian historian Nicolae Iorga revealed the significance of European or world reverberation in the history of the Romanian people. If we mention his work here it is only to point out that the international significance of the event of August 23, 1944 had its antecedents which we have considered useful to approach in the first chapter. To say that Romania has made a decisive contribution to the defeat of Hitler's Germany might seem hardly believable to someone who does not know the historical sources. However, equally unbelievable might have seemd the fact that in the 6th century B.C. of all Thracians the Gatae alone put up resistance to the Persian army of King Darius I; that in the 1st century B.C. the Geto-Dacian King Burebista turned his State into one of the great powers of the ancient world; that during the Middle Ages, of all the peoples of South-East Europe which had been faced with the Ottoman expansion, the Romanians alone succeeded in preserving their own State structures and in securing, through victories won on the battlefield, an autonomous status to Muntenia, Moldavia and Transylvania. Through their long resistance in front of Ottoman expansion, the Romanians formed a true barrier in the way of Ottoman attacks, actually being a shield to Central and Western Europe; the favourable conditions thus created enabled the latter to develop and helped the flourishing of the cultural and artistic Renaisance.

In this book we have tried to show that the setting up of the regime of military-fascist dictatorship in September 1940 and Romania's participation in the war alongside Hitler's Germany in 1941-1944 was the outcome of the international circumstances, of the sequence of events which occurred between August 1939-August 1940, which tore Romania away from the path of her traditional policy of defence of national independence and territorial integrity, of fighting expansion, aggression and territorial revisionism, a policy of collaboration with all the states interested in the setting up of a climate of peace and cooperation, and of a security system. In autumn 1940, when France was being overrun by German armor, Great Britain threatened with the landing of the Wehrmacht and bombed by the Luftwaffe and the Soviet Union bound by the non-aggression pact of August 23, 1939, Romania, a victim of serious territorial amputations in the summer of 1940, was completely isolated politically. Romania's entering the orbit of Berlin was not a free option, but a decision made under the constraint of some inexorable political and military realities. Romania did not choose the alliance with Germany, but was thrown into the latter's arms.

That collaboration, "against the grain," was in total contradiction with the entire policy Romania had promoted to that moment and with the feelings of the immense majority of the Romanian people. It was opposed by all the political forces of the Romanian society, in agreement with the communits. Under the leadership of the Romanian Communist Party, the broadest coalition of political parties and organizations ever known in the history of Romania was achieved, which on August 23, 1944,

through the anti-fascist and anti-imperialist revolution for national and
social liberation, overthrew the dictatorial regime and brought Romania
back to the side of her natural allies.

Through the disintegration of the whole German military system in
South-East Europe, through cutting off the Reich's supplies of fuel from
the vast oil fields of Ploieşti and of other products, through a string of
political crises which broke out in Bulgaria, Hungary and Croatia, through
Romania's joining the anti-Hitler coalition, the event of August 23, 1944
shortened the war by 200 days. It is easy to understand what those six
months meant in terms of saving the continent from further victims,
destruction and suffering. The fact should be stressed here—for it has
been too often overlooked that—that half a year denied to the German
war economy and output actually prevented the achievement and mass
production of a series of weapon projects and prototypes which might
have prolonged the war in Europe long after May 9, 1945.

This book is the final part of a larger work, a monographic research
devoted to August 23, 1944, which will make a multilateral approach of
the crucial event. Until there, here is this book, written with the sole
desire to serve the historical truth, in other words, to resort to the often
quoted but, unfortunately, not always observed formula of Leopold von
Ranke, to show things the "way they were."

CHAPTER I

PRELUDE TO 23 AUGUST 1944

"Romania's undertaking is an act of great courage which will speed up the end of the war. The situation of Germany in the Balkans is so close to a terrible catastrophe, which will surpass by its proportions the one caused by the pocket of Falaise [. . .] The collapse of the Hitlerites draws near with great strides, while the days of the Germans in the Balkans are running out."[1] The above-quoted lines belong to the commentary broadcast by Radio London on August 24, 1944, on the overthrow of Antonescu's dictatorship and Romania's turning weapons on Nazi Germany. There were many such comments, and as a matter of fact we shall further dwell upon them. We only wish to say here that they reveal in an impressive unanimity the exeptional political and strategic importance of the event accomplished on August 23, 1944, the surprise aroused by the minuteness and secrecy of the preparations, by the vigor and promptness of the Romanian actions, and also by the scope and impact of their consequences.

Indeed, it is hardly imaginable that over a few days alone an entire army, with an effective strength of over half a million men, disentangled itself from the interposing larger German units and in getting regrouped, for its greater role with extraordinary swiftness, in areas assigned beforehand; that, meanwhile, a part of the Romanian forces, supported by the broad masses of the people, were fighting to clear the country's territory of German occupation troops; that, concommitantly, the cover of the frontiers against the German and Hungarian troops in northwestern

1

Transylvania was ensured, and some very strong Romanian military groupings were shifted beyond the Carpathians with a view to reinforcing the
new front there and of mounting the liberating offensive in Transylvania.

The historic event of August 23, 1944, whose implications were commented upon by the foreign press and broadcasting stations, naturally
raised a number of questions. For instance, how was it possible for Romania to break off the "alliance" with Hitler's Germany "overnight"—as
some historians abroad still keep saying—and then join with her entire
army, actually her entire combat capability, the anti-fascist coalition?
How could an eintre army, whose combat force was considerable, "make
a 180° front change" without the least organizational command or operational fault.

Such questions and many similar ones seem the more so legitimate as
it is hardly conceivable that an army such as the Wehrmacht, so powerful
both in terms of combat strength and war materiel, which only a few years
before had succeeded in defeating, rapidly and with few losses, the Polish,
Norwegian, Belgian, Dutch, French, Greek and other armies, and in reaching the outskirts of Moscow and the banks of the Volga, and whose reaction to the Italian defection of September 1943 had been prompt and
efficient, was "close to a terrible catastrophe," due to the course of the
events in Romania, as radio "London" commented in its above-mentioned
broadcast.

$$* \quad * \quad * \quad * \quad *$$

The crowning of a century-old aspiration, the completion of Romania's
national unity in 1918 was acknowledged by the peace treaties concluded
over 1919-1920.[2] Those treaties sanctioned the victory of the struggle for
emancipation or for national unity carried on by a whole train of European peoples which, under the circumstances of the downfall of the Tsarist
Empire and the Austro-Hungarian monarchy, laid down—or restored—the
groundwork of their national states, or, as it was the case of Romania,
completed their unity. Therefore, the new European political system took,
from the very beginning, two aspects: on the one hand, it was the result of
the outcome of a war between two blocs of imperialist great powers—the
Entente and the Central Powers—while on the other hand, it recorded the
success of some long revolutionary-national struggles.

As an expression of the will of the Romanian people to defend the territorial integrity and national sovereignty of its country, Romania's foreign policy made of the maintenance of the status quo, the setting up of a climate of peace and security, and the observance of the League of Nations —as an expression of international lawfulness—its fundamental aims.

In order to defend her integrity and sovereignty, Romania, alongside the other small and medium-sized states, preoccupied to defend their status quo, had to fight with equal vigor both the revisionist trends—which were not late in showing themselves soon after the conclusion of the treaties—and the tendency of the Great Powers—even if allied ones—to exert, more or less explicitly, a sort of "surveillance right" upon her foreign policy. That twofold imperative led to the setting up of an alliance between Romania, Czechoslovakia and Yugoslavia, known as the Little Entente.[3]

The alliance of the three countries meant by no means some isolation into a narrow zonal perimeter; on the contrary, persuaded of the fact that their interests coincided with the interests of peace on the continent, Romania, Czechoslovakia and Yugoslavia saw the instrument of collaboration they had organized as an efficient means for collaboration between all the states in Central and South-East Europe, and for strengthening the League of Nations.

While defending the ideals of peace and security for all countries, irrespective of the latter's size, Romania had constantly promoted the need for collaboration grounded on the full equality of states and on the wide adhesion of the people's masses to the efforts for safeguarding peace. Nicolae Titulescu, who in the interwar years, particularly as Romania's Foreign Minister, acted as a relentless defender of the principles laid down in the Pact of the League of Nations, pointed out in a conference held in Cambridge in 1930: "And while countries are not equal in terms of strength, and experience, statesmen can be equal in their love and care for peace. And all the so-called small countries know better the exigencies of peace than the big countries, because they are more afraid of war and more vulnerable than the latter." And the Romanian diplomat went on asking his audience: "How could the edifice of peace be built without the support of the masses?"[4]

Equally guided by the care for her own security and for world peace, Romania signed the Briand-Kellogg Pact on September 4, 1928, which pursued to eliminate war as a means of solving interstate differences from international life. Vitally interested in the speediest implementation of that treaty, on which so many hopes for an everlasting world peace were pinned, Romania later signed the Moscow Protocol (February 9, 1929) together with the USSR, Poland, Estonia and Latvia, which expressed the resolve of the signatory parties to "contribute to maintaining peace among their respective countries and, to this aim, to make effective between these peoples the treaty on renunciation of war as an instrument of national policy, signed in Paris on August 27, 1928."

Respect for international law—as a condition for world security and peace—also underlay Romania's stand regarding the Sino-Japanese conflict (1931). While recommending the immediate cessation of hostilities and the negotiation of an armistice without political conditions as a premise for negotiations between the parties involved in the conflict with a view to solving the respective differences, Nicolae Titulescu pointed to the need of rigorously observing the territorial integrity of the member-states of the League of Nations—provided for in Article 10—as a fundamental prerequisite for maintaining the agreements of Geneva: "Any weakness in relation to Article 10, any hesitation as to its integral implementation would deal a fatal blow to our institution."[5]

A natural aspect of Romania's posture with respect to the issues of world peace and security was the stand she adopted at the conferences on the reduction and limitation of armaments. The main principle underlying that position was that disarmament was an "absolute requirement of peace;"[6] Romania's representatives upheld the renunciation of sterile talks on the relationship of precedence between security and disarmament in favor of the adoption of some practical measures able to contribute to the setting up of a climate of confidence. In Nicolae Titulescu's opinion, who also made a valuable contribution to the talks on the limitation of armaments and on disarmament—both in terms of principles and of their implementation—disarmament had to rely on a triad consisting of the "degree of disarmament, the degree of security and that of applying the principle of equality."

When after more than a year's talks the goal of the latter seemed as remote as ever, Titulescu concisely formulated the cause of the failure: "Whenever there is a serious conflict hindering the natural course of things, there is always a great power involved."[7]

The talks on disarmament had, however, a positive outcome through the drawing up of a convention on the definiton of aggression signed on July 3-4, 1933, by the USSR and the countries surrounding it, among whom Romania as well, which saw in that document the first "bold, frank and clear"[8] definition given to aggression, and evasion from the sphere of "vague idealistic aspirations" in order to set the question of peace on a "practical, solid foundation which is the starting point of a completely new life."[9]

The setting up of the Nazi regime in Germany (January 30, 1933) brought instability and threat into international life, the share of which permanently increased, ultimately leading to a crisis that would find its issue in World War II. The new regime in Germany overtly proclaimed its intention to obtain a revision of the Versailles Treaty of 1919 and thereby attacked the very groundwork of the European status quo. The foreign policy of the Nazi Reich actually spurred all revisionist forces on the continent which finally came to see Germany as the leader of a true anti-Versailles coalition.

To Romania, the course imprinted by the Nazi regime to German policy spelled a twofold threat. First and foremost, there was the danger that the great Western democracies—France and Great Britain—might not be able to arm themselves adequately, which would have been a deterrent to the revisionist and expansionist intentions of Hitler's Germany, and consequently be led into a compromise formula within a directorate—established or de facto—including France, Great Britain, Germany and Italy. Secondly, located in an area traditionally considered by Berlin as one of its own areas of economic expansion, Romania, whose economy felt the effects of the economic crisis of 1929-1933 and which had close exchange relations with the German market, might be exposed to pressures from the Third Reich, to which the "Süd-Ost" (South-East Europe), even if not included in its "Lebenstraum" (vital space) meant to be conquered and colonized, still belonged to the so-called "Wirtschafts-raum" (economic space), which was to be controlled economically.

In 1933, when upon the insistence of Magyar Prime Minister G. Göm-bös Germany had concluded a trade and payment agreement with Hungary that favored the latter's exports of cereals, she definitely refused to grant similar advantages to Romania, stating in unequivocal harsh terms that such concessions could only be granted to those states which did not lend "political support" to the Reich's enemies.

Romania was thus among the first countries—if not the very first—upon which pressure was exerted by the Reich with a view to leading them into changing their foreign policies. By firmly sticking to the principles of defense of national independence and territorial integrity and by faithfully fulfilling the obligations she had assumed through international treaties, Romania did not yield either to the tempting economic advantages offered by exchanges with Germany or to the threats formulated by the representatives of the Reich and of the Nazi Party.[10]

The worsening of the international situation and the increased threats hovering over the status quo called for finding new means and formulas in order to cope with the new circumstances: on February 16, 1933, a document was signed on the reorganization of the Little Entente, meant to consolidate the alliance of the three states and give it a new status in the international arena; in the preamble of the pact one affirmed first of all the "firm will [of the signatories—a.n.] to intensify economic relations with all states without any discrimination whatsoever and particularly with the states of Central Europe," as well as the "concern to see peace safeguarded in all circumstances, to ensure a course toward lasting stability of affairs in Central Europe."[11]

In the following year, the same preoccupation for protection against aggression lay at the bottom of the setting up of the Balkan Entente. On January 22, in Zagreb, the foreign ministers of the states making up the Little Entente—N. Titulescu, E. Beneš and B. Jeftić—examined the clauses of the future alliance, also analyzing the possibility of two other countries' joining the alliance—Bulgaria and Albania. The goal of the alliance was to be clearly defined by the Romanian foreign minister: "a comprehensive association of states, aiming at maintaining peace through the setting up of a collective, impressive force, placed at the service of the fairest and most amicable international practices."[12]

In only a few months, the structures of the international system were so much shattered in the heart of Europe and in the Ethiopian deserts that the League of Nations, its guarantor, was dealt a deadly blow. The introduction of military service in Germany (March 16, 1935)—the first flagrant violation of a clause in the Versailles Treaty—and Italy's aggression against Ethiopia questioned the very foundations underlying European and world peace.

Through the voice of her foreign minister, Romania asked for a rigorous applying of the sanctions stipulated in the Pact of the League of Nations. The bloody events in Ethiopia had a very obvious European reverberation: what was then taking place in a remote corner of Africa—the Romanian diplomat pointed out—might happen in Europe too, had the aggression been left unsanctioned. Under pressure of an indignant public opinion, the League of Nations voted, for the first time, the application of a set of sanctions. Their results would have tested the efficiency of that international institution which had identified itself with the very status quo. However, the efficiency of the sanctions was not the one banked on by their promoters: only a few states—among them Romania too—took a firm stand as to the application of the sanctions. In the absence of wide international adhesion to the principle itself, they could not yield the contemplated results.

Encouraged by the passivity of the Western Powers, Hitler, in his turn, made a further step toward creating the necessary premises for revanche: the remilitarization of the Rhineland (March 7, 1936). Through its strategic consequences—covering the vital zone of the Ruhr, creating a bridgehead against France and denying the latter any possibility of intervening in favor of her allies in Eastern Europe—the remilitarization of the Rhineland provided the Nazi Reich with those indispensible elements for carrying through its aggressive plans. The failure of the Western Great Powers to fulfill the international responsibilities they had assumed proved fatal to the whole world. From this viewpoint, one can say that the "prewar," to resort to a term used by B. Liddell-Hart, started in 1936.[13]

The changes occurred in the strategic balance of forces had—as was but natural—serious political effects. An obvious thing to anyone, the fortifications of the Rhenish frontier "undoubtedly rendered difficult the effective validity of the remote alliances France had concluded." Nicolae Titulescu voiced the feelings of those allies perfectly well when he said that the friends of France had in Eastern Europe were addressing her an S.O.S. and were inviting her to take a firm stand.[14]

In the meeting of the Council of the League of Nations held on July 18, Nicolae Titulescu depicted the situation created by the Nazi Reich's act of force in memorable words: "If the unilateral denunciation of a treaty might be accepted without consequences, this would mean the end of collective security and of the League of Nations. We would enter a world we thought we had left for ever, a world governed not by the force of law, but by the law of force."[15] The lenient reproof expressed by the Council of the League of Nations, followed by no concrete steps against the aggressor, actually meant the acceptance of the fait accompli.

Within the context created by the remilitarization of the Rhineland, Nicolae Titulescu, who had identified himself with a firm policy against the Nazi revanchism, fell a victim to the intrigues of the right-wing groupings, which demanded an accommodation with this new state of affairs.[16]

Nicolae Titulescu's removal from the lead of Romanian diplomacy brought no change in the latter's foreign policy. The fundamental aims remained the same as before; only the tactics were altered, as a result of the political conjuncture entailed by the political-military changes occurring on the Rhine. At the same time, the policy of appeasement promoted by the Western cabinets rendered the checking of the Reich's disguised or overt aggression ever more difficult.

The Anschluss, followed by the Munich Pact, brought new changes of the territorial status of the Versailles Europe acquired by those powers which used to be regarded as the symbols and guardians of the system itself: France and Great Britain. The phantom of the quadripartite pact—passed away in 1933—found a tragic embodiment in the capital of Bavaria: the directorate of the Western Great Powers imposed on the Czechoslovak peoples—in the latter's absence and against its will—the alteration of its country's frontiers. The statesmen in London and Paris, who thought of themselves as partners of the Führer and the Duce in deciding upon the destines of the people were to be soon disappointed. The dismemberment of Czechoslovakia, followed by the annexation of Bohemia and Moravia (March 15, 1939), as a protectorate annexed by the Reich, marked Germany's moving away from what had been thought to be a program for bringing all German people within the frontiers of one single State.

During those months of strain and danger, Romania maintained the by then traditional trend of her foreign policy. Aware of the fact that, after Czechoslovakia, Germany would not delay in trying to disintegrate Yugoslavia and Romania,[17] the latter used every possible means to come to the succour of her jeopardized ally. By granting Soviet planes permission to fly over the Romanian territory on their way to Czechoslovakia, by having rolling stock concentrated along the eastern frontier in order to allow—had the circumstances required it—the transportation of Soviet troops, the official circles in Bucharest showed their desire to cooperate in granting military assistance within a joint action, in which Great Britain, France, the USSR and Poland were expected to participate. Romania's loyalty toward Czechoslovakia was the expression of her adherence to the principle of observance of national sovereignty and territorial integrity, of each people's right to self-determination. Even after the dismemberment of Czechoslovakia had begun, Romania continued to take steps for attenuating the blows dealt at the allied neighbor State; she turned down the proposals of the Polish government to join Poland and Hungary in the annexation of some territories belonging to the Czechoslovak State, and made demarches in the capitals of a number of Western countries in order to make them act, at least at the eleventh hour, for checking the wave of fascist aggression.

In the autumn of 1938, the pressures of the Nazi Reich upon Romania intensified: the failure of the four-year plan for the production of synthetic fuel made Romanian oil one of the essential goals of German expansion. An economic partner of utmost importance to the Reich in South-East Europe—through her yield of cereals and industrial raw materials— Romania belonged politically to the forces opposing the revisionist and expansionist policy promoted by Hitler's Germany. In order to make the best of Romanian resources to the benefit of the Reich's economy and its efforts for armament, the ruling circles in Berlin enhanced pressures through stipulating and capitalizing on the Romanian-Hungarian disputes regarding the frontiers fixed by the Trianon Treaty. What had been but an occasional weapon until then became an essential component of the Reich's policy vis-à-vis Romania.[18] Political and economic blackmail, the threats with the use of force countered Romania's determination to remain faithful to her policy of defending national independence and sovereignty, of observing each people's right to decide upon its own destiny. The Romanian-German economic treaty concluded on March 23, 1939, was but another tactical concession meant to save the fundamental assets: national sovereignty and territorial integrity.[19] Already on January 23, 1939, the Romanian Foreign Minister Grigore Gafencu had pointed to the need for the Romanians to be ready "to make some concessions to Germany, yet to stick to our viewpoint on all matters that might jeopardize our independence and sovereignty."[20]

Romanian-German economic negotiations were accompanied by strong political and military pressures exerted by the Reich upon Romania. The Romanian-German economic treaty of March 1939 was seen in Berlin as the decisive element in ensuring the success of the German endeavors to secure economic control over South-East Europe. H. Wohlthat, the main German negotiator, would write on February 27, 1939, that "by orienting Romania's economy toward Germany through a joint planning spanning several years, Germany will acquire supremacy in South-East Europe, as it is expected that similar treaties with the Balkan powers should follow."[21] As it has been observed, the "Germans saw Romania as a potential fulcrum of anti-Nazi activities in the Balkans and, consequently, they considered Bucharest as the key to their political intentions regarding the South-East."[22]

In the tense climate set in following German pressures and the concentration of Hungarian troops on Romania's western frontier, a possible prelude to a German-Hungarian military action (nor was Bulgaria's joining ruled out), the Romanian government signed the treaty with the intention of avoiding its stipulations and to counterbalance it through enhancing and enlarging its economic relations with Great Britain and France. The sudden change for the better that occurred in British policy after the blow in Prague thus coincided with Romania's efforts toward checking the Reich's "Drang nach Süd-Osten" (Drive to the South-East), and led to granting Romania the Anglo-French guarantee on April 13, 1939. The reason which led the political decision-making forums in Bucharest to conclude the above-mentioned treaty was clearly expressed by the Romanian premier in his writings: "If we concluded the economic agreement with Germany, it was to buy time and get some economic advantages rather than get closer to her politically."[23]

Once the treaty was concluded, Romania resorted to every possible means to escape the German grip and facilitate the consolidation of the economic position held by Great Britain and France in her national economy with the view to strengthening her anti-Hitler resistance front,[24] and carried on sustained diplomatic activity in order to bar the way of the Third Reich's expansion.[25] From among the interlocutors of the Romanian diplomats, Ismet Inönü, President of Turkey, perfectly synthetized Romania's stand when he stated in June 1939, that this country "does not accept peace at any cost, being ready to defend her independence and integrity arms in hand."[26]

After the outbreak of the second world conflagration, the fall of Poland in the autumn of 1939, followed by that of France in late spring of 1940, Romania which had been faithful in her collaboration with Great Britain and France with a view toward maintaining the Versailles settlement, found herself completely isolated diplomatically, with all the tragic consequences derving from that position: territorial amputations, the setting up of the military-fascist regime with the Reich's help and the coming of German troops to the country. It was only in such a wholly unfavorable international conjuncture that Romania, a steadfast enemy of the Reich's expansionist and hegemonic policy in the interwar period, could become an "ally" of the latter between September 1940-August 23, 1944. That "alliance" ran in complete and total contradiction with the two-decade orientation of Romanian foreign policy, which all throughout that period had remained true to the fundamental principles of international law—respect for national independence and territorial integrity, non-interference in internal affairs, security and cooperation. Each time the Reich made a step toward the war it was preparing and violated those principles, Romania's reaction was quick and firm, blaming aggression and acting for its sanctioning and for preventing further actions of the kind. In the international context of the time, such a policy could only yield fruit through the joint action of all the states interested in the maintenance of the status quo. Instead of such a salutary orientation, some powers preferred to reach an understanding with the aggressor—in exchange for some temporary advantages—which resulted in the latter's encouraging and the failure of every attempt to thwart its plans. In that way, Romania herself fell a victim to that "Drang nach Süd-Osten" which, with the ascent of the Nazis, acquired unprecedented dynamism and brutality. Despite all her endeavors to check the advance of aggression and servitude, Romania in whose rich resources of oil and cereals the Nazi Reich took a considerable interest, was pushed, against her will, into the economic, political and military orbit of Nazi Germany, becoming thus associated with an enemy she had ceaselessly fought.

Romania's efforts to defend national independence and territorial integrity in the face of the Third Reich's aggressively dynamic foreign policy were paralleled at home by the struggle of the social-political forces, true to the democratic principles, were carrying on against the fascist organizations. Until the ascent to power of the Nazis, fascism had been a marginal

phenomenon in Romanian political life.[28] Mysticism, nationalism, jingoism and anti-Semitism were the ingredients of an ideology that was looking for its sources—despite the exaltation of antochthonism—in Berlin
and Rome rather than in the native land. The great Romanian historian
Nicolae Iorga harshly blamed the "dangerous aping of foreign ways, which
could neither be brought to us, nor adopted here."[29] The illustrious
scholar also revealed the incompatibility between the acts of violence
perpetrated by the iron-guardists and the peaceful nature of the Romanian people: "One comes to be ashamed of the state such banditlike behavior has brought to this country, a country famous for its lofty toler-
ance, for its Christian, specifically Romanian leniency."[30] It was he again
that pointed out that fascist aggressiveness was only present within a
narrow section of Romanian society: "Fortunately, as it has been seen on
the occasion of the recent sad circumstances, the bulk of the Romanian
people from all levels and, particularly, in its so-wise lower stratum, is
indifferent to all passionate cries and all urgings to blood-stained acts of
violence. As in other fields too, the groundwork of the nation has remained healthy and no matter what happens with the other strata of the
society, so long as this fundamental one keeps on being the way it is
[. . .] our century-old traditions, our future can be regarded as completely safe."[31]

Therefore, in Romania fascism was an imported phenomenon, a characteristic which did not make it less dangerous. In a country in which the
univeral suffrage had only been introduced in 1923 and, consequently,
parliamentary democracy was in its infancy, in which social conflicts
sharply cropped up, in which the agrarian issue—despite the land reform
of 1921—was still unresolved, nationalistic demagogy could seem appealing to certain segments of the population. More serious though was the
support Nazi Germany lent to the Iron Guard. After a period of soundings and waverings (1933-1934) between various small fascist and right-
wing groupings, the Nazi leadership decided to make the Iron Guard its
main agency in Romania. The Iron Guard, in its turn, through the voice
of its chief, Corneliu Zelea Codreanu, proclaimed its adhesion to the
principles underlying the collaboration between the dictators in Rome
and Berlin, stating that Romania would join the Rome-Berlin Axis within
48 hours from the "iron-guardist victory." The foreign, aberrant nature
of the Iron Guard when compared to the Romanian people's traditions

and psychology, as well as the former's orientation toward the Nazi Reich, the main revisionist force, made the overwhelming majority of the Romanian public opinion openly and relentlessly show hostility toward the pro-fascist elements in Romania.

Within the wide arc of the social-political forces opposing internal and world fascism, the Romanian Communist Party showed such firmness and consistency that would confer upon it the role of initiator and leader of the anti-fascist struggle in Romania. The Romanian Communist Party has the historic merit of having been the first to understand the essence of fascism and the danger the latter represented both to Romania's existence as a State and to its essentially bourgeois parliamentary-democractic regime. Setting out from that premise, the RCP called all parties and organizations, in their capacity as representatives of the social-political forces whose interests were jeopardized by the setting up of a fascist dictatorship and the Nazi Reich's hegemonic policy, to unite within a united front, able to bar the way to fascism at home and to defend national independence and territorial integrity from without. In that struggle the interests of all those social classes and categories were actually in agreement with the interests of the nation itself, and that concordance ought to be the strongest binder of the antifascist people's front in Romania.

Of utmost importance for defining the political line of the Romanian Communist Party in establishing the people's front tactics were the plenums of the Central Committee of the RCP of February 1935 and July 1936. The Plenum of 1935 made a through analysis of the ratio of forces between the classes and categories of Romanian society showing that in the confrontation between democracy and fascism the former had the upper hand, rallying workers, peasants, craftsmen, clerks and intellectuals under the banner of defense of the great assets and principles of democracy. The rallying of the working class within the United Workers' Front was to provide the Antifascist People's Front with a polarizing leading center. The enlarged Plenum of the CC of the RCP of July 1936 warned against the threat the practices of expansionist policy in general of the Third Reich's in particular were to Romania: "Romania"—the plenum showed—"may become the object rather than the subject of a new imperialist redivision of Europe." Nazi Germany's efforts for "Lebensraum" —a pretext-label for securing continental hegemony—could only result in the country's dismemberment, in the enslaving of the Romanian people and the seizure of its economic resources. Contemplating a possible joint attack of the Nazi Reich and Horthyst Hungary on Romania, the Plenum stressed the complete identification of the communists with the highest interests of the people: the Party members "consider it necessary to defend each strip of this country's land" and "will go to the first lines of fighters in order to repel fascist aggression."[32]

Aiming at ensuring a wide popular character to the antifascist struggle, the RCP, then acting underground, carried on ample activities for rallying all social classes and categories hostile to fascism, taking the initiative in setting up a whole number of mass organizations such as "Comitetul Naţional Antifascist" (The Antifascist National Committee), "Liga muncii" (The Work League), "Blocul Democratic" (The Democratic Bloc) and others.[33] During the same period a great number of newspapers and magazines were brought into circulation—"Arena" (The Arena), "Blocul" (The Bloc), "Cuvîntul liber" (The Free Word), "Dacia nouă" (New Dacia), "Era nouă" (The New Era), "Horia" (the name of a national hero), "Înainte" (Forward), "Korunk" (The Morning), "Omul liber" (The Free Man), "Orizont" (The Horizon), "Reporter" (The Reporter), "Spiritul vremii" (The Spirit of the Times), "Torţa" (The Torch), "Vremuri noi" (New Times)—the columns of which carried articles blaming fascist ideology, denounced as an offense to human dignity and a jeopardy to the freedom of the individual and of the nations.

In the political establishment of the country there were personalities such as Nicolae Iorga, Virgil Madgeru, Armand Călinescu, Victor Iamandi, Demetru Dobrescu and others who acted as firm opponents to the Nazi Reich and to the latter's agents in Romania, the iron-guardists. The ideology of the extreme right-wing and, first and foremost, of the Iron Guard, the exaltation of mysticism and death, of jingoism, the denial of the principles of democracy and progress, all of which belonged to the ideological arsenal of the Legion, were vigorously fought, while exposing their evil consequences for Romanian society. The sterility of that ideology of the extreme right-wing naturally associated with the brutality of the political action, murder becoming the substitute for the political argument: statesmen such as prime ministers Ion Gheorghe Duca and Armand Călinescu, or personalities of Romanian and world culture, such as Nicolae Iorga, were assassinated by the iron-guardists.

Notwithstanding the hostility showed by the greatest part of the Romanian public opinion to fascism, the policy of the RCP aiming at setting up an antifascist people's front yielded but modest results: on September 24, 1935, a collaboration agreement was concluded between the Ploughmen's Front and the Union of the Magyar Working People in Romania (MADOSZ) at Băcia (Hunedoara county), followed, on December 6, by the agreement of Țebea[34] (relevantly concluded under the oak trees of Horea[35] and by the grave of Avram Iancu[36] between the RCP, represented by the Bloc for the Defense of Democratic Freedom, and the Ploughmen's Front, the Socialist Party and the MADOSZ, setting up a minimal action program: fighting the "fascist dictatorship, irrespective of the form it may take," defense of democratic freedoms, amnesty, fighting war and the like. The call addressed to the other parties did not enjoy a nation-wide response; it was only in the partial parliamentary elections held in Hunedoara and Mehedinți counties that collaboration, at the local level, was achieved between the democratic forces, resulting in the victory of the latter's candidate (February 18, 1936): that was a clear proof of the great political advantages of the people's front formula, envisaged by the RCP, advantages that were not capitalized politically on account of the refusal of the "historical" great parties to collaborate with the communists.[37]

In March 1939, when the dismemberment of Czechoslovakia brought the Wehrmacht units to Romania's frontiers and German pressures threateningly intensified, the RCP issued a manifesto to the nation, in which it solemnly declared: "the communists will fight, weapons in hand, in the first lines. Unite, all of you, in one powerful front against Hitler and his revisionist allies."[38] A few weeks later, on May 1, 1939, the RCP organized a number of massive antifascist demonstrations under the slogans "We wish a free independent Romania!", "Down with fascism!". Young Communist Nicolae Ceaușesau made a decisive contribution to the organization of that demonstration, which ranked among the best organized in Europe.

Fascism failed to become a mass movement in Romania; the political share of the organizations of the extreme right-wing and particularly of the Iron Guard kept being low (in the 1937 elections the Iron Guard carried the highest number of votes in its history, i.e. 15.58% of the votes cast), though their demagogic agitation gained ground in some quarters of the petite bourgeoisie, the peasantry and the university youth. In the conditions of the parliamentary regime, the iron-guardists had no chance of ascending to power: their taking the helm of the country in September 1940 was the result of the changes that occurred in the balance of forces in the international arena. The political weakness of fascism in Romania was proved by its late ascension to power with the assistance— and this should be again emphasized—of forces from outside (Hitler's Germany and fascist Italy), which took advantage of the favorable international circumstances and of the ephemeral character of the fascist regime in Romania, discredited as a result of the murders, incompetence and anarchy the latter had brought into the country. The victories scored by the Wehrmacht in the spring of 1940 led to the setting up of a military-fascist dictatorship in Romania, in which the Iron Guard shared power with General Ion Antonescu.

The attempts of the Iron Guard to secure a power monopoly—with the assistance of some elements in the Nazi Party and the SS—brought it into conflict with General Ion Antonescu, who, after the abdication of King Carol II, had become the "ruler of the State." The conflict between the two partners in the regime set up in September 1940, knew its acme in early 1941: the iron-guardist rebellion of January 21-24, 1941—during which the bestiality of the iron-guardists took paraxistic forms (massacres, captured soldiers were burnt alive, robbery)—put an end to Ion Antonescu's collaboration with the iron-guardist movement. Preoccupied with preparations for the attack on the Soviet Union (Directive No. 21 of the "Barbarossa" plan had been signed on December 18, 1940), Hitler would not tolerate an unstable situation in a zone lying right in the rear of his future front; his preference—and the OKW's too—mainly dictated by pragmatic reasons, which in that way went before his ideological affinities, went to General Ion Antonescu, the man able to ensure the conditions and cooperation needed for the "Barbarossa" operation.[39]

Considered by Hitler himself as a matter of life and death,[40] Romania's participation in the anti-Soviet war was deemed as absolutely indispensible to the Reich. The motorized units of the Wehrmacht, as well as the planes of the Luftwaffe—the two groupings on which the Blitzkrieg relied—could not work without Romanian oil, which had become the keystone of the fuel supply system within the German war economy.[41] The geo-strategic position of Romania in South-East Europe made of the former an element of utmost importance within the military disposition both as regarded the Reich's control over that part of the continent and the future operations making up the "Barbarossa" plan.

Romania's joining the anti-Soviet war was followed by the declarations of war of Great Britain (December 5, 1941) and the United States (June 6, 1942), which thus showed solidarity with the Soviet ally. Romania's entering World War II, against the will of the Romanian people, was the direct consequence of the political-military context in Eastern Europe in 1939-1940; therefore, it was not an option—as in World War I—but rather a submission to a brutal force—that of Nazi Germany—which was in control of a large area of the continent, Romania included.

Seen against the policy she had promoted all throughout the interwar decades, Romania's participation in the war alongside the Third Reich appeared as tragically nonsensical: Romania could neither be the ally of a country which had presided over her territorial amputation, nor the partner of a great power advocating the setting up of a "new order" based on denial of the independence and sovereignty of the peoples and states, a principle with which Romania's policy had associated to the point of close identification.

It goes without saying that, under the circumstances, the war waged by the side of Germany could not enjoy popular support. The main enemy of Romania's national independence and territorial integrity was the German "ally" itself, and it was against it that the social-political forces of the Romanian society unanimously raised. The existence of such a wide political spectrum is easy to explain if one takes into account that the Third Reich's policy of expansion and domination seriously endangered the interests of all social classes and categories in Romania.

The subordination of the Romanian economy to the Reich's material exigencies considerably narrowed the sphere of the transactions concluded by the capital owners, obliged as a matter of fact to accept the terms set by their German partners, with hard repercussions upon the living standard of the mass of the employed. The war years witnessed a progressive worsening of the material conditions: scarcity of food, high prices, forced loans and the like.

In the opinion of the well-known Swiss daily "Neue Züricher Zeitung" "in no other countries of the world have the prices gone so high as in Romania",[42] a comparison of the data regarding the ratio between prices and wages obviously shows a rapid decrease of the real wages index:

Date	Nominal wages index	Price index	Real wages index
August 1939	100	100	100
December 1941	168.5	412	40.8
December 1942	212.4	712	29.9
December 1943	275.5	1,158	25.3
August 1944	275.5	1,392	19.7

It goes without saying that the precarious economic situation in Romania brought about a climate of discontent which aggravated with the continuation of the war—with the latter's whole train of suffering—and the economic depression caused by the war effort and German spoliation. Grafted on the almost unanimous conviction that Romania's participation in Hitler's war ran counter to the national interests, that climate gave rise to manifestations of opposition and protest. The report of the police, gendarmerie and of other repressive bodies are full of information regarding the population's manifestations of discontent, its hostility toward the continuation of the war. Petitions, protests, strikes, acts of sabotage—all those symptoms of the social-political strain in the country actually filled the confidential reports addressed by local agents to the central bodies; all of them reveal a state of tension and agitation evolving toward an explosive unfettering.

* * * * *

The setting up of the military-fascist dictatorship with the generous assistance of the international fascist forces—which had followed the territorial amputation presided over by the same foreign circles—the occupation of Romania by the Wehrmacht troops and the former's precipitated entering the political and military orbit of Hitler's Reich spelled a highly serious situation for the Romanian people. It was imperative to regain Romania's independence and sovereignty, to remove the political regime then in power with outside support, to drive away or annihilate the foreign troops, to win back Romania's political and military freedoms in the international arena. Those priority exigencies of the historical moment were also the main objects of the strategy of the Romanian resistance movement, initiated and carried on by the whole nation, under the leadership of the Romanian Communist Party, ever since the autumn of 1940. Through program-documents with a powerful mobilizing and organizational character—"Our Viewpoint," September 1940; the "Circular of the CC of the RCP" of January 15, 1941; "From the Iron-Guardist Regime to Military Dictatorship,"[43] issued after the rebellion of the Iron Guard—the communists provided the national resistance with a comprehensive theoretical "arsenal," mapping out the main directions for its actions, the ways of rallying all patriotic forces within a broad national front.

Ever since the first days of the anti-Soviet war, the RCP made a remarkable analysis of the internal and world political context in order to find out the ways and means for preventing the national tragedy that was looming ahead. The conclusion deriving from that analysis was that the salvation of the nation could only be achieved by the forces of the nation itself. Those forces had to be mustered and organized within a national front that should include the entire range of democratic anti-Hitler forces, and should act for overthrowing Antonescu's regime, for taking Romania out of the war waged against the United Nations and for turning its weapons on the Nazi Reich. Historical sources peremptorily show that the RCP was the first party in the country preoccupied with finding a political formula able to ensure a joint basis for cooperation to the parties and other political groupings whose outlook on home organization was still divergent. Already in the circular of the CC of the RCP of July 8, 1941 there were two basic ideas that would guide the alliance policy envisaged by the RCP. "The communists have to work daily on the formation of the unity of struggle and of the united front of the working class, the social democratic workers, members of the National Peasant Party and non-party people;" the circular went on to say that "the communists have to concentrate all their forces for the setting up of a National United Front." The circular therefore set two goals: the establishment of the National Front as a coalition of all forces hostile to the German occupation and to Ion Antonescu's dictatorial regime, and the setting up of the

United Workers' Font, the solid groundwork of the National United Front, because, as pointed out in the above-mentioned circular, "without the unity of the working class one cannot successfully organize the unity of struggle for the Romanian people's unfettering either."[44]

The policy put forward by the circular of the CC of the RCP of July 8, 1941 turned to good account—as can easily be seen—the principles and exigencies of the antifascist people's front tactics used with notable results in the thirties. However the RCP considered that in the struggle against the Nazi Reich, which was threatening by its expansionist and hegemonic policy the sovereignty and integrity of the Romanian State, it was possible and necessary also to secure the collaboration of the non-proletarian social-political forces. The efforts for setting up a wide anti-Hitler, patriotic front required, first and foremost, the finding of that common denominator able to make possible the collaboration of the communists with the social-democrats, national-peasants, national-liberals, and the like. The struggle for the rescue of the nation, which called for the unity of all anti-Hitler democratic forces, also required that priority should be given to the making up of the anti-Hitler national front, as compared to the other specific goals of the working class.

On September 6, 1941, the RCP issued the program-platform entitled "The Struggle of the Romanian People for National Freedom and Independence" which listed the targets of the struggle of the country's political forces, which agreed to coalesce within the National United Front in order to save the country from a disaster: Romania's getting out of the anti-Soviet war and the driving of the German troops out of the country; the overthrow of Antonescu's regime; the annulment of the Vienna Diktat, the restoration of civic and democratic rights and freedoms; the raising of the living standard of the working class. "In the interests of the National United Front, for crushing the invading fascism, for winning democratic and civic rights and freedoms, the Romanian people's independence"—the document showed—"the communists give up any slogan or action that might *separate* [italics in the original text] them from the other political parties and groupings, upholding the national liberation of the Romanian people. Yet, they do not give up their program, the promotion of their program and of their ultimate goals."[45] Those principles were summarized and thoroughly developed in the resolution of the CC of the RCP of January 1942, which emphasized again that the Party was ready to collaborate with any political party or personality "for the achievement of any claim in the Platform, the only criterion of that collaboration being one's attitude toward German fascism and its bandit-like war."[46] Therefore, the RCP promoted a policy of the stretched hand, asking and waiting for the collaboration of anyone ready to commit himself to the work of national salvation.

The Social-Democratic Party (SDP), banned too following the setting up of the royal dictatorship, unofficially continued, though obviously on a more restricted scale, its political activity. At the time undergoing reorganizations—which would last until mid-1943—the SDP could not envince its antifascist stand through a constructive political action. The serious matters facing the country were approached within some small groups (for reasons of conspiracy), and it was only after the reorganization of the party staff had ended that the socialists could act as a political factor in terms of sharing responsibilities.[47]

Among the forces opposing Antonescu's dictatorial regime, there also were two "historical parties": the National-Peasant Party (NPP), led by Iuliu Maniu, and the National-Liberal Party (NLP), presided over by C. I. C. (Dinu) Brătianu. Representing the town and rural bourgeoisie, the two parties, which shared the principles of parliamentary democracy and had backed Romania's alliances with the anti-revisionists powers—first of all with France and Great Britain—were in disagreement with Ion Antonescu's regime on matters of principle. During the dramatic circumstances in the autumn of 1940, both parties has assisted General Ion Antonescu in taking over the power, being convinced that, in the internal and international context, he represented—through the position he enjoyed at home and through his connections with Germany—the most suitable formula able to spare Romania serious political convulsions. The separation of the general from the Iron Guard had likewise been welcomed by the NPP members and the liberals. However, aware of the fact that, notwithstanding the victories of the Wehrmacht, the issue of the war was to be unfavorable to Germany, they were reticent about the steps made by General Ion Antonescu toward strengthening relations with the Axis. Romania's joining the Tripartite Pact was outrightly blamed on the two parties. In a joint petition. Ialiu Maniu and Dinu Brătianu straightforwardly asked Ion Antonescu: "For what reason and for whom have you signed the pact? What have you got in exchange for the pledge you have assumed that may throw us into a war in which we might have quite a lot to lose? Then, no matter how much influenced we are by Germany, can she compel us to defend countries that are enemies to us, and join a war against those who have been our friends?"[48] The leaders of the two parties would stress that Romania's joining the Tripartite Pact was the action of the government alone, and therefore it involved in no way the Romanian people, which had not been consulted and rejected the idea of coalescing with those who had contributed to the amputation of its national territory.

The position of the two parties was clearly formulated by Iuliu Maniu during a conversation he had with Prince Rohan, a German emissary, in July 1941: "As far as I am concerned, I cannot follow the politics of Germany. In the first place, I cannot side with Germany because I am convinced that she will lose the war. In the second place, I cannot side with her because I am not able to forget, not even for a moment, that Transylvania's joining the motherland was only possible thanks to England and France [. . .] All this I cannot forget, and it is this that guides my political conduct [. . .] I step in line with England and France."[49] Those views of the chief of the NPP were fully shared by the liberal leaders who, holding important offices in the industrial and banking fields, were alarmed at Romania's progressive integration into the German "economic space" (Wirtschaftsraum).

The attitude of the two parties toward the anti-Soviet war also derived from their opposition to the alliance with the Nazi Reich. "It is unacceptable for us"—Iuliu Maniu wrote to Ion Antonescu—"to act like aggressors toward Russia, today an ally of England, probably a winner [. . .] in botherhood-in-arms with Hungary and the Axis, which through an arbitrary act, sanctioned by no one, have torn off an important part of this country, encroaching upon our territory, and hurting our national pride and dignity."[50] The NPP and NLP declared for the re-establishment of the eastern frontier previous to 1940, but they opposed pushing military operations beyond that frontier, and, even more so, any annexation of Soviet territories, in which they saw a German attempt to turn Romania's attention away from the serious injustice done to her through the Vienna Diktat by offering her "territorial compensation" in the east for the loss of northern Transylvania. In a joint letter addressed to Ion Antonescu on August 12, 1943, the chiefs of the NPP and NLP reminded the former that "after the 1941 campaign had ended, when some of the commanding

officers had declared against the participation of our armies in the eastern
fighting, we again insisted on the need not to exhaust the stamina of the
Romanian army in battles far from this country's frontiers and from its
natural goals, and also on the need to keep its strength for the complete
achievement of our national claims, threatened and infringed upon by our
closest neighbors."[51] Winning back northern Transylvania was constantly
among the fundamental demands included in the petitions submitted by
the chiefs of the two parties to the head of the State. As a matter of fact,
Iuliu Maniu gave an outright wording to the demand-expressing a national
consensus—when he wrote to Ion Antonescu: "It is unacceptable that we
should assist those who are aiming at pushing us eastwards, thereby
removing us from the natural stronghold of Transylvania, the cradle of
the Romanian spirit, with arguments and motives [for doing it] [. . .]."[52]
The opposition of the "historical parties" actually limited to a "war of
petitions," with no efficiency; their disagreement on matters of domestic
and foreign policy would not be followed by any practical action, both
parties rejecting the offers for collaboration made by the communists in
1941-1943.

However, as the military situation of the Axis powers worsened, Antonescu's regime looked for a way out from the political and military crisis
that showed its symptoms ever more vigorously.

The soundings taken by Mihai Antonescu, as Romania's Foreign Minister, first in Sofia and then particularly in Rome, where he hoped to find
a more responsive and politically-minded interlocutor—in the person of
Mussolini—were followed by as feverish as sterile demarches made in
Madrid, Ankara, Bern and Stockholm with a view to getting in contact
and negotiating with the Anglo-Americans, reckoning on the differences
allegedly existing between the Soviet Union and her Western partners.[53]

In late 1943, secret negotiations were opened, upon the initiative of the
Soviet Union, between Alexandra Kollontai, her ambassador to Sweden,
assisted by V. Semionov, and Frederic Nanu, Romania's minister in that
country. During the negotiations, the Soviet side accepted the proposals
forwarded by Romania's representative to the effect that a fifteen day-
term would be granted for the withdrawal of the German troops from Romania—a free zone, with no foreign troops—while the Romanian government would benefit by facilities of payment as regarded the war compensations.[54] Relations between Hitler and Ion Antonescu had worsened under

the impact of the repeated military failures that highly strained Romanian-German military collaboration.

On receiving Barbu Ştirbey before his departure for Cairo, as secret emissary of the opposition, the marshal had admitted that he was "one hundred percent convinced that the Germans cannot win the war any longer," but that, by shortening the front on the Riga–the Carpathians–Nămoloasa-Focşani-Galaţi line, they might put up prolonged resistance.[55] Even a German interlocutor–such as C. Clodius, who used to have frequent talks with Ion Antonescu–had been able to notice: "the marshal is persuaded of the fact that the war cannot finally be won militarily, but has to be ended through a political compromise."[56] Until June 6, when the hope of an Anglo-American landing in the Balkans vanished, the marshal, convinced that England would not tolerate the crushing of Romania, had believed he would succeed in avoiding a dialogue with Moscow and in reaching an agreement with the Anglo-Americans. After that date, as rightfully observed by Frederic Nanu, the marshal contemplated the possibility of an armistice with the Soviet Union as long as it seemed a remote prospect, only to recoil as soon as military developments made of the armistice the topic of the day. The marshall's vacillations between March-August point to the confusion of the diplomacy of Antonescu's regime and to the failure of the latter's attempts to arouse the Western powers' joint interest in Romania's fate.

The month of March was highly strenuous for the marshall. On March 5 a great Soviet offensive began that would be subsequently known as the Uman-Botoşani operation; on March 26 the troops of the 2nd Ukrainian Front reached the Pruth river on a 85 km-long segment of its course; on March 29 they occupied the town of Chernowitz. In late March mid-April, the same troops had reached the Rădăuţi-Paşcani-Dubăsari line. It seemed as if nothing could check the advance of the Red Army in Romania's territory. In mid-March Ştirbey left for Cairo, but the Anglo-Americans' deliberate leaks within the "Bodyguard" plan alerted the Germans, making them turn a more attentive eye to the situation in Romania. The occupation of Hungary on March 19 created great anxiety in Bucharest, which turned into panic with Marshal Antonescu's summoning by Hitler. On March 22, on the eve of Marshal Antonescu's departure for Klessheim, Mihai Antonescu asked Alexandru Cretzianu, Romania's minister to Ankara, to find out on what assistance might the Romanian government count had it turned down fresh German demands regarding Romania's participation in the war.[56] "Romania is faced with either still closer collaboration with Germany or resistance to Germany without knowing upon what immediate assistance she can count and what she may expect in the future from a political standpoint."[57] General Maitland Wilson's answer was anything but reassuring; first, he asked Antonescu not to go to Hitler ("If he goes, this will be seen as a proof of Romania's intention to take all consequences") and then to order the cessation of Romanian resistance on the front and immediate surrender. When the message arrived the marshal had already left for Austria. Threats were coming from everywhere: from Germany, there was the possibility of Romania's being occupied the way Hungary had been; from the Anglo-Americans—Maitland Wilson's message; on the front—the Soviet offensive. After much hesitation, also noticed in the Wilhelmstrasse, the marshal decided to leave. Ion Gheorghe left us a description of the gloomy atmosphere in Salzburg on the marshal's arrival: his first questions were: "Well, what's this all about? What's in store for us? Do they intend to treat me the way they treated Horthy?"[58] Ion Antonescu's fears proved unjustified, but the alarm had not yet passed. Through the agency of Colonel Teodorescu, Romania's military attache to Ankara, the marshal asked the Anglo-Americans to answer the following questions: 1) What were the Allies' airborne or air forces he could count on had the Germans come up with new demands in written form? 2) Could the Allied governments assist him in his struggle against Germany through a declaration regarding Transylvania or at least through applying the Atlantic Charter in Romania's case? On informing the Western allies that he had kept the bulk of the army (fifteen divisions) west of the Brașov-Ploiești-Bucharest line, Ion Antonescu hinted at the possibility of a military conflict with the Germans: "If he decides to resist and is hard pressed by the Germans, he intends to withdraw into Yugoslavia and co-operate with the Allies and Tito. Airfields and high octane will be made available if the Allies send air support." Given the large number of troops the Germans had in the Ploiești area, he did not think that significant damages were possible.[59]

These declarations of Marshal Ion Antonescu are understandable against the military background in the spring of 1944. His referring to anti-German resistance aimed at wining Anglo-American support at a time when the Soviet offensive was in full swing (the same day, on March 29,

Charnowitz had fallen). Yet nothing indicated that the marshal, back from Klessheim, was making preparations for turning Romanian weapons against his recent host. As a matter of fact, the only concrete promise he made in the same message was his refusal to send any further divisions to the front besides the thirteen already there, under the pretext that his men lacked training and equipment, with the obvious aim of buying himself a respite ("breathing space"). The marshal's demarches did not yield the expected results. "I hesitate to be optimistic with the Romanians, parrticularly Antonescu's gang,"[60] a British official wired from Cairo.

British skepticism, however, was no unjustified. Once the front stabilized—on May 6 the Soviet troops had passed over to the defensive—Marshal Antonescu no longer showed the same eagerness to . . . withdraw to Yugoslavia! The measures taken by General Schörner restored his confidence in the German's capacity to hold the front. The negotiations in Cairo had reached a deadlock. The center of gravity of the negotiations with the Allies seemed to have been moved to Spain and Portugal and took on two aspects. In Lisbon, Mihai Antonescu was trying to set up a Romanian national committee with second-rate and even lower diplomatic officials (Antoniade, a former minister with the League of Nations, his son, trade secretary at the legation in Madrid, Scarlat Grigoriu, first secretary at the same legation—also suspected of being an agent of *Siguranța*, the Romanian political police department—Cădere and N. Dianu).[61] More important were the talks carried on at the American Embassy in Paris by a group of Romanian representatives—legation secretary Coste, first secretary Grigoriu and Barbu, Mihai Antonescu's principal secretary.[62] The relation between the Soviet-Romanian negotiations in Stockholm and the Romanian-American talks carried on in Madrid is conveyed in a telegram Mihai Antonescu sent to Barbu on June 30, the next day after a violent Anglo-American bombing of Bucharest: "I would like to know if I am supposed to understand that this is the assistance granted to us, namely that one wishes Romania'a anarchization before her rallying [. . .] Nanu has been again asked to give an answer [an allusion to the Soviet demarches in Stockholm—a.n.] which we have not, in the hope that with you things are pondered over in an earnest European-minded way," emphatically concluded the Romanian diplomat.

The worsening of the situation on the eastern front—the Soviet offensive in Byelorussia, followed by the collapse of the "Center" Army Group, the withdrawal of some large German units from the Romanian front, the German failures in France, the lack of efficiency of V1 bombings— again faced Marshal Antonescu with an impending disaster. The alarm signals given by the German ethnic group (Andreas Schmidt had left for Germany to warn Hitler personally about the danger of a switchover in Romania's policy) and by the German units, worried over the anti-Hitler frame of mind of the Romanian army and population, brought about Antonescu's summoning to the Führer's headquarters (Rastenburg). After his return from Wolfschantze, the marshal unequivocally told Turkey's representative: "if the English came to Romania he would be faithful to his decision to receive them as friends, but as long as Hitler was in his present state of fury and so long as there were 800,000 German soldiers in Romania it was neither possible nor in Romanian interests to undertake military operations against Germany."[64]

Feverish activities were resumed with a view to convincing the Anglo-Americans not to let Romania down. The marshal's primary emissaries were Colonel Teodorescu and Professor Contantin C. Giurescu. On August 12, the Foreign Office was informed that the two had got in touch with the American agents in Istanbul and said they were authorized by the marshal and Mihai Antonescu to declare, on behalf of the Romanian government, that the latter a) was ready to send a new embassy to Cairo, given the failure of the Ştirbey-Vişoianu team; b) the new representatives were authorized to make any concessions in the areas of oil, extractive a.o. industries that would be asked for by Great Britain and the Americans if the two countries pledged to pay the war compensations asked by the USSR; c) the Romanian troops were ready to cooperate with the Anglo-American forces had they been landed on the Black Sea coast or airdropped. In a talk with Colonel Teodorescu had with Commodore Wolfson and Lieutenant-Colonel Harris Burland, in addition to specifying that the surplus of cereals from the previous year as well as the two-million tons crop of that year were kept in store for the Allies, the former also conveyed the marshal's political views. He ruled out any understanding with the Soviet Union alone and rejected Molotov's declaration of April 2, 1944, on the grounds of making no distinction between the terms of an armistice and those of a peace treaty, or, because of the territorial cessions it claimed, of running counter to the Atlantic Charter.

"The Marshall would on no account turn against the forces of his allies the
Germans at the behest of Russia alone." He wanted the armistice to be
discussed with all three powers, while "at the Peace Conference Romania
would gladly abide by any terms provided they were imposed by the Western Powers in addition to Russia." The marshal—Colonel Teodorescu
showed—believed that Churchill wanted Romania to keep on resisting in
order not to let the Soviet Union penetrate into South-East Europe.[65] Ion
Antonescu—and he was not alone—could not imagine that, for attaining
that goal, Churchill had bartered with Stalin: Romania in exchange for
Greece. It should be said, however, on behalf of the British premier that
his public statements should have brought the representatives both of
the dictatorial regime and of the bourgeois opposition back to reality.
On August 2, speaking in the House of Commons, Churchill had said:
"It seems to me now that before anything else, the Romanians should
reach an understanding with Russia, whom they attacked so meanly and
at whose mercy they will be soon. Russia has offered generous terms to
Romania and has no doubt that they would be accepted with gratitude
by the Romanian people." That passage, which had aroused bitter be-
wilderment in Bucharest because it did not coincide with the image the
bourgeois parties had created of the British premier, was interpreted by
Antonescu—with a naïveté—as being meant for public consumption!"

On August 19, on the eve of the Soviet offensive in northern Moldavia, a violent discussion took place between Ion Antonescu and C. Clodius,
reproduced by General Hansen (whom Clodius informed the following
day) as follows: "Antonescu [. . .] had told him, in a state of extreme
agitation, that unless one German division at least, an armored division
to the extent such a thing was possible, were brought back without delay,
he would have to take, given the great—impending, in his opinion—Soviet
offensive, full liberty of action."[66]

On August 20, the Soviet offensive allowed no further time for discussion. The front broken, the army in confusion were signs of a catastrophe
approaching with great strides: Antonescu's regime was agonizing; it hoped
to prolong its existence by announcing its readiness to negotiate an armistice. Mihai Antonescu asked Turkey's representative in Bucharest: "Can
Turkey mediate between ourselves and the belligerent Anglo-American
armies? I have the consent of the Marshall, the King and heads of all the
opposition parties. I appeal for an answer within 24 hours from the British

and the USA Governments to the following points: 1) Will despatch a
Romanian delegation to Moscow for conclusion of an armistice; 2) Put
ourselves in contact with Russians and Anglo-Americans at the same time
to fix armistice conditions; 3) Discuss armistice conditions in Cairo with
Allies; 4) The President of the Council is desirous of knowing which of
these three alternatives would be preferred by the Anglo-Americans."[67]
Therefore, the formula was a resumption of a dialogue in which, it was
hoped, the Anglo-Americans would be the main partners. As on other occa-
sions, the Romanian vice-premier proved presumptuous. On August 21, he
self-confidently tol the director of the broadcasting station: "I will be the
signatory to the peace;"[68] what were the real chances of an armistice
singed by Antonescu's government?

On the evening of August 21, Ion Antonescu had informed Clodius
that he would commit all reserves to battle, but that, given the situation
on the front, he might assume "freedom of action." Clodius himself was
of the opinion that the marshal would resort to such freedoms only if
the front had collapsed.[69] The following day, a diplomatic courier left
for Stockholm with a mandate for the negotiation of the armistice, and
the marshal asked Gheorghe Brătianu for a written agreement of the opposition that he should start negotiating an armistice. From what Neagu
Djuvara—the courier—told Nanu, the marshal indicated that he was ready
"to leave the scene as soon as this would be necessary." The scenario he
contemplated was, therefore the following: resistance on the Focșani-
Nămoloasa-Galați line (on August 23, 11.20 a.m., Hans Freissner informed General Heinz Guderian that the front could be maintained along
that line), negotiations with the Soviet Union, securing Anglo-American
assistance and, possibly, the Germans' agreement. At any rate, he wanted
to let the Germans know about the steps he would take.

Antonescu's stand was seriously detrimental to Romania's interests:
he did not think of ceasing hostilities, but of continuing them in conjunction with the armistice negotiations (the government was to move
to the Hațeg area, and a line of resistance to be organized on the Olt
river); the whole country would thus be turned into a battlefield. On the
other hand, had the Germans been informed about those negotiations,
the Reich would have had time to prepare a response, which might have
led to the occupation of the country, repressive actions against the population, damages and, obviously the overriding of the national territory by
the war roller.

Marshal Antonescu's foreign policy revelas the deep crisis of his dictatorial regime. The political options he made over the last months of power
stand as proof to a complete deadlock: he would turn weapons against
Germany only under the circumstances of significant Anglo-American
assistance to or presence in Romania, in which he saw the guarantee of
the survival of the bourgeois regime. However, the division into spheres
of influence, a policy initiated by Churchill, considerably reduced the
interest of Great Britain and the USA (on October 6, 1944, it would be
quantified to 10%) in Romania. In the absence of Western support, Antonescu was determined to remain true to the Reich, under whose banner
he had come to power. The crisis of Antonescu's diplomacy was nothing
but the crisis of a regime, one of the characteristic symptoms of the
revolutionary situation preceding, as a prerequisite, the revolution proper.

The government crisis was paralleled by an intensification of the population's hostile frame and mind and resistance: the acts of protest and
sabotage considerably increased. The calls of the RCP to overthrow
Antonescu's regime and to turn the nation's weapons on Hitler's Germany
met with an even wider response. In June 1943, after the self-dissolving
of the Comintern—which opened great opportunities for the communists'
collaboration with other political forces—the Central Committee of the
RCP suggested the setting up of a National Fight Committee for the
liberation of the country, the task of which was to "muster up and rally
all national forces, irrespective of party membership and confession, in
the People's Anti-Hitler Patriotic Front,"[70] aiming at restoring national
independence and the democratic freedoms, and at taking Romania out
of the war waged against the anti-Hitler coalition.

On the basis of those proposals negotiations were carried on, following which the Anti-Hitler Patriotic Front was set up, joined by the RCP,
the Ploughmen's Front, the Patriots' Union, the MADOSZ, the Socialist-
Peasant Party and, temporarily, by the Social-Democratic Party (SDP).[71]

Though a success along the line of rallying the democratic forces, the
Anti-Hitler Patriotic Front confined itself to the left-wing political groupings, and even so not to all of them, given the withdrawal of the SDP.
Under the circumstances, the RCP intensified its political actions in two
directions: on the one hand, to secure the collaboration of the SDP to
the setting up of the United Workers' Front, meant to be the solid groundwork of any coalition of the anti-Hitler forces (the bourgeois parties

included), and on the other hand, to persuade the "historical" parties of the need to give up, in the country's interest, their anti-communist feelings and to cooperate with the left-wing forces.

As far as the first goal was concerned, in November 1943 the RCP resumed proposals for collaboration with the SDP, so that, through joint efforts, they should attain the second goal: by suggesting that the SDP should "immediately join the Anti-Hitler Patriotic Front, made up of the anti-Hitler forces in Romania, and the all-national Patriotic Committee of his front," the communists asked the social-democrats: "join us and the other anti-Hitler organizations in the struggle for winning over the leadership of the national-peasant and national-liberal parties, for the fighting platform we have recently proposed to the latter."[72]

While negotiations between the communists and the social-democrats were under way, the RCP also got in touch with King Michael I and his entourage. Already in 1940-1941 in the palace quarters there had been a certain reserve as to Ion Antonescu, which, as the crisis of the dictatorial regime deepened, had grown into a latent conflict. The royal quarters began to realize that, in order to outlive the war storm, the monarchy had to dissociate itself from the dictatorial regime. Laying stress on the need for the king to tak part in the change of the country's policy, a petition drawn up on May 15, 1944, clearly showed the consequences of the inactivity of the bourgeois opposition and the monarchy: "It is not only the Allies but Romanian public opinion itself that would be entitled to maintain, with good reason, that through its inactivity, the democratic opposition has proved to be powerless. The Romanian people will naturally tend to look for a new form of political and social organization."[73] Therefore, persuaded of the fact that its presence in the coalition of the anti-Hitler forces was required by its own interests, the monarchy opened talks with the RCP; getting a more comprehensive image of the political-military circumstances, of the fact that it was more threatened by its association—even if only formal—with Antonescu's regime, the monarchy showed responsiveness to the collaboration proposals of the RCP, thereby breaking away from the so-called "historical" parties. During the conversation he had with the British agent G. de Chastelain on the night of August 23-24, 1944, the king himself complained about the "lethargy" of those parties, pointing out that "whever the plans appeared to be maturing he was prevented from taking action by the objections raised by the Opposition."[74]

In the spring of 1944, the efforts of the RCP for achieving the unity of action of the working class scored a remarkable success: in mid-April, following negotiations carried on by delegates of the RCP with representatives of the SDP, the United Workers' Front was set up; on May 1, the latter issued a manifesto mapping out the goals of the struggle of all forces opposing the dictatorship and the Nazi Reich: "Immediate peace, the overthrow of Antonescu's regime, the setting up of a national government made up of representatives of all anti-Hitler forces in this country, the sabotaging and destruction of the German war machine. Lending assistance to the liberating Red Army. Alliance with the Soviet Union, Great Britain and the USA. For a free, democratic and independent Romania."[75] The setting up of the United Workers' Front actually meant the achievement of a first goal, set as early as 1941, namely to pave the way for the rallying of all anti-Hitler forces in Romania; that front had to be the backbone of the envisaged coalition. In the spring of 1944, the RCP appeared as the main factor able to rally those forces, a fact which —given the differences between the bourgeois parties (the NPP and NLP refused to collaborate with Gheorghe Tătărăscu's grouping and with the Radical Peasant Party led by Mihai Ralea)—was still late in becoming a reality. Persuaded of the fact that only a national front could save the country from catastrophe, on May 26, 1944, the RCP concluded an agreement with the two political formations "ostracized" by the "historical" parties, and with the grouping led by Dr. P. Topa—a remnant of the National-Democratic Party founded by Nicolae Iorga—thus setting up the National-Democratic Coalition.

As long as they hoped that an Anglo-American military presence would have been a guarantee of the preservation of the bourgeois structure of Romanian society, the NPP and NLP evinced reservations—if not hostility—to the prospects of collaborating with the communists. In order to sound out the intentions of the Western Allies, they sent Prince Barbu Știrbey and then Constantin Vișoianu as emissaries to Cairo to negotiate the conclusion of an armistice with the representatives of Great Britain, the USA and the USSR.[76] The hope of capitalizing on the possible disagreements between the three great allies quickly vanished, and so did that of an Anglo-American landing in the Balkans (similar hopes—actually illusions—were also harbored by Ion Antonescu). On May 25, George Duca (son of former Prime Minister Ion Gheorghe Duca), an official with the

Legation of Romania in Stockholm, opened secret negotiations, on behalf of the opposition, with Alexandra Kollontai and Vladimir Semionov (Frederic Nanu, Romania's minister to Sweden, was not informed of those negotiations). The endeavors of the Romanian negotiator to secure, for the opposition as well, the concessions granted by the Soviet government to Marshal Ion Antonescu did not yield the expected results. The only concrete outcome of the negotiations were the communicatin to Moscow of the plan for the overthrow of Antonescu's regime, a plan Alexandra Kollontai considered as "very interesting and also thoroughly worked out," and the agreement of the Soviet government—as late as on August 23, in the morning, though it had been asked since August 8—on the arrival of General Aldea for discussing the details of Romania's action.[77]

Inexorable political and military realities finally persuaded the NPP and NLP into accepting a dialogue with the communists within a Central Action Committee, made up of representatives of the RCP, SDP, NPP and NLP, which led to the setting up of the National Democratic Bloc on June 20, 1944, the platform of which was actually the common denominator of the most comprehensive coalition of political forces in the history of the Romanian people: "1. The conclusion, without delay, on the grounds of the suggestions made by the Allies, of an armistice with the United Nations (the Soviet Union, Great Britain and the United States of America), trying to secure the best possible terms for this country's interests. 2. Romania's leaving the Axis, the liberation of the country from German occupation, Romania's joining the United Nations and restoration of her national independence and soverignty. 3. To this end: the removal of the present dictatorial regime and its being replaced by a democratic constitutional regime to grant civic rights and freedoms to all the citizens of this country."[78]

Concommitantly with preparations for a political action, aiming at achieving a radical turning point through revolutionary means—an insurrection—in Romania's life, the RCP also carried on intense military preparations. Preoccupied with providing the resistance movement with a wide popular basis, the RCP set up patriotic fight formations intended to make up the organizational and military framework of the anti-fascist and anti-Hitler struggle. In conjunction with arranging armament depots for those formations that were to engage in battle at the right moment, the RCP organized partisan detachments in the Prahova Valley, Vrancea Mountains,

Semenic Mountains, in Bîrzava Valley, and so forth. A significant moment
of the military preparations for the insurrection was the meeting held on
the night of June 13-14, 1944, when the representatives of the RCP, the
army and the Royal Palace discussed and adopted the plan worked out by
the RCP for overthrowing Antonescu's regime and for turning Romania's
armament against Nazi Germany. While the democratic forces led by the
RCP declared, therefore, for a military and political action of an insurrectional nature, the NPP and NLP upheld, as late as August 23, the idea
of an armistice signed by Ion Antonescu himself. However, notwithstanding those disagreements, the Romanian political scene had under-
gone a fundamental change, noticed by the Germans themselves: "the
entire population has moved leftwards and the leadership of this opposition has been assumed by the Communist Party."[79]

On August 23, 1944, there were all objective conditions for turning
the revolutionary situation into an anti-fascist and anti-imperialist revolution for social and national liberation. Approaching the events that took
place four decades ago against that background, one is led to an indubit-
able conclusion: the historic act achieved on August 23, 1944 was not a
mere change of political regimes through a coup d'état, the latter itself
precipitated by a military crisis on the front—in short, a conjectural
phenomenon—but the acme of a long struggle for the restoration of
national independence and the democratic renovation of the country,
things which the entire Romanian people aspired after.

CHAPTER II

THE SUCCESSFUL COURSE OF THE REVOLUTION

On August 23, 1944, around 5 p.m. the Romanian people's insurrection broke out, the starting point of the anti-fascist and anti-imperialist revolution for the social and national liberation in Romania. Its political and military plan, drawn up with responsibility for the destinies of the Romanian people by the Romanian Communist Party was immediately and faultlessly carried into effect. Dictator Ion Antonescu and his close collaborators were arrested by a group of military in the Royal Palace, and then taken over by a patriotic fight unit organized by the Communist Party to be kept under surveillance under house arrest.

Tha was also the signal for carrying through the plans regarding the armed rising of the entire Romanian nation against the fascist occupiers.

"The achievements of the historic act of August 23, 1944"—Romania's President emphasized—"under the favorable international circumstances brought about by the victories of the Soviet and Allies' armies, by the fight of the peoples in Europe against German fascism ushered in a new era in the history of the people."[1]

A new government, made up under the political aegis of the National Democratic Bloc, with Army Corps General Constantin Sănătescu as Prime Minister, immediately took over the levers of State power. Starting at 10.20 p.m., the fundamental political documents outlining Romania's new political and military stand both at home and in the international

35

arena, worked out beforehand—the Proclamation to the country of the
head of the State, the Government's Proclamation and the Declaration of
the Central Committee of the Romanian Communist Party[2] —would be
broadcast and printed in mass editions.

At home, the overthrowing of Antonescu's dictatorship concomitantly
entailed the setting up of a democratic regime, the reintroduction of the
democratic Constitution of 1923, the granting of civic rights and freedoms.
Romania declared herself ready to conclude an armistice with the United
Nations and to start the fight for the liberation of the national territory
from Hitlerite and Horthyst occupation.

Under the new circumstances, deriving from Romania's changeover, an
essential role devolved upon the Romanian army, which had to break away
from the German troops, to turn weapons on the Wehrmacht, to defeat
the German troops in the interior of the country and those in the operational rear of the Moldavian front, and to prevent the Germans or their
allies from bringing in fresh troops from beyond the frontiers. The tremendous complexity of that operation is illustrated by the amount of
Wehrmacht forces and combat means deployed in the territory of Romania which the Romanian army were to face soon (see Table 1).

TABLE 1

The German Forces in Romania on August 23, 1944[3]

Deployment area of the German forces	Effectives
On the front	390,873
Halting places	128,682
Inland Romania	70,842
Air Force and Navy	36,248
Sum Total	626,635

The massive quantum of the German forces in Romania was substantially
enhanced by the way they were deployed inside the country (west of a
hypothetical line running between Cislău and Olteniţa, separating the

front and its immediate rear from the rest of the national territory), actually located in almost 800 points (commands, depots, repair shops, airports, military schools, telephone, watch and air surveillance stations, barracks, antiaircraft artillery batteries or battalions, and the like), spread over the entire national territory, all of them being potential enemy resistance points (see Table 2).

TABLE 2

German Forces Deployed in the Inland Area[4]

No.	Area	Effectives	Occupied point
1	Bucharest and the surrounding area	13,414	173
2	Prahova Valley	29,199	223
3	Brașov County	8,968	68
4	Vlașca County	4,509	31
5	Dolj County	3,307	42
6	Sibiu County	2,035	34
7	Arad County	1,809	24
8	Teleorman County	1,301	24
9	Mehedinți County	1,297	17
10	Caraș County	800	5
11	Other Areas	4,193	119
	Sum Total	70,832	770

To these forces one should add some 40,000 men from the paramilitary groups organized by the Nazis from among the German ethnic population.

Concomitantly, in Romania's close vicinity, i.e. in Bulgaria, Yugoslavia, the ceded northern part of Transylvania and in Hungary, there were considerable German effectives which made up a true hostile "belt" around Romania (see Table 3).

The carrying into effect of the national insurrection, a task which devolved upon the standing troops, patriotic fight formations organized beforehand by the Communist Party, on the fighting groups spontaneously

TABLE 3

German Forces in the Vicinity of Romania[5]

No.	Area	Effectives
1	The Balkans (Yugoslavia, Greece, Bulgaria)	25 (2 armored) divisions + 11 Bulgarian divisions
2	Hungary	2 German divisions + 16 Hungarian
3	Occupied northern Transylvania	divisions and 3 Hungarian brigades
	Sum Total	54 divisions and 3 brigades

set up by citizens, actually on the entire Romanian people,[6] required a fast turning of weapons, an effective front reversal, without the least hesitation. The Romanian army (see Table 4) had to stop fighting againt the Soviet forces unilaterally, ceasing fire, to disentangle itself from the German disposition and immediately to open hostilities with the Hitlerites. All these missions were to be carried through under the circumstances in which on the 654 km-long frontline at the southern wing of the Soviet-German front, strectching from the Eastern Carpathians to the mouth of the Dniester, one single huge battle was being carried on.[8] On August 20, 1944, two strategic groups—the 2nd and 3rd Ukrainian Fronts—totalling about 1.1 million military, had mounted a broad offensive, with the final goal of reaching the Maritime Danube and the Eastern Carpathians.[9]

On the evening of August 23, 1944, Division General Gheorghe Mihail took over his office as Chief of the General Staff appointed by the insurrectional government. The missions of the national armed forces were immediately mapped out in a strategic directive passed to all commands and large units. The fundamentals tasks outlined by the directive were the following: clearing the national territory of German troops and preventing them from setting up a defensive front on the peaks of the Romanian Carpathians; recovering the operational armies at the southern wing of the Soviet-German front; regrouping those forces and the interior

TABLE 4

The Deployment of the Romanian Armed Forces, August 23, 1944[7]

No.	Arm	On the front	Inland troops	Commands	Remarks
1	Army	20 divisions + 5 brigades	30 divisions* + 57 battalions**	23***	* 21 training divisions ** 5 detachments, 37 military schools, and 20 training centers *** 3 army and 20 army corps commands or their equivalent
2	Air Force	30 squadrons*	28 squadrons**	2 air corps***	* 249 aircraft ** 259 aircraft *** there were another 1,131 training aircraft in military bases, centers and schools
3	Antiaircraft Artillery	16 batteries*	168 batteries** + 14 searchlight batteries	4 brigades***	* 96 muzzles ** 1,268 muzzles and 168 searchlights *** 10 AAA regiments
3	Navy	34 ships 11 coast batteries	37 ships + 17 artillery batteries + 4 infantry battalions	3*	* The Navy Command, the Maritime and Fluvial Command, the Fluvial Forces Command

ones with a view to triggering off the offensive for the liberation of northern Transylvania; covering the offensive as well as the massing of Soviet troops. According to the directive, the Romanian army had to "cease fighting alongside the German troops in order to secure peace from the United Nations, and engage in combat alongside the forces of the latter for the liberation of northern Transylvania." During an earlier stage, the two Romanian armies on the front were to withdraw to the Focşani-Galaţi area with a view to preventing the Wehrmacht from retreating and getting reshuffled on the Focşani-Nămoloasa-Galaţi fortified line; subsequently, the Romanian armies were to reach the Ploieşti-Bucharest area, so that they should be able to go on to the offensive in Transylvania. The interior armed forces were assigned specific tasks. The Romanian First Army was to drive the enemy out of southern Transylvania and the Banat and to check the pouring of enemy troops from beyond the frontier into Romania, being also entrusted with the overall carrying through of the cover operations. In Oltenia, the same missions were assigned to I Army Corps. East of the Olt river, Muntenia was divided into two areas: the V Territorial Corps was assigned the northern part, while the II Territorial the southern one, both large units having to clear them of enemy troops. The Bucharest area was assigned to the Military Command of the Capital, whereas Dobrudja, the territory lying between the Danube and the Black Sea, to the II Army Corps. Specific missions were assigned the Air Force, Antiaircraft Artillery and the Navy. The insurrectional strategic directive specified that the military actions "had to be carried out with lightening speed," while the attitude toward the Soviet troops "should be friendly, though not servile."[10]

The carrying through of the tasks incumbent upon the national military establishment started at once. In Bucharest, in the Prahova Valley, in Oltenia and the Banat, in Dobrudja and eastern Muntenia, southern Transylvania and southern Crişana, actually the entire country, the insurrectional forces took up their positions and, self-denyingly supported by the entire population, immediately initiated hostilities against the Hitlerites. The Romanian commands and troops in the German disposition, at the southern wing of the eastern front, acted in a similar way, depending on the circumstances. A telling example of the conduct of the Romanian troops faced with such a situation starting the evening of August 23, 1944, was the way in which the "Bukovina" Frontier-Guard Detachment, interposed in the German positions, engaged in battle. No sooner had the political documents of the insurrectional government been broadcast than Colonel Nistor Teodorescu, the commander of the detachment, articulated his disposition in the Mălini-Valea Seacă zone, southern Bukovina, and opened the attack on the German 3rd Mountain Division. On August 23, at 11.15 p.m., Romanian subunits developed a surprise attack, managing to seriously upset the disposition of the large German unit during the night and the following day. Several years later, a former enemy fighter would recall the way in which, through suprise and determination, the Romanian frontier-guards had thrown the enemy troops into the area into a "hellish cauldron."[11] On August 25, Colonel Teodorescu contacted the commander of the Soviet L Corps and, once the cooperation forms were agreed upon, joint actions were undertaken, across the Bukovinian hills toward the northern passes of the Eastern Carpathians.[12]

The case of that detachment was not unique. In many places the broadcast news was the signal for rapidly passive on to offensive actions. On the evening of August 23, 1944, the Romanian commands and troops broke away from the German commands and unilaterally ceased hostilities with the Soviet army practically everywhere. The entire Romanian army, without the least defection or hesitation, showing no symptoms of disintegration or lack of discipline, promptly answered the requirements and orders of the political insurrectional forces, their turning weapons being rapidly effected, uttering taking the enemy by surprise.

In some areas, cooperation with the Soviet allies began immediately, in accordance with some understandings that had been reached by the commanders of the large units. Thus, on August 27, 1944, plenipotentiaries of the Soviet Seventh Army asked the commander of the Romanian 1st Armored Division the following questions: "1. Is the Romanian 1st Armored Division contemplating to take action alongside the Russian Army for conquering Romanian Transylvania? 2. In case of an affirmative answer, is Lieutenant-Colonel Gheorghe Matei [at the time commander of the division—a.n.] taking the risk that might crop up during the fight as a result of certain defections?" Both questions were answered in the affirmative, the Romanian commander showing, on the other hand: "We are very keen on enjoying the status of an allied partner and not a lower one, a fact that would enormously bear on the morale of the officers and of the troop. Due assurances have been given [. . .]."[13]

The blow dealt at the Wehrmacht by the Romanian army's "turning
weapons" was an extremely heavy one. Here are two accounts dated
August 23, 1944, belonging to the German strategic commands in Romania or in her immediate vicinity: on August 23, the file of orders of
the "Southern Ukraine" Aarmy Group operating at the southern wing of
the Soviet-German front, recorded: "By the evening, things have considerably turned for the worse as a result of Marshal Antonescu's overthrow and Romania's getting out of the war."[14] The same day, the file of
orders of the German Army Group "F", deployed in Yugoslavia, related:
"[. . .] Romania has broken up her alliance with Germany and has concluded an armistice with the Bolsheviks. In an appeal to the Romanian
people the king has stated that Romania would fight alongside the Allies
against the Vienna Award. This spells quite a predicament for the German
troops fighting in Romania."[15]

In Berlin, Hitler, who was immediately informed of the change that
had occurred in Romania, ordered the German forces there "to suppress
the putsch [the term used by the Nazis to designate the Romanian insurrection—a.n.], to take hold of the king and the palace camarilla, and to
set up a new government headed by a pro-German general in case Marshal
Antonescu has been lost."[16] The implementation of that directive from
Hitler came up against the unflinching determination of the Romanian
people and army to hold on, against the unconditional loyalty of all Romanian commanding officers to the new government, to the supreme
interests of the nation. As regards the last part of the above assertion, a
German document of August 30 recorded: "As for the time being, there
is no territorial basis for a Romanian national [pro-German—a.n.] government [an implicit acknowledgment of the Wehrmacht's having been
eliminated from the insurrectional area—a.n.], and as at present there
are no prominent Romanian statesmen or military in the area under our
control [north of the Romanian-Hungarian demarcation line imposed
through the fascist Diktat of Vienna—a.n.] who might assume the task
of forming such a government, there is no question of its being set up, at
least not for the time being."[17] How can the Romanian army's rapidly and
efficiently "turning of weapons" on August 23, 1944, be accounted for?

Without entering into details, one should point out the main determinants underlying that operation, a unique one in the records of Romanian
military history.

First and foremost comes the intense organizational and propaganda work carried on by the antifascist political forces headed by the Communist Party. That work aimed at enhancing the anti-Hitler and anti-dictatorial frame of mind of the Romanian army and at guiding it toward a clearly defined goal: the antifascist and anti-imperialist revolution for social and national liberation. In the platform the Romanian Communist Party suggested to all parties and political organizations in the country, to all Romanian patriots in June 1943 that the army was called upon to play an outstandingly important part in the struggle for the liberation of the country. The first point of the platform explicitly stated: "Saving the army through sending out fresh troops and bringing back the troops from the eastern front. Winning officers and soldiers over to the side of the People's Patriotic Front. Setting up groups of partisan patriots."[18] The action of the antifascist forces, mainly of the Communist Party, found a highly propitious basis in the ranks of the army. The command staff as well as the rank and file had become fully aware that, unless decisive political action was taken, a national disaster, which might have also entailed the destruction of the army, was impending. Likewise, it should be pointed out that, just like the entire people, the army too was actuated by the desire to liberate the country from foreign domination.[19]

Quite relevant, on the morning of August 23, 1944, Colonel Nicolae Dragomir, Chief of Staff of the Romanian Fourth Army, telephoned Army Corps General Constantin Sănătescu, the future Prime Minister of the insurrectional government, and told him that "our foremost purpose now is to move southwards as quickly as possible in order to occupy the F.N.B. [Focşani-Nămoloasa-Brăila—a.n.] fortified line, and not to make for the mountains and cover the territory occupied by the Hungarians [. . .] Everything is ready. In the approaching military and political circumstances you can rely on our absolute loyalty to the Romanian cause."[20] In short, the army in its entirety, from private to general, had become aware of the compelling need for a political action that should ensure the fulfillment of that desideratum. On the other hand, one should point out the strong Romanian military traditions, the fact that the army has always been on the side of the entire people in fighting foreign aggression throughout the centuries. Likewise, mention should be made of the fact that throughout the history of the Romanian nation the army has never been split by diverging interests that might have engendered a civilian war; it has always acted in full and unbroken unity.[21]

I. Victory in the Capital

The effectives of the Wehrmacht in Bucharest and its surroundings amounted to almost 14,000 men. In the city proper—in commands and special services, in hotels or private houses—there were some 8,000 military, of whom 2,000 officers and NCOs. As early as the night of August 23-24, a powerful German combat unit was organized north of the Capital, in the Băneasa-Otopeni area.

The General Staff would have some large units and units quickly shifted to Bucharest with the obvious purpose of ensuring a ratio of forces favorable to the Romanian side and of denying any opportunity of achieving surprise to the enemy, who could have brought and actually did bring in airborne reinforcements. Consequently, the Romanian troops fighting in the Bucharest area raised to the effectives of an army corps.

The Military Command of the Capital worked out the planning of the combat actions: annihilating the enemy forces inside the city; denying the Wehrmacht units penetration on the main approaches to the city; pinning down the German combat group north of the city; encircling and crushing the enemy group with the help of two Romanian detachments: one attacking south-northwards from inside the Capital, while the other one—an armored detachment—manuevering its flanks and rear east-west wards.

After the first hours of surprise and confusion, the enemy proceeded to arrange some strong resistence points in the Capital: at the seat of the German Military Mission of the Luftwaffe, lodged in a building on the left bank of the Dîmbovița river; at the Higher War School, an edifice located on an overlooking height in the south-western part of the city; at the "Ambassador" Hotel, at the German Legation, and other points. Outside the city, powerful groups and nuclei of Wehrmacht forces were organized and assigned the task of forcing a way into the city in order to get control over the latter. The most powerful group supplied, on the night of August 23-24, with fresh and battle-tried forces brought over from the Ploiești oil field area, and on August 25-26 with troops air transported from Yugoslavia or from the "South Ukraine" Army Group— was the one formed in the north, its center being in the Băneasa forest. Initially, the group was led by Lieutenant-General Alfred Gerstenberg, Chief of the German Military Mission of the Luftwaffe in Romania, and

later, starting August 26, by Lieutenant-General Reiner Stahel, who had
the reputation of a specialist in retaliating insurrectional movements (he
came directly from Warsaw, where he had conducted the suppression of
the Polish patriots' insurrection).

During the evening and night of August 23-24, the Romanian troops
took complete military control of the entire Capital. Once a firm military
control was secured, the German resistance points were successfully
eliminated.

Hard fighting took place at the seat of the German Military Mission of
the Luftwaffe, a building defended by large numbers of enemy troops
while the approaches to it were mined. On the morning of August 24, at
4.30 a.m., part of the Second Calarashi Regiment opened a lightening
attack, after having encircled the building. By 11.00 a.m., after a brisk
exchange of fire, the enemy was forced into surrendering. At about the
same hour, the German groups in the buildings located in the southern
part of the city had also been rendered neutral, either by being forced
to surrender or crushed in battle.

On August 24, in the afternoon, the Romanian military started to
storm the Higher War School, where considerable German troops had
been assembled, turning the building into a strong resistance point. That
enemy target was neutralized on August 25.

In other places, the Romanian troops succeeded in taking control of
the seats of the Wehrmacht commands in the Capital, of various services
of the Gestapo, ammunition depots, repair shops, and so forth, by blending the classic modes of fight—encirclement and attack—with forms of
psychological warfare—intimidation, ultimatum, challenge—and those of
the popular war, with the assistance of patriotic fight formations and other
groups spontaneously set up by the citizens. As a consequence, by the
afternoon of August 25, 42 German targets in the city had been neutralized. In the evening, Bucharest was generally cleared of any German
armed presence. The few small remaining resistance points were annihilated the following morning.

The citizens of the Capital actively participated in defeating the Nazi
enemy. There were many groups of armed patriots who disarmed the
enemy blocked up in some buildings, fighting alongside the regular troops
for getting rid of some German "islands" in the Rahova district, or taking
part in preventing the enemy troops from entering the city through the

Colentina barrier. The patriotic fight formations arrested stray German soldiers, ensured the guard of some targets and contributed to maintaining order and discipline in the Capital. The participation of the civilian population alongside the army in the fighting against the Hitlerite occupant was a form of the entire people's war, with such old and valuable traditions in the history of the Romanian people.

Concurrently with street fighting in Bucharest, the insurrectional forces successfully carried out some other tasks too. First, they thwarted the attempts of the German units to enter the city. Starting August 24, in the morning, the enemy troops tried to force their way into the Capital through the northern, south-western, western and southern barriers simultaneously. Most dangerous proved to be the action undertaken by the forces under General Gerstenberg's command at the northern approach to the city. On August 24, at 6.30 a.m., a German motorized column (some 20 trucks), preceeded by 6 aircraft cannon, tried to force its way into Bucharest. The firm resistance of the Romanian troops stalled the German attack.

The enemy was stopped at the other gates to the city, also. Faced with the circumstances, General Gerstenberg decided to resort to terrorist air attacks on the city, in order to undermine the morale of the insurrectional forces; at the same time, he asked his higher echelons for fresh troops to break through the Romanian defenses at the gates of Bucharest.

The Luftwaffe came in sight on August 24, at 10.35 a.m. The bombing was aimed primarily at the center of the city, the Royal Palace and its vicinity with most of the civilian establishments and military commands, and was carried out both by day and by night (August 24, 25 and 26); among the targets of the Luftwaffe pilots there were also the positions held by the Romanian troops in the northern part of the city. The damaging air attacks resulted in great devastation in the Capital. The National Theater, the Romanian Athenaeum, the Romanian Academy museums and cultural establishments, hospitals, industrial enterprises, a few barracks, were destroyed or damaged. The effects of the air bombings were limited to a considerable extent by the efficient counteraction of the Romanian antiaircraft artillery and fighters. For instance, on August 25, the 3rd AA Brigade rendered four enemy aircraft unserviceable on the Otopeni airfield. Moreover, in various other places they shot down three aircraft of the "Giant" type, carrying one hundred task troops each, brought in from Yugoslavia to reinforce the German troops in the Băneasa area. Likewise, during those days, the Romanian 9th Fighter Group, its base on the Popeşti-Leordeni airfield (west of Bucharest), shot down nine enemy bombers.

The smashing of the German combat group north of the Capital began on the very morning of August 24, with its encircling.

Starting August 26, when the enemy in the northern surroundings of the Capital was being hit from several different directions by the Romanian troops, the decisive attack was mounted. The disposition of the Wehrmacht troops had been seriously shattered as a result of the continuous fire of the Romanian soldiers, and, on the morning of August 26, of the heavy bombing carried out by American aircraft which had taken off from airfields in southern Italy. The defense perimeter of the Wehrmacht troops was drastically narrowed. The enemy, massed in the Băneasa forest, was actually surrounded by a true belt of Romanian fire.

During the night of August 27-28, the enemy remnants broke off combat and retreated northwards, under cover of night, in a desperate attempt to escape. The effectives of the German combat group had seen a considerable decrease falling down to some 1,900 men. A Romanian armored group immediately set out in pursuit of the enemy. The bulk of the enemy group was disarmed at Gherghiţa (25 km southeast of Ploieşti) by units of the VI Army Corps (the Fourth Army), which had marched all the way down from the front in north-eastern Romania, in order to get massed in the Bucharest-Ploieşti area, in keeping with the strategic Directive of the General Staff of August 23.

The battle of Bucharest, the brain of the revolution, was fully won by the Romanian military and popular forces.

On August 30, 1944, the first columns of Soviet troops entered the liberated Capital, warmly welcomed by its inhabitants. After having delivered the battle of Jassy-Kishinev and after passing without significant encounter the Focşani-Nămoloasa-Galaţi fortified line on August 27, 1944, the forces of the Red Army crossed the territory of eastern Muntenia, which had already been cleared of German military presence through the fight of the Romanian troops, substantially assisted by the civilian population (it was only in the Ploieşti area that the Soviet troops had small-scale clashes with remnants of German units).

II. The Battle for Oil

All oil extractive and processing facilities were located in the Prahova
Valley and partly also in the Dîmboviţa county. Ploieşti, Cîmpina, Brazi,
Moreni and the adjoining localities were the main centers of Romania's
most important industry at the time. Attributed vital importance for the
development of the war by the Germans, the oil-field in the Prahova
Valley was crammed with Wehrmacht troops. In addition to the 29,000
German troops there, various other military formations retreating from
the Moldavian front were brought over to that area.[22] The most powerful
Wehrmacht force in the area was the 5th AAA Division, under the command of Major-General Kuderna, which boasted 30 heavy batteries, 18
medium and light batteries and 5 searchlight batteries. Apart from Kuderna's division, also deployed in the area were a passive defense brigade,
construction and repair battalions, auxiliary troops, two fighter groups
(on the Strejnic and Tîrgşor airfields), and so on.

The command of the Romanian V Territorial Corps decided to proceed first to the disentangling of the Romanian troops from the enemy
disposition, and then to have the "islands" of German resistance in various
points of its operational area isolated and crushed. Particular importance
was attached to having a safe Ploieşti-Braşov communication line, by
which the Wehrmacht troops might have poured beyond the mountains,
in Transylvania, through the Predeal pass. In the oil-field area, the Romanian Command had over 23,000 men, effectives which were to be considerably increased through bringing in Romanian troops from elsewhere
in the country.

On August 24-25, the enemy resistance points in the Azuga and Buşteni
areas were neutralized, with over 300 German military taken prisoner, and
then those in the area around the Breaza, Posada, Scăieni, Bucşani, Zam-
fira, Plopeni a.o. communes, with more than 1,000 enemy prisoners and
several train loaded with tanks and various war materiel.

On August 24-25, under Romanian pressure and fire, lorried German
troops started to retreat across the Carpathians. Some of the these troops
would be annihilated as they fled.

In order to check their withdrawal, the Romanian command had the
railway heading through the Prahova Valley and the Predeal pass beyond
the mountains dismantled and blocked up in several places. Likewise, units

of the 1st Mountain Division barred the approaches to the pass. As a consequence, on August 26 the division made 800 German prisoners and captured 150 transport vehicles, while at Comarnic, as a result of the dismantled railway, Romanian troops, supported by the local population, managed to pin down and capture over 1,500 enemy officers and troops.

On August 26, Romanian units brought over from the north-eastern part of the country and other areas started pouring into the Ploieşti-Prahova Valley zone, bringing about, in only two days, a substantial change in the ratio of forces in favor of the Romanian side.

During the same day, the Romanian troops intensified their attacks on those still existing enemy points of resistance. In some places, enemy units putting up extermely strong resistance were encircled and isolated or attacked with reinforced troops.

A bloody clash took place in the Moreni area (some 30 km west of Ploieşti), on August 25. The hedgehop enemy disposition there was crushed by the insurrectional forces, who took a great number of prisoners.

An important episode was the liquidation of the enemy forces in the Cîmpina area and west of Ploieşti. Fierce encounters occurred south of Cîmpina, in the Slobozia flat area, with a German motorized column made up of over 60 vehicles. The German antiaircraft artillery batteries on the heights overlooking the Bucharest-Braşov national highway opened fire. On August 26, in the afternoon, the enemy was forced into surrendering through a lightening attack carried out by subunits of the Romanian 10th Roshiori Regiment and artillery men equipped with portable arms, assisted by the local population. Concomitantly, many enemy formations in the surrounding area of Cimpina were also crushed.

West of Ploieşti, the Germans had fighting groups around the Tîrgşorul Nou airfield, in the Tîrgşorul Vechi and Crîngul lui Bot forests and at Strejnic. From there, over August 24-27 they mounted several attacks on Ploieşti which were repelled, the enemy being utterly annihilated during the following two days.

On August 28, 1944, the two counties in which the oil fields lay were, for the most part, freed of any German military presence. That day, all the German resistance points in the localities south of Ploieşti (firmly held by the Romanian troops) were smashed and 1,300 German military were made prisoners. In addition, the bulk of the Romanian Fourth Army (which up to August 23, 1944 had fought on the German front in north-eastern Romania) and units of the Romanian Mechanized Corps (which were pouring from Bucharest on several approaches to Ploieşti and Cîmpina, sweeping away all enemey remnants on their advance route) were brought over to that area. As a result of it, by August 28, 1944, some 40,000 Romanian military had added to the V Territorial Corps. The German forces in the oil-field area had been massed in a camp located in the Păuleşti forest, 12 km north of Ploieşti. They had articulated strong defensive dispositions there, being provided with armor and air support.

The Păuleşti Lagerwald was attacked by three tactical groups set up by the command of the V Territorial Corps. The attack, triggered off from three directions, was opened on the morning of August 30, 1944. The Romanian assauting waves were faced with desperate German resistance. Lieutenant Jakab, a German officer on the staff of the Training School of the German Eighth Army, whose retreating from the front had been contained by the Command of the 5th AAA Division on August 24 and who had joined the Păuleşti disposition with all his men, would later recall that uncommonly violent clash. "Around 1.00 p.m. [August 30–a.n.] and then at 6.00 p.m. we were thrown two kilometers back from our positions," the German officer reported on October 4, 1944. "It was onlythrough an immediate counterattack that we managed to reclaim a new line."[23]

However, during the following night, the German fight group at Păuleşi assumed the offensive. Some enemy columns forced a breaking out of the encirclement northwards, but were soon scattered by the Romanian troops. The bulk of the Păuleşti group, transported in some 130 lories, forced a breakthough on August 31, at dawn, and headed, in two-column formation, for the mountains. The Romanian troops quickly established positions in the Slănic area, behind which the German column could have reached the Bratocea pass and get into Transylvania. The cadets of the Reserve Infantry Officers School No. 1 took up positions at the southern end of the Slănic town.

The fighting started at 11.00 a.m.; the position favoring the defense, the heroism and bravery of the cadet-officers surpassed the indisputable superiority of the enemy forces. The enemy was compelled into suing for a ceasefire, asking through messengers, to be allowed free passage across the mountains into Transylvania. The request was turned down by the school commander and, seeing no way out of that predicament, the enemy was forced into surrendering. The second German column, closely pursued by Romanian troops, was caught up and taken prisoners near the town of Vălenii de Munte.

In this way, the "battle for oil" delivered in Prahova county throughout the eight days of the insurrection ended in the victory of the Romanian army. The brave troops of the Romanian army were joined in action by patriotic fight formations made up of oil-industry workers. They enthusiastically and efficiently backed the actions of the regular troops at Tîrgşor, Moreni, Mărgineanca, and around Cîmpina. Here is a telling example of the role played by the patriotic fight formations in the oilfield area: on the night of August 24-25, about 30 armed workers, supported by peasants and by the military subunits deployed in the area, initiated and developed an attack on the enemy troops massed around the Tîrgovişte airport; during the ensuing days, the enemy was considerably prevented from using the airport as a result of that daring and efficient action, a typical one as far as the insurrectional fights in Romania were concerned.

During the final stage of the battle in the Prahova Valley (August 29-31) advanced elements of some Soviet armored units also joined the action. On the afternoon of August 29, Soviet armored vehilces and units of the Romanian 18th Infantry Division, the latter just withdrawn from the Moldavian front, advanced from east of Ploieşti and entered the town. During the following days, the Soviets, closely cooperating with the Romanian forces, contributed to the final smashing of the enemy "Lagerwald" at Păuleşti.

The Wehrmacht's losing the Prahova oil field area meant a heavy blow dealt at Hitler's war machine. As far as the fuel supplies were concerned, the German war economy was now left only the poor oil-fields of Hungary and Austria, and the synthetic oil plants, the latter being the target of repeated Anglo-American bombings. In an interview granted to the New York broadcasting station on May 4, 1945, German Field Marshal Gerd von Rundstedt stated that one of the major causes leading to the collapse of Hitler's Reich was "the loss of raw materials, especially of those in Romania" (other causes being the inferiority of the German air force, the disorganization of the Wehrmacht's logistic system and the massive bombing of the industrial regions of Germany).[24]

III. Mopping Up Other Areas in the Country

In Dobrudja. The troops of the II Army Corps and the Romanian Navy forces had to face powerful Wehrmacht effectives. Suffice it to say that the German naval forces—the Admiral Schwartzes Meer Command—amounted to 80 combat ships—of which four were submarines. These were rounded off by strong coast artillery batteries and ground troops. The German "Tirpitz" battery on the coast kept under control with its 280 mm-caliber guns a great part of the maritime area (up to 40 kms. from the shore) as well as the habor and city of Constanța.

The operations carried out by the Romanian troops in Dobrudja spanned two stages. First, till August 25, the Romanian navy, river and ground forces fought against the stationary German units and subunits in that part of Romania. After that date, the effort was directed against the German columns retreating from the German-Soviet front north of the maritime Danube, and against the German ships on the Danube. Also attacked were the stationary German troops in the towns of Tulcea, Hîrșova, Cernavodă, Medgidia and in several other localities. The German forces there were defeated and, for the most part, taken prisoners. The towns and villages on the shore were simultaneously cleared of any enemy units. Kept under permanent surveillance by the insurrectional forces, lacking fuel as a result of the supplies cut off from the Prahova Valley—under Romanian control—and unable to go upstream on the Danube because of strong Romanian barrages, the German fleet on the Black Sea was foced into scuttling. After having annihilated the stationary German troops in Dobrudja, the Romanian II Army Corps was ordered to move to Bucharest, leaving behind the maritime and river forces, the coast units and a training-infantry division. While carrying through the order (August 26-28), the Romanian troops came across retreating German columns. In the vicinity of Tortoman, Cernovodă, Gherghina, Medgidia and in other places the enemy columns were intercepted and smashed or captured after heavy fighting. Thus, the entire area of Romanian Dobrudja was liberated.

As an outcome of the operations carried out in that area, the Romanian troops made some 12,000 German prisoners, a general included. Actually, thanks to the Romanian victory, the basin of the Black Sea was cleared of any German troops. The maritime habor facilities, the Romanian fleet in its entirety could be quickly and efficiently employed to back the anti-Hitler coalition.

In the Bărăgan Plain. During the days of the insurrection, eastern Muntenia, the fertile Bărăgan Plain, was turned into a true "boiling cauldron." The sui-generis nature of the battles waged there lay, on the one hand, in the fact that the Romanian garrisons had to face, besides the stationary German troops, many enemy columns (provided with armored vehicles) retreating from the eastern front. On the other hand, on the main communications in that vast flat area German and Romanian troops would frequently run into each other, the former being on the retreat, while the latter moving toward the ordered build-up area. Consequently, the encounter engagements—short but extremely violent—were far more frequent than elsewhere.

The Romanian troops gained control over the railways and roads in the area from the very outset, denying the enemy, through stopping battles, the possiblity to move, and diminishing their combat capacity or capturing them.

Grim battles took place in a series of villages and towns as part of the plan regarding the development of military actions. For instance, at Stîlpu the 5th Infantry Division, on the move, violently hit an enemy motorized column trying to make headway from the south to Buzău. After short but fierce fighting, the German column was scattered. At Albeşti, Romanian units grimly fought a German armored column. At Slobozia, a German column was partly crushed, while 200 military were taken prisoners; at Urziceni some 1,000 enemy soldiers were disarmed and confined in camps; at Ţăndărei, after a few hours' fighting, over 300 military were captured, while at Feteşti—almost 400; at Bucu, 114 Germans were killed and almost 400 were taken prisoners in an ambush; some 500 Germans were disarmed at Ciocăneşti and a few other hundreds at Pogoaneie and Brădeanu.

The enemy forces the Romanians had to face in the Bărăgan Plain were, as a rule, made up of motorized armored columns. The latter would be permanently chased, attacked and split by the Romanian troops. The German forces which, that notwithstanding, succeeded in reaching the Danube were smashed or captured in the towns of Olteniţa and Călăraşi. A German document drawn up by a staff officer of the powerful enemy group a few weeks later speaks of its zig-zaging across the Bărăgan Plain, under the continuous surveillance of the Romanian troops. It was the case of the fight group under the command of Lieutenant-Colonel Görres, made up of some 1,400 military, 140 officers included, cadets of the Reserve Officer School of the German Sixth Army (the battalion commanders' reserve of the Sixth Army, batches of company and battalion commanders, numbers of officers trained for special arms, and the like). After a brief encounter with the Soviet troops at the eastern end of Reni (north of the maritime Danube), the Gorres fight group retreated across the Danube and took hold of the Şendreni (a village on the Siret river) bridgehead. Powerfully attacked by the Soviet forces, it abandoned the bridgehead and retreated toward Baldovineşti (4 km northeast of Brăila), wherefrom it continued its retreat to Cilibia (20 km south-east of Buzău); on August 30, the German column, split into battalions, was seriously harassed by the Romanian troops. On August 31, a Romanian lieutenant-colonel demanded the "disarming of the fight group," promising that "all soldiers will be transported by a special train from Călăraşi to the Romanian-Bulgarian frontier." Two small fight groups surrendered. "The Romanians"—the officer who managed to escape further reports— "insistently demanded the disarming of the fight group [. . .] At Olteniţa there are powerful Romanian forces equipped with heavy artillery; these Romanian troops evince hostility and have taken up positions at the outskirts of the town."[25] Faced with a predicament, part of the group surrendered, while the rest found escape across the Danube, into Bulgaria.

A similar fate was shared by parts of the German 13th Panzer, 10th Panzer-Grenadier and 153rd Field Training Divisions. Substantial effectives of those divisions, who had escaped being crushed on the Soviet-German front, were to be taken prisoner by the Romanians.

In that area too the popular elements made a notable contribution to the insurrectional fighting. A great number of citizens heroically joined the fighting carried on by Romanian regular units against enemy mechanized columns. The Special Bulletin of the Gendarmerie General Inspectorate, issued on August 29, 1944, reported: "At Slobozia the population fought a German column,"[26] the enemy combat strength being detailed in another document of that time: "some 2,000 German military are moving to Călăraşi and are now fighting against the population of the Slobozia-Ialomiţa communes."[27]

Along the Danube. The encounters carried on along the Danube had a specific nature. First, because they were joined in by all arms: infantry, artillery, air force, pontoneer and naval troops, etc. Second, because they were waged on water, on land and in the air. Last but not least, because in the Danube harbors the Romanian insurrectional forces fought against the local German garrisons, against ships retreating upstream, and against columns which, withdrawn from the German-Soviet front and harassed by the Romanian troops all along the way, reached the Danube with heavy casualties and tried to cross the river and get on the Bulgarian shore.

At Tulcea, for instance, the main targets were the German subunits in the garrison and their military depots. Most of the German fighters were disarmed and taken prisoners by the Romanian troops of the local command. On the night of August 24, the rather few German troops in Galați, attacked by a Romanian subunit and by forces of the local gendarmerie, blew up their own depots and, after damaging a number of buildings, made a hasty retreat to Buzău, leaving a completely free town behind. Setting out from Brăila harbor, the Romanian monitors would chase and intercept the German ships retreating upstream along the Danube, sinking many of them or forcing them into unconditional surrender. In the Brăila-Șocariciu Danube sector alone the Romanian monitors captured 108 enemy ships. At Hîrșova, Romanian subunits attacked the German troops in the town, whom they chased away, or took prisoner, also capturing a few enemy ships.

At the 3 km-long railway bridge over the Danube at Cernavodă the fighting lasted several days on end. First, the German garrison was encircled by the 2nd Frontier Guard Regiment in the town; following a resolute Romanian ultimatum, the German soldiers surrendered; yet, heavy fighting would continue on the Danube between German ships and the Romanian artillery, infantry and ship crews which defended the bridge and the harbor. Simultaneously, the Romanian troops crushed a German column retreating on land.

Bloody clashes on water and land would take place in the harbortowns of Giurgiu, Zimnicea, Turnu Măgurele, Corabia, Calafat, and so forth; the Romanian troops came out victorious everywhere, completely sweeping away the German forces. In four of the abovementioned towns alone the Romanian troops took over 2,350 German prisoners and captured or sank 48 enemy ships. The enemy forces which had chosen the

Danube course as a retreat route were bombed or machine-gunned by squadrons of the Romanian air forces.

During the insurrection, of particular importance proved to be the Iron Gates area of the Danube. The plans of the Wehrmacht High Command considered control over that part of the Danube as indispensible to the successful stabilization of a defensive front on the peaks of the Carpathians, further extended to the Balkans, as a bulwark for prolonged resistance against any enemy (the OKW strategic directive of August 28, 1944, saw it as a junction point between the "South Ukraine" Army Group in Romania and the responsible command in the Balkans—the "South-East" Theater of operations). The Iron Gates-Cazane area was assigned, according to the strategic directive of the Romanian General Staff, to the Romanian VII Territorial Corps. There, units of the 19th Infantry and 5th Motorized Divisions—the sedentary part—were committed to action.

During the first days of the insurrection, the fights against the enemy in that perimeter assumed the so frequent forms of striking, splitting, and capturing the German motorized columns, which attempted to squeeze out beyond the frontiers or to reach areas where there were more powerful fight groups. On the evening of August 25, a German motorized column (some 1,600 men and 10 artillery muzzles) drew near Drobeta-Turnu Severin coming from Craiova. As challenges to surrender were left unanswered, an attack was opened to crush the enemy.

After almost half a day's fighting, the enemy troops, hit from several sides, were forced into surrendering, with the result of some 900 German military being taken prisoner. On August 27, the town of Drobeta-Turnu Severin was again threatened by a German military detachment of about 1,000 men. After a grim clash, the detachment was defeated and partially annihilated, with further prisoners being taken. Romanian sailors of the "Upper Danube" Detachment also took part in the actions carried on against the two German columns. Using the artillery aboard ships, they successfully supported the attack, hitting the positions held by the enemy and his remnants who tried to escape by running. Likewise, workers from the shipyards in the town, organized in a patriotic fight unit, took an active part in the hostilities.

Most violent clashes occurred in the town of Orşova and at Gura Văii. At Orşova, the fighting went on for two days, being actually carried on from house to house, and the Hitlerites were finally defeated. An attempt to land German troops brought over from the opposite bank of the Danube at Moldova Veche (also aiming at taking hold of the Iron Gates) was thwarted by the Romanian units there. By August 31, the entire abovementioned Danubian sector and the adjoining territory up to the Carpathians had been brought under the control of the Romanian troops. Consequently, the Hitlerite troops failed to "lock up" the Iron Gates.

In the Banat. One of the most violent battles in that part of the country was delivered in the area of the Arad city, an important support point for getting control over the valley of the Mureș river. During the first days of the insurrection, the enemy set up a powerful fight unit around the airport in the vicinity of the city, bringing over fresh lorried troops (over 100 vehicles) from beyond the frontier. The Romanian VII Territorial Corps articulated a defensive disposition there, by quickly shifting infantry units to the area. The attack was opened on August 27, after intense artillery preparations. Despite the intervention of German Stukas (the enemy had some 50 fighters in the area), the Romanian troops repelled the enemy in the north-western part of the city step-by-step, throwing him beyond the frontier by the end of August 28. The strong, well-trained enemy troops—about 2,700 men, of whom 2,000 had arrived later—were faced by Romanian units made up of recruits who had barely completed their group training term (that is two and a half months' training). Although benefitting by considerable advantages in terms of battlefield configuration and equipment, the enemy forces, which were opposed by 2,789 Romanian fighters, were nevertheless defeated.

Actions aimed at defeating and chasing away the German troops in the Banat were also carried on—besides those at Orșova and Moldova Veche—at Lugoj, Caransebeș, Reșița, Anina, Oravița and in other places, where the Romanian troops took almost 900 German prisoners and captured a great deal of war materiel. At Șofronea, the documents recorded a new episode testifying the the entire people's war nature of the insurrection. With the assistance of railway workers, who faultlessly cooperated with the regular forces, an important German train loaded with troops and war materiel was captured.

In southern Transylvania. The Romanian troops belonging to the First Army, the VI Territorial Corps and the Mountain Corps were assigned a threefold mission· to check the penetration of enemy forces from beyond the Romanian-Hungarian demarcation line in the Transylvanian Plateau, to mop up the assigned territory, to crush stray Wehrmacht groups that had escaped from the southern part of the country across the mountains. Likewise, in the event of an enemy offensive operation carried out with superior forces, they had to block the passes in the Southern Carpathians, holding bridgeheads north of the mountains.

The action undertaken by the Mountain Corps in the Brașov area starting August 23, 1944, is a typical example of faultless implementation of an assigned task. All German targets were blocked, while connections among them were cut off; the military guards at the Romanian targets, particularly those at the factories in the area or at the broadcasting station at Bod, were reinforced. Then, all nuclei of enemy resistance in the city of Brașov, at Prejmer, Ghimbav, Bod were crushed, an operation which was completed by August 25.

During the following stage, the units of the Mountain Corps arrested the advance of the enemy columns westward of the Buzău pass (through which some of them tried to retreat from the German-Soviet front and cross the mountains toward western Romania) and annihilated enemy penetrations in great force from noth of the Romanian-Hungarian demarcation line in the Transylvanian Plateau (at Araci, Doboli, Bod). Finally, toward the end of the insurrection, troops of the Mountain Corps launched an attack in the Ormeniș-Aita Seacă direction in order to clear a block of the Brașov-Sighișoara railway track. That operation, resolutely carried through on August 30, 1944, the very day the hateful Vienna Diktat had been imposed four years before, also entailed the liberation of a strip of land from the territory occupied by the Horthysts. The news of that victory, which also marked the beginning of the struggle for completing the liberation of the national territory, was passed on without delay to the General Staff by the commander of the Mountain Corps: "Today, August 30, 1944, four years since the first towns in northern Transylvania were ceded, the border was crossed in the Brașov area and the first target was carried through fighting."[28]

In the central and western parts of Transylvania, the insurrectional actions devolved on the VI Territorial Corps. There, local small-scale enemy attacks were repelled at various points of the demarcation line or near the frontier, while reconnaissance parties were sent over to get rid of the German transmission and listening stations, and of isolated subunits. German columns retreating to north-western Romania, at the time under Horthyst Hungary's occupation, were intercepted and attacked. As part of those actions, the Romanian troops crushed a section of a German tank regiment in the vicinity of Aiud. Several German formations were intercepted and disarmed by Romanian soldiers near Vinţu de Jos. At Alba-Iulia and Sebeş-Alba, subunits from four Romanian regiments attacked the columns of three German regiments, which they scattered capturing 1,300 German soldiers and officers. By August 30, the entire area assigned to the VI Territorial Corps had been completely cleared of German troops, the Romanian forces coming out victorious everywhere.

Withdrawal through fighting. A major component of the insurrectional operation carried out by the Romanian army was the fallback of the Third and Fourth Armies from the front toward the Romanian interior. The first stage of the fallback was carried out between August 23-25, 1944, when Romanian large units and units belonging to the two great armies were ordered to get reshuffled in an area stretching between Focşani and Galaţi. The aim to be attained during that stage was the setting up of a defense alignment running from the springs of the Putna river (the curvature of the Carpathians) to the Focşani-Nămoloasa-Galaţi fortified line, and further on to the maritime Danube that should check the pouring of German troops from Moldavia into Muntenia, and prevent the possible organization by the latter of a resistance front in the way of the advancing Soviet troops.

The Romanian soldiers carried out the first stage tasks in a rapid tempo, avoiding as much as possible meeting the German troops retreating in the same direction. Troop fractions that did not manage to carry out the ordered fallback engaged in combat with the interposing German units, such as the detachment under the command of Colonel Nistor Teodorescu. A salient characteristic of that operation was that the greatest part of the two Romanian armies disentangled from the German front succeeded in reaching the ordered regrouping areas. On August 25-26, part of the Romanian large units were caught up by Soviet motorized columns. The Romanian commanding officer got in touch with the Soviet commanders, suggesting that they should jointly act against the Wehrmacht. Cooperation with some Romanian units was accepted. Such was the case of the 7th Heavy Artillery Regiment, of Lieutenant-Colonel Gh. Matei's Detachment from the 1st Armored Division, of the 6th Artillery

Brigade from the 4th Infantry Division, and of the 103rd and 104th Mountain Brigades, which cooperated with the Soviet Seventh Guard Army in the forthcoming battles for crossing the Eastern Carpathians through the Trotuş pass. On August 27, 1944, other large Romanian units on the front in Moldavia were ordered to concentrate south-west of Roman in order to get reorganized "with a view to cooperating with the Soviet army, more precisely with the command of the Seventh Guard Army."[29]

On the evening of August 25, orders were issued for the second stage of the withdrawal, with the Red Army's being expected to cross the Focşani-Nămoloasa-Brăila line during the ensuing days. The General Staff ordered that troops be rapidly shifted to the Ploieşti-Bucureşti area, where they had to be massed by August 29 with a view to mounting the overall offensive in north-western Romania.

During that stage, while withdrawing to the ordered areas on routes in the eastern Romanian plain, large units and units of the Third and Fourth Armies frequently had encounter clashes with parts of the German divisions retreating from Moldavia southwards. As it has been shown, starting August 27 the clashes between Romanian forces and the Wehrmacht troops acquired a general scope, actually occurring throughout the Bărăgan Plain. However, the fighting in the Bărăgan Plain did not prevent the Romanian troops from marching to the Bucharest-Ploieşti area, which they reached between August 26-31, 1944.

Withdrawing the troops of two strongly-equipped armies, during a short span of time and under particularly complex military circumstances, meant a novel experience in many respects, a unique one in the records of Romanian military history: starting August 23, 1944, the Romanian troops on the front unilaterally ceased fighting against the Soviet troops, immediately opening hostilities, on their own during an earlier stage, with the German army; likewise, they had to make a rapid move southwards, often on parallel routes with those taken by the Soviet or German forces, sometimes forcing their way through by fighting, while other times directly engaging in combat, alongside troops of the Red Army, against the common enemy. And all those actions were supposed to meet a priority exigency which was that of preserving the combat strength of the divisions and regiments as high as possible, as that was absolutely necessary for the liberating offensive the General Staff had planned to mount in Transylvania.

The military characteristics of the "withdrawal through fight" show the highly complex military conjuncture in Romania, the original and daring way in which the Romanian High Command and its intermediate command echelons carried through the difficult tasks assiged to them.

Ensuring a safe insurrectional perimeter. In addition to defeating the German forces in the interior of Romania, the Romanian large units were also assigned the strategic mission of covering the demarcation line in Transylvania and the 1,400 km-long south-western and southern frontiers. The Romanian covering forces were entrusted a twofold mission: to prevent fresh German troops from penetrating into the national territory and to crush or capture them. The strategic covering operation was carried through in the record time of 48 hours, starting the night of August 23-24. Three army corps comands, 11 divisions—made up mostly of recruits—and several training centers, that is a total of 64 battalions, 16 squadrons and 37 batteries were assigned the defense of the Romanian-Hungarian demarcation line in Transylvania and of the south-western frontier between Intorsura Buzăului and Orşova. The eastern sector of the covering front, otherwise provided with most important forces, was deemed the sore point on the covering front, as it was crossed by the most favorable invasion routes leading to the Prahova Valley and to Bucharest. An element of utmost interest in the covering operation, showing the deep historical roots of the national military strategy, was the idea according to which the Hațeg depression, surrounded by mountain heights, which the hero-king Decebalus had once linked through an ingenious system of fortifications, was to become, in the event of overwhelming enemy superiority, the last redoubt of national resistance. That decision—motivated both by historical traditions and by the presence of a large and combative workers' contingent in that area—was grounded on the fact that the Hațeg depression firmly closed the Mureş, Jiu and Bistra passes, blocking the approaches to the operational areas in central Transylvania and the west of the country. The planned resistance in Hațeg was to be rounded off by the fight carried on north of it in the powerful natural stronghold of the Apuseni Mountains.

By August 31, 1944, the Romanian large units had successfully carried through the two missions assigned to them. They generally succeeded in defeating and disarming the German troops in the covering zone or in driving them away. Likewise, they smashed some small-scale attacks delivered by enemy units from beyond the frontier: for instance, in the sector of the Mountain Corps, in the neighborhood of Nădlac, at Moldova Veche and Giurgiu, where German troops attempted an assault crossing of the Danube, trying to establish bridgeheads on the Romanian bank. Such attempts were swiftly thwarted by the Romanian troops. Under protection of the covering operation, the Romanian troops inland could fight unhampered, with no outside intervention threatening them. Moreover, the covering units barred the way of the German columns trying to get out of Romania.

During the latter stage of the insurrection, the troops of the Romanian Fourth Army started pouring on the covering alignment so that, conjointly with those of the First Army, which had already taken up their position in the area, they should be able to pass on to the offensive for the liberation of north-western Romania. During the first ten days of September 1944, Soviet troops would arrive on the new front opened by the Romanian troops through the strategic covering operation. On September 7, 1944, the Romanian forces, closely cooperating with the Soviets, mounted the offensive for the elimination of the "Szeckler salient," while until September 20, the frustrated the enemy offensive in the Transylvanian Plateau and west of the Western Carpathians, favorable premises being thus created for the final stage of the liberation of the country's entire territory.

The fights carried on by the Romanian army within the framework of the covering operation were decisively important for preserving a safe Romanian Carpathian arch, as well as a vast bridgehead in central Transylvania and the Banat, where in an area of some 50,000 sq km the necessary forces could be massed for the victorious advance through the valley of the Middle Danube toward Germany. General I. M. Managarov, commander of the Soviet Fifty-Third Army, who fought in the Arad-Timişoara area, would point out in an order of the day, the outstanding importance of the performances achieved by the Romanian army during the covering operation: "The Romanian units... holding out against the pressures of the German and Hungarian troops, have covered the movement of the Red troops toward the Hungarian Plain.... During these fights, under difficult reshuffling, the Romanian units and subunits evinced resoluteness and boldness, creditably fulfilling the lofty mission which they had been entrusted with."[30]

A "popular war" type of fight. The complex military developments in Romania on August 23, 1944, lent an utterly distinct nature to the insurrectional fights. Some characteristics of that background point to the form the clash between the Romanian and Hitlerite troops had necessary to take, to a number of peculiarities that made it look different from a classic war, where there are a contact line of established dispositions, an operational rear, and a "no man's land."

First, the Romanian army had to detach from its former combat "partner," and simultaneously, to open hostilities with him. The operation was to take place under three aggravating circumstances: fire against the Soviet forces was ceased unilaterally, without an understanding being previously reached with the Red Army on the Romanian army's "front change"; on the front, the Romanian large units had been interposed between German forces, an expression of the safety measures taken by the Hitlerites who, particularly over July-August 1944, did not trust the loyalty of the Romanian troops; at the strategic group, army, and cometimes, even at army corps and division levels the command had been exclusively vested in the German side.

Second, the deployment of German troops in the interior of Romania ruled out the possibility of establishing a classic type. Throughout the national territory there was a multitude of places (zones) occupied by the Wehrmacht (some 800) which automatically turned hostile to the Romanians, making up a true "network" of military control over Romania. In that case too there was an aggravating circumstance: their annihilation called for a great dispersion of forces, some of them—and not few by all means—as it was the case of the AAA batteries or battalions, the airports or the fortified camps, requiring a considerable number of troops belong ing to various arms. The dispersion of the Romanian forces was also required by the need to ensure control over the localities, thereby denying the enemy any possibility to turn them into support points, and over communication lines of any kind, with a view to preventing the enemy network from working and to turning it to Romanian benefit; moreover, troops were needed for opening the new front—this time of a classic type— in southern Transylvania and in the Banat, wherefrom the general offensive of the Romanian and Soviet troops toward Budapest and Vienna could be mounted.

Third, throughout August 23-31, 1944, remnants of the Wehrmacht large units falling back from the southern wing of the front—some of which boasted very high combat strength—penetrated into the insurrectional perimeter, and the permanent movement of their columns was hardly foreseeable. Those German units followed the same routes on which the Romanian troops were carrying through the strategic withdrawal from the Moldavian front ordered by the General Staff. Consequently, the scattering, capturing and smashing of those enemy columns became the purpose of a "string" of military actions carried on with no respite whatsoever.

Last but not least, there was the German commands' tendency to build up important forces in the close vicinity of Romania's vital political and economic centers—particularly around Bucharest and Ploieşti—by merging various neighboring "points," and to withdraw the forces that had managed to escape the deadly blows of the Soviets on the front through the insurrectional perimeter, toward the new front in Transylvania. Therefore, there was an urgent need for a permanent control over the country's moves, for concentrating considerable forces meant to destroy the agglomerations of enemy troops, and for choosing the right moment for triggering off mopping-up actions.

As a result, an exceptionally fluid military situation cropped up, which called for an equally exceptional layout, and that was the popular fight which the Romanian High Command resorted to. The "islands" of German resistance were soon isolated, and communications between them cut off with forces from their close vicinity and the assitance of the local population. A firm control was set over localities by clearing them of any enemy presence. Communications of all types would be either "opened" by continuous patrolling or "closed" in case of need, in the unavoidable passage points ("ambushes," as it had been laid down in an order of the General Staff of August 25, 1944), or kept under permanent air suveillance (the case of the Danube and of the road running through the Întorsura Buzăului pass). The shifting of the divisions needed by the new front beyond the mountains started in keeping with minutely worked-out railway transport plans. Ad hoc military units—detachments, tactical groups—would be set up, consisting of near-by troops belonging to various arms, which, benefitting by the considerable support of the local population, passed on to liquidating (by crushing or capturing) the "knots" of the enemy network in the national territory. Resorting to popular forces proved opportune and efficient everywhere. When facing strong enemy groups—in Bucharest, Ploieşti or the ship convoys on the Danube—various forms of military action—air and artillery bombings, diversion, ambushes, and the like—or psychological warfare—ultimatum, intimidation, and so forth—would be chosen, followed by general concentric attacks, carried out successfuly, in full force.

All these military actions—for chasing, splitting and crushing enemy columns, for checking their advance through ambushes and encounter engagements—entailed intense movement of the Romanian troops, high density of engagements to each square kilometer, and against one and the same enemy group. The sui-generis characteristics of the military developments during the insurrection were grasped at that very time by the military commanders supposed to fight under such uncommon conditions. "It is for the first time in the history of the Artillery Training Center"—the latter's commander wrote in a retrospective battle account of September 7, 1944—"that the cadets of the NCO artillery school and the recruits in the garrison have been compelled to engage in *guerilla warfare* [our italics] in ad-hoc set up units and with utterly improvised vehicles."[31]

To fulfill its tasks during the insurrection, the army needed the wide support of the population, which the latter granted unreservedly. Watching enemy movements was indispensible and the totally hostile attitude of the Romanian population was an efficient solution to the matter of utmost military importance. The chasing of insignificant enemy fractions —even of some stray soldiers—could be and actually was achieved by largely using the popular element. The enemy "points," isolated and attacked by the Romanian forces, found in the spontaneously set up groups of armed citizens another redoubtable enemy. On the whole, the wide-scope popular military effort—which implied blending the actions carried on by the regular troops with those of a popular type carried on by the population—led to the isolation and smashing in a record time of the "islands" of Hitlerite resistance, depriving the latter, from the very outset, of any chances of success.

The nuclei of that tremendous popular effort were the patriotic fight formations, organized underground by the Communist Party, which would see a numerical growth during the days of the insurrection. No sooner had the insurrection broken out that a great number of citizens reported to the seat of the Central Command of the Patriotic Fight Formations, volunteering for enlistment. A newspaper of the time, dated August 27, 1944, testifies to the daily flow of thousands of people to the seat of that command: "workers from factories, the citizens who have borne the brunt of an oppressive regime for four years know how to fight in defense of their Capital. At the command of the Patriotic Fight Formations, Alexandru Street, thousands of citizens reported yesterday to enlist as volunteers for the final crush of the last remnants of Hitler's army."[32] In many othe towns, particularly in those with a powerful industry, the workers rapidly set up fight groups. In the Hunedoara county, a document recorded, patrols were set up "to keep order,"[33] at Turda the people demanded the "arming of the workers"[34] and the phenomenon would rapidly spread to the Banat[35] as well as to Oltenia, Dobrudja, southern Transylvania and other areas.

The patriotic fight formations were equipped with armaments coming either from the depots secretly organized by the Romanian Communist Party, or from captures following clashes with the enemy. The feats of valor performed by such military units of a popular type were truly remarkable. Here are two telling examples in this respect. Starting the evening of August 23, 1944, such a patriotic fight formation was entrusted with the highly important task of ensuring the guard of the chief leaders of Antonescu's regime, who had been arrested. Taken over from the Royal Palace by armed workers, the former potentates of the dictatorial regime would be safely guarded in a secret house of the Communist Party for almost two weeks. A conclusive example of the active commitment of the patriotic fight formations was the action carried on by workers of the Regifer-Tohanu factory, who organized an artillery battery and joined the fight against the enemy. In acknowledgment of its feats of valor, the workers' battery would be cited in a general order of the day for the "steadfastness with which it has withstood the enemy, setting an example of what fulfilling the duty to one's country means."[36] The regional fixed battalions, the military units of a popular type in the frontier mountainous area, the pre-military fight formations, the gendarmerie posts, and so forth, were further nuclei rallying the pople's military effort. Not only were the army non-combatant elements (military schools, rear or pre-military troops), of the State apparatus (gendarmes and police forces) or the fight formations of the Communist Party committed to combat, but the need arose to organize the local population from the military point of view, in accordance with place and time requirements. Here is a relevant example. On August 25, a German formation attacked the Chiselet frontier guard post near Olteniţa. A NCO "has immediately set up a group of pre-military fighters and civilians, whom he armed, and hastened to succor the picket."[37] And that was an opportune and successful action.

The massive involvement of the population in the insurrectional effort would project the latter as an original form of popular war against the background of World War II.

During the fight against the German troops in Romania, the army was the mainstay of the Romanian war effort, the conception of the military operations naturally devolving, at the strategic level, on the Romanian High Command, whereas—at the tactical level—on the commanders of the units and large units deployed in the field. Yet, the scope of the liberation military effort was much wider; the army was joined by the patriotic fight formations, organized by the Communist Party, and by units and formations of a popular type, so that the military energies of the entire people should be conjoined with the highest purpose of driving the occupants away.

The political and military changeover energetically achieved by the entire nation in August 1944 had overwhelming consequences in Romanian military history.

Politically, what occurred on August 23, 1944, was not a mere change of government. The vital forces of the nation, headed by the working class, started a process that would bring deep-going transformations in the Romanian society. For the first time in the national history, State power was taken over by a wide coalition of political forces, the significant role being played by the Communist Party. That historic turning point in yielding State power opened wide prospects to the development of the Romanian nation, as the Communist Party became a coparticipant in decision-making, right after two decades' underground activity, gradually winning, as the revolution ran deeper and deeper, all levers of State power. As the starting point of the antifascist and anti-imperialist revolution for social and national liberation, August 23, 1944, also triggered off an objective

historical process which was to make of the Romanian Communist Party
the leading political force of the nation, the only one entitled to represent its sovereign will.

The insurrectional coalition government, which immediately passed
the political documents required by the restoration of a democratic, constitutional political life, had a patriotic, antifascist and anti-Hitlerite character. It replaced Antonescu's dictatorship, resolutely breaking with a
past of oppression that had been highly detrimental to the Romanian
people.

The insurrectional government was the political expression and instrument of the wide-scope coalition of patriotic and anti-Hitlerite forces,
organized and led by the Romanian Communist Party. Its composition
mirrored the participation of all socio-political forces in the effort for
overthrowing the dictatorial regime and for restoring national independence by taking Romania away from the Nazi Reich's enslaving orbit.

The presence of Lucrețiu Pătrășcanu, the representative of the Romanian Communist Party, in the government—in his twofold position as
State Minister and ad-interim Minister of Justice—a position that none of
the representatives of the other parties enjoyed, was indicative of the
decisive share held by the Romanian communists in preparing and carrying out the insurrection, as well as of the role they assumed in further
promoting the revolutionary process initiated on August 23, 1944.

On August 23, 1944, by the change effected in its domestic and foreign
policy, the Romanian people firmly asserted its will to be free and master
in its own country, to remove imperialist or any kind of foreign domination, and not to allow of its being at the mercy of the Great Powers. Started without an agreement being previously reached with the Soviet Union,
the United States and Great Britain, the insurrection of August conclu-
sively illustrates the constant vocation of the Romanian people to shape
its future in accordance with its own aspirations.

The act of resolute self-determination carried out by the Romanian
nation in the thick of World War II considerably told on the latter's progress. Under the circumstances in which the Wehrmacht was fiercely defending the European "Festung" (fortress) built up by Hitler, the Romanian insurrection, through its military-strategic results, made a wide break
in the fortress, thereby greatly diminishing the German's possibilities of
prolonged resistance. The Romanian army, taking part in fighting alongside

the patriotic fight formations, the spontaneously set up groups of armed citizens, actually the entire people won a brilliant victory. The table below (Table 5) makes a detailed presentation, per amrs, of the Romanian military forces taking part in the insurrection.

TABLE 5

Romania's Armed Forces Committed to Battle
Between August 23-31, 1944

No.	Arm	Combat strength
1	Army	383,222
2	Aeronautical forces (Air Force and AAA)	73,667
3	Navy	9,468
	Sum total	466,357

Sustaining but minimal losses, the Romanian army put out of action over 61,000 Wehrmacht military (killed and prisoners), a strength equivalent to six divisions, which means 18 percent of the total losses of Hitler's armed forces over July-August 1944 (see Tables 6 and 7 below).

During the nine days of grim fighting, the Romanian forces liberated the central and southern parts of the country, that is an area of 150,000 sq km, the equivalent of the territories of Belgium, Holland, Switzerland and Denmark taken together. Likewise, a considerable amount of armament and war materiel (222 intact aircraft and 438 ships) were captured and others were destroyed in action. Table 8 (below) details the results obtained by the insurrectional forces in the main battle areas.

The international reverberation of the Romanian revolution. Already in August 1944, the remarkable military impact the Romanian revolution had upon World War II was largely commented upon in newspapers and broadcasts, by new agencies, military personalities and statesmen to name a few. Those comments unanimously emphasized the decisive importance

TABLE 6

The Army Effectives Taking Part in the Insurrection
(August 23-31, 1944)

No.	Name	Number	Effectives	Remarks
1	The General Staff	1	2,882	Command staff, signal unit, pontooneer units, etc.
2	Armies	2	582	The effectives of the commands, units and army rear formations
3	Corps	15	28,350	
4	Divisions*	38	241,321	* 14 training divisions and one detachment with the strength of a division
5	Separate units*	39	110,087	* Regiments, detachments, officer and NCO training schools, regional fixed battalions, gendarmes legions, depots
	Sum total	95	383,222	

of Romania's changeover for the general progress of the world war, a true "bolt from the blue" for Hitler's Reich.

"Romania's leaving the Nazi camp is a great political and economic victory," London broadcasting station commented on August 24, 1944, at 7.15 a.m., after having pointed out only a few hours earlier that "Romania's undertaking is an act of great courage which will speed up the end of the war. [. . .] The collapse of the Hitlerites is drawing near with

TABLE 7

Losses in Manpower Inflicted Upon the Enemy by the Romanian
Army During the Insurrection (August 23-31, 1944)

No.	Losses	Effectives	Remarks
1	Prisoners	56,455*	*Subsequently taken over by Soviet commands
2	Killed	5,048*	*Only those identified by the Romanian side
	Total	61,503	

great strides."[38] At about the same hour, the Reuter News Agency would comment that the insurrection in Romania and the liberation of Paris, which had taken place on August 23, 1944, "write down a black page in the war waged by Germany [. . .]," that "the entire Nazi edifice in the Balkan Peninsula begins to crumble," while the "consequences for the future development of the war are incalculable."

Such commentaries would become more frequent with every passing hour, showing that "Romania's action will be an example to be followed by Bulgaria, Finland and Hungary,"[39] that "Germany has now lost its single oil source, a fact that would be badly felt [. . .]," while "Hitler's days are running out."[40]

Quoting further commentaries broadcast by the BBC or carried by the British press during those days, mention should be made of military commentator Thomas Cadett's opinion, according to whom the Romanian changeover was an "amazing event," which, alongside the liberation of Paris, confronted the Nazis "with utter destruction." "To the Germans" —Cadett concluded—"the military bearings of Romania's leaving the war are incalculable."[41] The "News Chronicle," appearing in London, while referring to the disintegrating political consequences of the Romanian insurrection for the German fascist bloc, showed in its August 24, 1944 issue that "Bulgaria has been left no choice whatsoever. Hungary has still some option."[42] In the opinion of another British military commentator, Edward

TABLE 8

The Results Obtained by the Insurrectional Forces in the Major Battle Areas

No.	Area	Date	Prisoners	German generals taken prisoner	Romanian participating forces
1	Bucharest and the surrounding area	August 23-28	some 7,000	E. Hansen A. Gerstenberg Busch Lilienthal R. Stahel K. Spalcke Tilesen	—The Military Command of the Capital (forces made available) —the Fourth Army (at Gherghiţa, Prahova County) —Armed popular forces
2	The Prahova Valley	August 23-31	some 8,600	Kuderna Hoffmayer Teschner Appel	—The V Territorial Corps —The Fourth Army (forces reshuffled over August 28-31) —Armed popular forces
3	Dobrudja	August 23-26	some 12,000	von Tschammer Osten	—The II Army Corps —The 2nd Frontier Guard Regiment —Forces of the Third Army —Armed popular forces

Continued on next page

TABLE 8 (Continued)

No.	Area	Date	Prisoners	German generals taken prisoner	Romanian participating forces
4	Călărași-Oltenița Giurgiu-Roșiori	August 29-30	some 9,000	Burckhardt	–The II Territorial Corps –Armed popular forces
5	Turnu Severin-Gura Văii	August 25-31	some 1,600		–The 19th Infantry Division (two regiments) –The 5th Cavalry Division –Armed popular forces
6	Oltenia (The Argeș County included)	August 24-28	some 2,400		–The I Territorial Corps –The III Territorial Corps –Armed popular forces
7	Teleorman (Alexandria, Zimnicea, etc.)	August 26	some 1,200		–The III Territorial Corps –The IV Territorial Corps –Armed popular forces

Continued on next page

TABLE 8

No.	Area	Date	Prisoners	German generals taken prisoner	Romanian participating forces
8	Southern Transylvania	August 23-31	some 1,700		–The First Army –The VI Territorial Corps –The Mountain Corps –Armed popular forces
9	The Banat	August 23-31	some 3,000		–The VII Territorial Corps –Armed popular forces
10	Gendarme formations assisted by armed popular forces, over the entire territory	August 23-31	some 7,000		
	Total 150,00 sq km		some 56,500	14	

Montgomery, the Romanian insurrection was to speed up the end of the war in Europe: "Really backed by the Romanians, the Russians will reach Vienna before long. Through the Carpathian Gateway that the Romanians opened, the Russians could reach Munich and march towards Berlin."[43] In its issue of August 25, 1944, the "Daily Herald" commented the events taking place in Romania under the heading "The Best News of the Day," unhesitatingly asserting that the insurrection was "an extraordinary event," whose strategic outcome would be, "from the military point of view, the collapse of the German defensive system, whereas from the political one the removal of German influence from South-East Europe."[44]

A commentary carried by the English press and released by the Reuter Agency on August 25 pointed to the fact that Romania's action was a "lethal blow dealt at the German Reich,"[45] and that the "deadly Romanian blow [. . .] took unawares all Allied governments."[46]

The British press highlighted the paramount importance of Romania's military and political action. The "Daily Express" of August 24, carried Morley Richards' commentary showing that Romania's new political stand "means that Germany has actually lost the war. And that for the reason that, without Romania's oil-fields, neither can the German army hold on in the field, nor the German economic life go on for more than three months." If the commentator was wrong in assessing the Reich's capacity to hold on, he nevertheless correctly estimated that Romania's action "means that Germany has lost the entire Balkan Peninsula, and the way through the Danube Valley to the very heart of the Reich lies open." The same day, the "Daily Mail" considered that the change effected in Bucharest "will considerably tell on the war in Eastern Europe." According to the "Evening Standard," "the only thing the Germans can do is to retreat through the Carpathian passes to Transylvania, but this means the abandonment not only of Romania, but also of Bulgaria and of the entire Balkan Peninsula. This is the most significant event entailed by Romania's changeover." The far-reaching consequences of the event of August 23, 1944, would also be noticed by the "News Chronicle" of August 25, which drew attention to the fact that the German flank was left open, while the military commentator Philip Gribble showed that Romania's action "undermines the groundwork of further resistance in the Balkans . . . The Russians are now benefitting by a safe 600 km-long communication, from Bessarabia to the Hungarian border." The "Statesman and Nation" of August 28 saw Romania's turning weapons on the Reich as a fact of "great and decisive consequence for South-East Europe." The "Daily Mail" of August 25 estimated that "from the political standpoint, it [Romania's action—a.n.] means the complete crumbling of German influence in the Balkans and this, in its turn, would undoubtedly lead other satellite countries into finding a way out of the German camp [. . .] From the military standpoint, Romania's action is a heavy blow dealt at Germany, and it should finally lead to the withdrawal of all German troops from the Balkans." The "Times" of August 25 showed that, in the opinion of some observers, "Romania's decision will eventually persuade both Bulgaria and Finalnd into putting an end to stalling and passing on to action. At any rate the blow dealt at German control over the Balkans and South-East Europe is more than obvious." The military correspondent of the "Evening Standard" contributed a pertinent analysis to the August 28 issue on the strategic consequences of Romania's changeover: "The Romanian Black Sea coast is open. The potential defense line between Focșani and Galați has been lieft behind. All this loses importance when compared to the Romanians' taking hold of the passes [in the Carpathians—a.n.] to Transylvania. The circumstances there resembled those at Monte Cassino, in Italy. The Germans could have retreated into the passes and held out on the peaks of the mountains. They could have withdrawn large effectives from Romania and held out with but a few covering in purely defensive dispositions. Yet, it is the Romanians who are controlling the passes. The Germans have been disarmed and the Russians are quickly carrying forward the advance." In the "Truth" of September 1, 1944, General Sir Hubert Gough concluded that Romania's action was "an almost crushing blow to the Axis."

To quote from the broadcast of August 24 (10.15 a.m.) of the New York Broadcasting station, the American Press commented upon that "important political military event," pointing to the fact that "Romania made that step before Bulgaria and Hungary, "being the first satellite nation to join the Allies."[47] Two days later, another American broadcasting station highlighted the outstandingly important fact of Romania's being the "first country in Eastern Europe which has done her utmost to break off ties with the Axis. On embarking upon this action, Romania has taken great risks [. . .]."[48]

In its issue of August 25, the "New York Times" underlined that to
Nazi Germany "control over the Romanian territory is of great importance
[. . .] Through this control not only is he [Hitler] defending the southern
flank, but also the oil supply—the most indispensable war material—is
ensured [. . .] The loss of this supply source will be serious blow dealt at
Germany that could cripple its military operations." "History may record
Romania's defection as one of the decisive events of the entire war." The
"Evening Star" of August 24 showed that through Romania's changeover,
Nazi Germany was deprived of her most important oil source and also of
the military contribution of the Romanian army. "It [Romania's action]
shatters the whole Balkan front and imperils whatever German forces are
in Greece, Yugoslavia, Bulgaria, Hungary, Czechoslovakia and Southern
Poland. Wholly apart from its effect on the fast-wavering Finns, this event
must surely hasten the decision of the Bulgarians and Hungarians to end
their unhappy partnership with Berlin and thus speed up the day when
Hitler will be obliged to fall back all the way into Germany." The "Washington Post" of August 25 expressed the opinion that "Romania's action
[. . .] will make wide gaps in Hitler's Balkan empire and will hasten the
end of the war. Romania's move will undoubtedly precipitate Bulgaria's
getting out of the war." For the "Wall Street Journal," Romania's action
surpassed in all respects the military disasters sustained by Germany in
France, Italy and Poland. In an article entitled *Disaster for Germany
Looms in the Balkans,* carried by the "New York Times" in its issue of
August 27, the well-known journalist Cyrus Sulzberger said: "Without
the Ploeşti oil, gasoline and lubricants, no matter how hard the Germans
try to develop their synthetic supplies, they just will not have enough. The
mechanized Wehrmacht and the Luftwaffe are bound to grind to a halt."

A highly competent military commentator such as Hansen E. Baldwin
wrote in the same newspaper on August 27 that Romania's changeover
meant "at least a serious weakening of the Axis military position on the
southern front; at most, the eventual collapse of the whole Balkan position. Immediate results are of great political significance; Bulgaria may be
encouraged to follow suit and resistance in Yugoslavia greatly encouraged."
On August 28, an article carried by the "New York Times" would make
the following comments on the changeover effected by the Romanian
people: "Romania's leaving the war leads to a considerable decrease in
the German strength in South Europe, perhaps even to the complete

downfall of Nazism. Notwithstanding the losses sustained, the Romanian army continues to be the stronger one among those belonging to Germany's former allies. Under no circumstances will Hitler's Reich be able to replace the thirty Romanian divisions [. . .]. At the height of the war Romania has had the wisdom to go there where she creditably belongs."[49]

As a crowning of all commendatory comments made in the United States here is the opinion expressed in a broadcast of February 9, 1945, of an American broadcasting station for listeners abroad: "when history is written, the event of August 23 will be recorded as an important factor in the development of this war."[50]

The comments of the public opinion in the Soviet Union were not late in joining those in the other Allied countries. On August 25, Moscow broadcast the statement of the Commissariat for Foreign Affairs of the USSR: "The Soviet High Command declares that if the Romanian troops cease military operations against the Red Army [actually ended by the Romanian side on the evening of August 23, 1944–a.n.] and if they pledge to wage the liberation war alongside the Red Army against the Germans, or against the Hungarians for the liberation of Transylvania, the Red Army will not disarm them, but will permit them to keep all armament and will assist them in carrying through this lofty mission."[51] The "Pravda" of August 27 read: "Romania's leaving the Axis has overwhelming importance not only for this country, but also for the entire Balkan Peninsula, because through this blow the whole German domination system in South-East Europe falls into pieces. The importance of the latter cannot be underrated."[52]

The same day "Trud" (Labor), the central newspaper of the Soviet Trade Unions, underlined that "Romania's breaking off the alliance with the Nazi Reich means the failure of Germany's political-military system in South-East Europe."[53]

The comments carried by the "Pravda" issue on the following day, August 28, 1944, rounded off the opinions expressed the day before: "Romania's leaving the war means the collapse of Germany [. . .] Romania's leaving the war at this very moment, and under such circumstances [. . .] is more than the heroic feat of a peaceful people; it is an example set to other peoples which are confronted with similar circumstances. By this noble gesture, Romania has ensured its national freedom and the sovereignty of her borders."[54]

Equally commendatory opinions on the Romanian insurrection would be expressed by various mass media in the neutral countries. Thus, the Swedish newspapers "Nya Dagligt Alehanda" and "Afton Bladet" of August 24, 1944 carried editorials characterizing the insurrection in Romania as a "terrible blow at the German war leadership, thereby decisively sapping German domination in the Balkans."[55] A commentary in the Turkish newspaper "Ullus" of August 27 pointed out that, through her action, "Romania has secured a free future, which is also a guarantee for the future of the entire Balkan Peninsula."[56]

The event of August 23 was paid due heed by a great number of other newspapers and broadcasting stations in Eurpe, South and North America, and Asia, to which the cause of defeating fascism, Hitlerism and militarism was an expression of the need for the people's freedom and independence to come out victorious.

Even the firmly censored propaganda in the countries belonging to the alliance patronized by Hitler's Reich or even in Goebbels' dens the Romanian insurrection was seen as an event of utmost consequence for the course of the war. On August 24, 1944, at 12.40 p.m., radio Budapest announced that the Hungarian government "has taken due steps"[57] in pursuance of Romania's changeover, while three days later news from the Hungarian capital emphasized that the Romanian action "could mean and bring about a serious turn in the current situation [. . .] Hungary follows, arm-in-hand and with the greatest attention, the progress of the events."[58] On August 25, in Helsinki, a spokesman of the Finnish Ministry for Foreign Affairs saw himself compelled, in order to calm down the Hitlerites' reaction, to declare that no official had stated that the news from Romania aroused "some reaction with the Finnish government."[59] Anyhow, on August 24, the Helsinki broadcasting station read the proclamation to the country of the head of the Romanian State[60] in extenso, announcing that Romania had gone to the side of the Allies. The public opinion in Bulgaria showed its "amazement" and "admired Romania's courage."[61]

In Berlin, the Romanian insurrection was first considered "a new coup of the Jews" (August 24), "branded [. . .] as treason to the loyalty owed to an alliance" (August 25), an event which Germany was not at all "willing to witness [. . .] without reacting" (August 26), a "second hand putch" (August 26).[62] Starting August 25, one could feel the Germans' concern over the military bearings of the Romanian insurrection. A commentary released by the Transocean Agency said that the "political events in Romania would be of some consequence for the situation on the southern front."[63] One day later one announced that the German Legation in Bucharest had been encircled by Romanian forces and that "heavy fights were being carried on against the Romanian armed forces"[64] in Romania's capital city. On August 27, what was an overwhelming reality cold no longer be concealed. That day the Berlin News Agency informed that "In Romania heavy battles are being fought against the Romanian troops [. . .] Particularly grim fighting has taken place at the northern end of Bucharest, as well as in the Ploieşti area."[65]

Beyond the "intoxicating " propaganda worked out by Goebbels' dens, there is the reality of the documentary records of various Nazi military or political command echelons. "The developments in Romania [a reference to the event of August 23, 1944—a.n.] has taken us completely unawares," the Wehrmacht High Command's file of orders recorded.[66] On August 25, 1944, the file of orders of the "South Ukraine" Army Group, operating in Romania, would note down that the fight of the Romanian forces against the Wehrmacht "has faced the German units and services in the rear with a difficult situation, and it is hard to foresee which of them might be evacuated or retreived from Romania."[67] The same file of orders contains the order put out by the Wehrmacht High Command with Hitler's approval to the effect that fighting in Romania had to be continued: "the mission [of the Army Group "South Ukraine"—a.n] is to get by advancing and maintaining a continuous front streteching from the Romanian-Bulgarian border, across the peaks of the Carpathians, to where hands are joined with the right wing of the XVII Army Corps [in Bukovina—a.n.]."[68] In this way the highest Nazi political and military authority recorded the complete success of the Romanian insurrection, and admitted that the territory under the authority of the government in Bucharest had been freed by the Romanian forces.

Hitler himself admitted the decisive consequence of the "front change" effected by Romania on August 23, 1944, considering it as a far-reaching military crisis in the general conduct of the Nazi war. During a talk the Nazi dictator had with Ante Pavelich, the leader of the fascist regime in Croatia, on September 18, 1944, the former listed the military crises that had confronted the Wehrmacht that year: the collapse of the Army Group

"Center" in Byelorussia, Romania's changeover and the disintegration of German defenses in France (following the breakthrough at Avranches).[69] Finally, here is the opinion of the Wehrmacht High Command after the success of the Romanian insurrection the way it follows from a report the chiefs of the OKW, Field Marshal W. Keitel and General A. Jodl, submitted to Hitler. According to them, "in addition to its immediate military consequences, it [the Romanian action—a.n.] has also brought about an extremely dangerous change of fronts that would entail not only the loss of Romania's territory, but also of the territories of Bulgaria, Yugoslavia and Greece, jeopardizing the entire German army in the Balkans. Besides losing positions in the Carpathians, the loss of the Romanian granary and oil is another heavy blow, as a result of which the Russian armies will be at the gates of Budapest in a few weeks' time [. . .]."[70]

The international consequence of the event of August 23, 1944—highlighted by the relevant documents above—was also acknowledged through the Romanian sovereign's being awarded the 'Victory' Order [. . .] "by the Soviets, whose armies were the first to benefit by the consistent results of the event of August 23, 1944, a historic one in all respects."[71]

The historical retrospect has even more convincingly revealed the tremendous impact the Romanian insurrection had on the development of World War II. We confine ourselves to quote there just two foreign military analysts who have compared the blow dealt by the Romanians at the Wehrmacht with the famous Stalingrad. In the opinion of a Swiss historian the political-military action of Romania was, through the consequences it entailed for the Third Reich, more important than the defeat sustained by the Wehrmacht at Stalingrad in the winter of 1942-1943: "To Hitler, Romania's getting out of the war meant a greater loss than the catastrophe at Stalingrad."[72] The same idea is shared by a former German combatant in Romanian in the summer of 1944. "The scope and military-political bearings of that German defeat [in Romania—a.n.] were no less serious than those of the battle of Stalingrad."[73]

* * * * *

An "amazing event," an "extraordinary act," a "terrible blow," "incalculable" consequences, an "example to be followed," a "great victory," a "fatal blow dealt at the German Reich," "deadly blow," "more than a heroic deed"—are only some of the comments made at the time in the international arena. Such appreciations might seem somehow exaggerated, even incredible, one may say. Have the military, economic and political bearings of the Romanian insurrection upon the development of World War II been that great? Or, to put it differently, has incredibility proved true? It is proper that the answer should come from the historiographic research, the chapters to follow provide arguments for such an undertaking.

CHAPTER III

UNSUCCESSFUL PLANS: THE HITLERITE REACTION TO THE ROMANIAN REVOLUTION OF AUGUST 1944

If the activity of the Romanian Communist Party in the preparatory and the actual stages of the insurrection, as well as the action of Romanian armed forces, have been studied in detail and with distinction the German countermeasures have been examined in a more perfunctory manner and on the basis of limited primary sources. The data contained in the records of the German Army Group "South Ukraine" or the establishment of the puppet-government of Horia Sima have been studied thoroughly but the reaction of Nazi Germany to the Romanian insurrection has not yet been analyzed in its entirety with a view to elucidating the three major components thereof—the political, the military, and the propagandistic. The following pages will attempt to fill these gaps.

* * * * *

Hitler was sipping tea at his headquarters in Rastenburg during the afternoon of August 23, 1944, around six o'clock German summer time, when Lt. Col. Erik von Ansberg, his adjutant for the Wehrmarcht's High Command, told him that an urgent telephone message was awaiting him.

The Führer was advised that Marshal Antonescu had been arrested while in an audience with the King. "Why didn't he listen to me. I knew that this would happen!"[1] was Hitler's initial comment. Are we to believe that this belated certitude was based on Hitler's earlier views regarding Antonescu's precarious position, ascribable to the lack of support from a political party of his own[2] or was it related to information secured through various channels indicating the imminent break with the Reich? Should the latter be correct one may well ask why were not the proper measures taken to prevent Romania's abandonment of the Axis, an act which would have extremely serious consequences for the successful continuation of the German war effort?[3]

The problem of the data available to various German institutions and networks on the preparations of the insurrection of August 1944 has been discussed in both Romanian and foreign historiography and, therefore, need not detain us.[4] Suffice it to say that the assurances repeatedly sent by the German legation in Bucharest regarding the improbability of a Romanian reorientation[5] and those despatched by Lieut. Gen. Alfred Gerstenberg, the German military attaché for the Luftwaffe, on the certitude of swift destruction of any such attempt[6] persuaded the upper political and military echelons of the Reich that a surprise from Romania was impossible. Even if on August 6 Hitler warned Antonescu "not to set foot in the royal palace under any circumstances"[7] we know now that two weeks later, on August 21, he expressed his displeasure to Gen. Werner Kreipe, the Chief-of-Staff of the Luftwaffe, in connection with the rumors which came to Kreipe's attention through his own sources regarding a proximate coup d'état in Bucharest, "Your air attaché should not stick his nose into matters which do not concern him. The SS says exactly the opposite."[8] In the discussion between Hitler and the commander of the South-East European front, Fieldmarshal Werner von Weichs, on August 22, the possibility of a Romanian change of attitude was not even mentioned.[9] It is evident, therefore, that the outbreak of the uprising took Hitler by surprise and that the strategic advantage, so essential for the success of the uprising, had thus been gained.

At Rastenburg the customary evening confernece was delayed until 2 a.m.. The upper echelons of the German command tried to secure through various channels—military, diplomatic, and news media—what was happening in Bucharest.

Around 8 o'clock in the evening, despite the attempted isolation of the German legation by those in charge of the insurrection, Manfred von Killinger, the Minister Plenipotentiary of the Reich in Bucharest, and Gen. Alfred Gerstenberg succeeded in establishing contact with Gen. Werner Kreipe. Kreipe summarized the conversation as follows: "Conversation with Minister von Killinger and with Gerstenberg in Bucharest. Both besieged in the legation; Killinger, totally dismayed, sends greetings to the Führer. Gerstenberg suggests an attack with Stuka bombers and using the anti-aircraft division located in Ploieşti for the occupation of Bucharest. I telephoned Hitler several times and he approved Gerstenberg's suggestions; he demands the King's arrest. Contact established with Bucharest, then interrupted."[10] Thus, the suggestions emanting from Bucharest, via Gerstenberg, for the "stabilization" of the situation in Romania, based on an optimistic appraisal of the relative strength of the opposing forces through ignorance of the actual situation (Gerstenberg himself believed, as shown, that a single anti-aircraft unit would be able to repress any Romanian attempt at defection), received Hitler's approval. His prompt consent is to be understood through their corresponding entirely with the Reich's strategic and political interests and with Hitler's own temperament.

At 11:25 p.m. Hitler had a telephone conversation with General Hans Friessner, commander of the "South Ukraine" Army Group. There are two sources on this conversation. The first, contained in the records of the above mentioned forces and, as such, more trustworthy, indicates that Friessner reported on "the assumption of the supreme command over all German military forces in Romania as well as on the immediate necessity for the withdrawal by the most direct route to the rim of the Carpathian mountains."[11] Surprisingly, this suggestion which meant the abandoning of the Focşani-Nămoloasa-Galaţi line and, as such, loss of the oil fields of the Ploieşti region, was agreed to by Hitler, who was to send directives.

The second version, which fits logically into the actual course of events, is contained in Gen. Friessner's memoirs. According to this version, Friessner informed Hitler of the assumption of the supreme command over the German forces in Romania—to which Hitler gave his consent—and of the necessity of an urgent transferring "onto Hungarian soil of everything that could be saved in men and materiel and setting up a new line of defense there."[12] (Hitler announced that he is sending directives). Thereupon, Hitler ordered Friessner to immediately remove the insurrectionist government and to set up a new cabinet. When Friessner stated that this order "could not be carried out" Hitler replied in an "irritated" manner: "Empower the most reliable Romanian general to set up a safe government!" In his memoirs Friessner alleges that even before his conversation with Hitler he had had telephone conversations with the Romanian generals Petre Dumitrescu and Ilie Şteflea, the commanders of respectively the third and fourth Romanian armies, who stated their loyalty to the new government. As a result, Friessner told the Führer that the Romanian generals refused to "renounce their oath of allegiance to their supreme military commander [the King]. Hitler was apparently disconcerted over this reply and reiterated his decision to send directives.

But also this second version—which, to repeat, comes from memoirs and, as such is not a contemporary source—is partly contradicted by a contemporary source. While recalling the fact that the records of the "South Ukraine" Army Group indicate that Friessner's conversation with the Romanian generals took place after his conversation with Hitler we note the report of Col. Nicolae Ivănescu to the Supreme Headquarters of August 27, 1944. Ivănescu, the translator of the conversations between Friessner and the Romanian generals, states in his report that "Before making telephone contact with the two Romanian army commanders in my presence, Gen. Friessner had a telephone conversation with the Führer in which he gave a brief account of the situation in Romania."[13]

Corroborating the data provided by these sources and eliminating, through critical evaluation of the sources, the inadvertencies and contradictions mentioned above we should be able to reconstruct the actual events as follows: (1) Through the Gerstenberg connection Hitler receives the first suggestion for resolving quickly and with minimal military effort the political-military crisis unleashed by the insurrection; (2) Through the Friessner connection Hitler receives the suggestion that all German troops in Romania be transferred inside the rim of the Carpathians; (3) Hitler won over by Gerstenberg's suggestion orders Friessner to set up a government headed by a pro-German general; (4) In carrying out Hitler's order Friessner sounds out the Romanian generals' attitudes. Hitler's order "to stifle the putsch, arrest the king and the royal court's camarilla and set up a new government, headed by a pro-German general should Antonescu be no longer available,"[14] represented the ultimate approval of Gerstenberg's proposal to end the insurrection by force. The first directives from Hitler comprised—as may easily be seen—two parts, a political one and a military one, which required the adoption of two sets of corresponding measures. Moreover, corresponding propaganda measures were to be adopted.

Political Countermeasures

Hitler's directives show that his faith in I. Antonescu had not been affected by Antonescu's mentioning, during the conversation which he had in the evening of August 19 with the German plenipotentiary Karl Clodius, the possibility of his seeking "freedom of political action" in the event that the front could not be strengthened (evidently, only if Hitler had become aware of this discussion by the evening of August 23, which is uncertain but not to probable).[15]

Certainly, Hitler was unaware of Antonescu's sending, on the very morning of August 23, an emissary to Stockholm[16] who was to deliver to Romania's ambassador to Sweden, Frederic Nanu, the *plein pouvoir* required to initiate the final negotiations for concluding the armistice with the USSR.[17] Thus, the reliability of Marshal Antonescu was, for Hitler, untainted and, not surprisingly, he wanted his immediate reassumption of the leadership of the Romanian state. Antonescu's status was, however, unclear as far as the Germans were concerned. During the audience given him on the evening of August 23, Killinger was unable to ascertain Antonescu's actual status and location. The records of the German Ministry of Foreign Affairs, dated August 24, state that the Marshal was in Predeal and that his attitude, as well as that of the king, was not "entirely clear."[18] The laconic character of the entry, the source of which is unidentified, obscures its meaning. It is certain, however, that the fate of the former leader of Romania continued to preoccupy the Germans (did they intend to repeat a Mussolini-type liberation from Gran Sasso in this instance also?). The records of the "F" Army Group entered on August 24, at 10:20 a.m., the rumor that the former Romanian marshal was free and that the king had left the country.[19] Clearly, the most far-fetched rumors are borne of confused situations but, in this instance, it is not unlikely that this optimistic picture, in such total contradiction with reality, was the product of German counter-propaganda particularly of the radio station Ilse II. In a message conveyed by Andreas Schmidt, on 3 September, it is stated that a secret agent looked up Antonescu's wife who "was uncommunicative" limiting herself to indicating that "her husband had been arrested."[20] With this bit of information Antonescu is no longer of concern to Nazi political and military strategists.

To carry out Hitler's directive to set up a counter-revolutionary government Gen. H. Friessner, who was ordered to find a military man to replace Antonescu, tried to sound out the intentions of Romanian generals in command of major units. The records of the "South Ukraine" Army Group show the failure to win over such commanders: "Not a single Romanian general is willing to continue the war on the German side" was the conclusion reached following conversations with generals R. Corne, commander of the "România Mare" division, P. Dumitrescu, commander of the Third Army, and I. Șteflea, commandant of the Fourth Army.

Hitler's desire to have a general as head of the government was dictated by political and pragmatic considerations. As previously shown, he regretted Antonescu's failure to establish a political party and even reproached the Marshal for it. The gap created by Antonescu's arrest could, therefore, not be filled by a leader of the same party; in Germany there prevailed the belief—shared by Antonescu, for that matter—that in the last analysis the Marshal's power was based on the army. It was therefore logical for Hitler to seek a general as replacement for Antonescu.

General Erik Hansen, chief of the German military mission in Romania, realized from as early as the night of August 23-24 that that perspective was wrong. Throughout that night discussions were held at the German legation concerning the establishment of a pro-German government in Romania. If the succinct account of Gen. Schultz[22] reveals only that extreme difficulties arose in the search for a military leader it is clear that the ultimate failure of this attempt was due to the strength and unanimity of purpose of the insurrectionist front established and led by the Romanian Communist Party. The failure of the attempts to establish a pro-Nazi puppet government in Bucharest was correctly explained by Gen. E. Hansen. In the early hours of August 24, at 4:05 a.m., Hansen called Friessner to dispel any illusions that might have been entertaining regarding a possible defection by generals of the Romanian army: "The new Romanian government must be taken seriously. We should not deceive ourselves in believing that we are dealing with a small clique of traitors. The government is backed by the entire Romanian people and, especially, by all generals."[23] This was clearly in accordance with reality.

Hitler had only one ultimate "reserve" to put into play, the remnants of the Iron Guard who had sought refuge in Germany. From as early as the winter of 1940-1941 Hitler, when faced with the alternative of Antonescu or the Iron Guard, chose Antonescu. The discrediting of the Legion because of the crimes and ravages commited by its members made it difficult, but not impossible, for that organization to retain power in Romania. However, and this was the deciding factor in Hitler's choice, the Iron Guard had shown itself during the brief period of participation in governance to be a fomentor of anarchy, to be inept and, as such, incapable of securing the proper functioning of the infrastructures and logistic systems which had to sustain the front which was to be established through the attack against the Soviet Union in June 1941. In August 1944, however, in a country which was on the verge of becoming a theater of war the Iron Guard, isolated politically and incompetent from an organizational standpoint, could only be a burden. Hitler, however, could not delay finding a substitute for Antonescu lest it would become evident that the act of August 23 was not the action of a "small clique" of the royal court but the insurrection of an entire people.

Faced with the failure of the attempt to find a pro-German general who would head a puppet government[24] and given the pressure of time, Hitler called on Horia Sima. Thus, on the afternoon of August 24, at 5:00, the German radio announced that "a leader of the Iron Guard, condemned to death in Romania" had become the head of a "national" government.[25] The announcement was more of a statement of intentions than a fact; the Minister of Foreign Affairs, the former legionary minister Mihai Sturdza, left his residence in Copenhagen on August 28 and arrived in Berlin the same day to receive instructions from the German foreign ministry. He was to meet the head of the "national" government, Horia Sima, only later in Vienna[26] in the company of 400 legionaries. The German government appointed Günther Altenburg as its representative to this make-believe Sima government[27] and as his counsellor, the former director of the German scientific insitute in Bucharest, Professor Ernst Gamillscheg.

The new "government" had to face two difficult problems—composition and residency. Neither the Nazi patrons nor their legionary tools deceived themselves into believing that the Guardist team constituted a representative government; as long as the "national" government was entirely a legionary team it had no chance of winning support in Romania not to mention the possibility of bringing about defections from the ranks of the Romanian army. The presence in the government of politicians with different orientations than that of the Guardists became essential. Therefore, a "hunt" for bourgeois politicians with known right-wing and pro-German proclivities was initiated. On August 28 Andreas Schmidt and Veesenmayer, the German plenipotentiary in Hungary, informed von Ribbentrop that the establishment of a "national" government with Gen. Dragalina is no longer possible since "in the meantime it has become impossible to land in Bucharest and take these persons out of the country."[28] The inquiries regarding politicians or military men who may be willing to collaborate with the Reich went on; on September 3 Andreas Schmidt reported that "it has been established through the mails that Manoilescu is living in Breaza, Cîmpina, and Gigurtu in Predeal. The residences of Valer Pop and Dragalina are unknown."[29] Shortly before that, the representative of the German Ministry of Foreign Affairs attached to the "South Ukraine" Army Group reported on rumors concerning the flight of Gigurtu and Manoilescu to Hungary,[30] rumors which proved to be false. The unity of the Romanian social and political forces which made possible the unleashing and victory of the insurrection made for the failure of Berlin's attempts to ever-so-vaguely represent the puppet government of Horia Sima as a "coalition" government.

The second major obstacle which faced the "national" government was the locating of its headquarters. On August 30 Horia Sima suggested to von Ribbentrop ". . . delaying the setting up of his government!" He deemed it appropriate to wait "until we are in possession of some Romanian territory lest we be compared to emigré governments."[31]

The securing of a territorial basis was, however, a major problem for the rulers of Germany. The Romanian territory which could have become the headquarters of the "national" government could belong, as a result of military developments, only to southern Transylvania, whose occupation was being contemplated to insure the closing of the mountain passes and, thus, to establish the front on the rim of the Carpathians. The successful military operation which protected the temporary Romanian-Hungarian border—imposed by the Vienna Diktat—insured Romanian control over the strategic access to southern Transylvania and over the Carpathian passes which allowed the Soviet armed forces to penetrate that region, without resistance, at the beginning of September.

As long as the German High Command contemplated the occupation of southern Transylvania the occupation was to entail a joint German-Hungarian effort involving the participation of Horthy's forces. The presence of the Hungarian forces would have made the instalation of Sima's government in southern Transylvania an impossibility for how could a national Romanian government be credible if it were established with the assistance of Horthy's military forces when Horthy's regime, through the Vienna Diktat, took northern Transylvania from Romania? But these were not the only problems as may be seen from an extensive report sent by Werkmeister on August 30: "In the event that, because of military requirements it would be necessary to use Magyar military units on Romanian territory (Transylvania, Banat), the setting up of a national Romanian government would pose serious difficulties since the Hungarians would surely regard their utilization as an indication of our recognizing their rights to southern Transylvania and the Banat." That belief was shared by Hungarian officers with whom he had a chance to talk.[32]

The situation was further complicated by Heinrich Himmler's instructions regarding the evacuation of the ethnic Germans from Transylvania so that, overwhelmed by the inextricable complications and contradictions resultant from the Reich's collaboration with two allies divided by a territorial conflict,[33] the two representatives of the *Auswärtiges Amt* attached to Gen. Friessner's headquarters sent the following message to the State Secretary on September 4: "As long as the situation in Romania continues as is we can see no possibility of making suggestions for the establishment of a genuine Romanian national government especially after we, on the basis of the decision of the *Reichführer* of the SS, are trying to remove the ethnic Germans from Transylvania and, through this, showing that we are giving up this area when in the ultimatum to the Romanians we had stated explicitly that we regard southern Transylvania as a future theater of war. Moreover, the Romanian generals with whom the *Obergruppenführer* Phleps had personal ties of long standing have not joined us, Horia Sima went back to Vienna (probably because he does not see any possibility for any action at this time), action by Hungarian troops in southern Transylvania is being contemplated, and, probably, the ("South Ukraine") Army Group will move its headquarters into the old Hungarian territory."[34] Therefore, the Reich's diplomatic representative in Budapest could henceforth perform the function of political advisor to General Friessner.

These circumstances, which reflected the rejection by all Romanians of the Iron Guard, prevented Horia Sima and his followers from being able to set up a government on Romanian territory. The eight traitors (five members of the Iron Guard and three non-members) who became members of Sima's government, formally established only on December 10, set up headquarters in the Lobkowitz Palace in Vienna.[35] The political countermeasures undertaken by the Nazi regime against the Romanian uprising thus failed completely.

Military Countermeasures

At midnight of August 23-24 the well-known directives issued by Hitler for the arrest of the new government reached Slănic-Moldova, where the headquarters of the German strategic unit in Romania had moved to. What military measures had caused Hitler's action?

At 1:05 a.m., on August 24, the headquarters of the "South Ukraine" Army Group ordered "the principal commander of the Luftwaffe in Romania," A. Gerstenberg, to carry out Hitler's orders by placing at his disposal "the totality of German troops from Bucharest and surroundings."[36] As it was then uncovered that Gerstenberg had no freedom of action, the command of the repressive action was entrusted to the SS brigade leader Hofmeier. A delay of several hours for the execution of this order was decided upon following a telephone message from Gen. Erik Hansen which was received in Slănic at 4:05 the same morning. Hansen stressed, as previously indicated, that the new government enjoyed the support of all people and of all generals.[37] Hansen further expressed his "conviction," shared for that matter also by von Killinger, Clodius, and Gerstenberg, that "by no means do we have the resources to secure Bucharest and dislodge the new government and one may expect such attempts to be bound to fail"[38] Initially, Friessner halted the execution of the ordered steps. Then, on Friessner's orders, Gen. von Grolman, the supreme commander of the "South Ukraine" group, contacted Lt. Col. von Amsberg of OKW informing him of what Hansen had related and suggesting reconfirmation of Hitler's directives. The answer came at 5 a.m. through a telephone call from Gen. Col. Alfred Jodl, the chief of staff of OKW. Jodl stated that Hitler's order stands because: "If we delay things are going to come out very badly. Only immediate action can help us." Ten minutes later, Gen. Gerstenberg, who had reached the quarters of Băneasa,[40] received the order to "unleash the action immediately."[41]

Thus, the carrying out of the attack on Bucharest had been delayed by more than three hours because of conflicting assessments by German military elements on the scene. Hansen's realistic appraisal was superseded by Gerstenberg's opinion according to which the new government in Bucharest was "shaking in its boots" and that only a "very thin curtain of Romanian troops" covered Bucharest.[42]

In anticipation of the forthcoming battle with Soviet forces on the Moldavian plateau members of the German command concerned themselves at all times with the tactics that were to be pursued vis-à-vis the Romanian troops. The King's declaration made so as to delay the Germans' reaction, to the plenipotentiary German minister von Killinger that "it goes without saying that the Romanian leaders will take no action directed against the German troops and citizens of the Reich in Romania,"[43] the hope that Romanian troops or commanders would support the German cause (Friessner "could not believe that the entire Romanian officer corps broke the fealty oath to Germany")[44] initially made for the adoption of an optimistic appraisal of the position of the Romanian troops on the German-Soviet front. During the night of August 23-24 firm orders were given by the German army group to the German forces in Romania that "all measures entailing violence should be suspended with respect to the Romanian army as long as it remains loyal."[45] The open hostility of the Romanian armed forces in the area of the German-Soviet battle—such as the well known case of the detachment of the border troops in Bukovina that found itself among German forces and which, upon hearing the proclamation to the country proceeded immediately to attack the new enemy—brought about a drastic change of attitude from the German side. At 1:30 p.m., on August 24, the "South Ukraine" Army Group ordered that "the armament, vehicles, and materiel of the large Romanian units that are loyal must be merely taken over without, within the limits of the possible, resorting to military violence; on the other hand, Romanian troops which engage in hostile activities or which perform acts of sabotage must be disarmed or exterminated by resorting without hesitation, to force."[46] On August 26, an order of the army group which spelled out new strategic directives issued by Hitler that very day—which is analyzed below—assigned to the forces under its command "the preventing by military force of the Romanian troops' moving beyond the Brăila-Focşani line."[47]

The crushing of the Romanian uprising was perceived, at Rastenburg, as the outcome of a joint military effort by the German forces located in Romania and adjoining territories. In accordance with this perspective the first directives were supplemented by a series of orders designed to "encircle" the area within which the insurrection had occurred. Thus, on the night of August 23-24 the headquarters of the South-Eastern war zone— which comprised the military groups "F" and "E" of Yugoslavia and, respectively, Greece—were instructed to mobilize all forces available in two zones, Nish-Belgrade and Skoplje-Nish. Priority was assigned to the assembling of forces in the Nish-Belgrade zone which was to include the 4th battalion of the Brandenburg regiment, the 468th tank company, an the 2nd division of the 201st artillery brigade.[48] The commanders in Hungary were to organize the movement from Budapest toward Romania of the 8th SS cavalry division, the German commander of the Romanian oil region was to safeguard the flow of petroleum products, via the Danube and the Predeal pass, while Admiral Helmuth Brinkmann, the commander of the "Black Sea Admirality," was to occupy Constanţa. The German troops in Bulgaria were placed on battle alert.

The carrying out of Hitler's first directive—putting down the insurrection and establishing a government loyal to Nazi Germany—was bound to fail. The assault unleased by Gerstenberg at 6 a.m. on August 24 met with strong resistance and ninety minutes later it was reported to have failed. To achieve his mission Gerstenberg resorted to bombing Bucharest, aiming primarily at the royal palace and government office buildings with a view to paralyzing governmental activities and intimidating the population,[49] and sought also the assistance of seasoned troops. German forces of the "South Ukraine" Army Group[50] and from the Nish-Belgrade[51] zone were flown to Bucharest and landed at the Otopeni airport, which was still held by the Germans on August 25 and 26. The Romanian situation was viewed with optimism at Rastenburg on August 24th: "Everybody is concerned over the situation in Romania. Hitler, very optimistic, he uses invectives against the SS intelligence service and the Ministry of Foreign Affairs ridicules Ribbentrop in the presence of Goebbels and Bormann." The next day the atmosphere changed, becoming tense, but the illusions persisted: "Ribbentrop invokes extenuating circumstances, he is certain that Killinger and Gerstenberg will stabilize the situation. Hitler agrees with this view."[52] On August 26 the command of the German forces in the northern suburbs of Bucharest was assumed by Gen. Rainer Stahel, who had flown in from Warsaw. On August 28, Stahel's even smaller forces, moved northward under pressure from Romanian troops. He was captured that very afternoon at Gherghiţa, 25 kilometers south of Ploieşti, by troops of the 4th Romanian Army, retreating from Moldavia. Hitler's first directives resulted, also from a military standpoint, in total failure.

As previously mentioned, in view of the German High Command the "treatment" applied to the Romanian insurrection was an integral component of the "prescription" imposed by the gradually deteriorating status of the Wehrmacht in Romania. To continue the German-Soviet conflict and "regulate" the political-military Romanian action the OKW, on August 26, issued new directives to the "South Ukraine" Army Group. At 3:05 in the morning the order was issued that "the mission of the armies comprising that group is to establish a new line of defense from Galaţi-Focşani-the Carpathians and to repossess the line on the Danube between its delta and Galaţi."[53] In effect, this represented the defensive front which Friessner had contemplated in his conversation with Antonescu on the afternoon of August 22, and for whose establishment Antonescu had issued preliminary orders.[54] At the same time, the directives stated that "the totality of German forces in Romania will have to be organized in combat units which will have to forcibly clear the area Galati-Danube (south of Bucharest)-Bucharest-Ploieşti-Braşov." In other words, while agreeing to the abandonment of Moldavia, the German High Command held on to the idea of annihilating, militarily, the Romanian insurrection and reassume control over the Dobrudja, Wallachia, Oltenia, the Banat, and southern Transylvania. With respect to southern Transylvania the Germans assigned the greatest significance to the area of Braşov, the terminal point of the Predeal pass and, therefore, the 4th German mountain division—which was to land at Sf. Gheorghe, was assigned the task of "conquering" Braşov. On August 25, at 11:50 p.m., the SS *Obergruppenführer* Arthus Phleps,[55] who was then in Yugoslavia, received Himmler's order to leave at once for Transylvania as "empowered general and superior chief of the SS and of police in Transylvania." His was a triple mission: (1) to cause, by using his old contacts within the Romanian

army, the defection of some of its commanders; (2) to handle relations
with ethnic Germans in Transylvania and the Banat; (3) to conduct specific
military operations (the 4th mountain division and the 8th SS cavalry).[56]
The failure of the new strategic directives was due to two related fact-
ors—the Soviet advance toward the Focşani-Galaţi area and the "opening,"
by the uprising, of the fortified Focşani Gate through which the forces
of the Red Army penetrated on August 27. On August 15, the Romanian
Supreme Command ordered that the active Romanian forces of the
Dobrudja, of the fortification battalions which manned the fortified
Focşani-Nămoloasa-Galaţi line, and of the service units of the Bucharest-
Ploieşti zone be moved.[57] In this manner, the proposed front which the
Germans intended to use against advancing Soviet armes was dismantled
by the Romanians on the night of August 25-26, 1944. In the evening of
August 26 the Soviet troops advanced, in several spots, beyond the Focşani
Gate. The assessment of the command of the "South Ukraine" Army
Group on August 24, at 7ͺ35 in the evening, that "the defense of the
Brăila-Focşani line is no longer possible"[58] was, given the defection of
the Romanian army, realistic. At the same time, the main *Widerstand-
gruppen*, located behind the front line—that of Bucharest and that of the
oil region—were either liquidated (the first on August 28), or encircled
and annihilated (the second as of August 27 when Ploieşti was taken over
by the Romanians). The German forces which withdrew from Moldavia
or were assaulted following the penetration of the Focşani Gate were
either destroyed or captured in the Bărăgan by the Romanian insurrectionary forces or used a Romanian "controlled" itinerary to move
into Transylvania. Using as a "turntable" the town of Buzău, which
the Germans had set up for defensive purposes, a few German troops
used the Intorsura Buzăului pass, which was outside the area of the
Romanian insurrection, for withdrawal purposes.

Consequently, the OKW, aware of the obvious lack of success of the
directives of August 26 issued, three days later, another order to the
Wehrmacht forces in Romania. The mission of the "South Ukraine"
Army Group was now to "secure and maintain a continuous defensive
line ranging from the Romanian-Bulgarian frontier, the Carpathians, to
the juncture with the right wing of the 17th army corps;" in other words,
defensive along the entire Romanian Carpathian rim.[59] The offensives unleashed by the Wehrmacht during the first half of September in southern

Transylvania and in the Banat—which also failed—were to facilitate the carrying out of these new directives.

Propaganda Countermeasures

The German propaganda machine sought to combat the Romanian insurection in two ways, depending on its addresses. Internally, for German public opinion, it was necessary to find a way of presenting and interpreting events which would not demoralize the population with the specter of another defeat; externally, for allies, enemies, and neutral countries, it was essential to depict the events in Romania in a manner which would demonstrate that any break with the Reich was, in fact, catastrophic.

As always in wartime, apprehensions and rumors—some incredible— engulfed the German civilian population. Under the circumstances, the place of Romania, and particularly the contents of rumors concerning Romania, is important with respect to German civilian attitudes toward this "involuntary ally." Thus, according to data secured by the SS security service in Karlsruhe, Braunschweig, Munich, Berlin, Bayreuth, and elsewhere, there was apprehension over the likely loss of the Romanian and Galician oilfields since the ensuing paralysis which would have hit the submarine and air fleets was equated with the loss of the war."[60] Two weeks later, the same service recorded apprehension over Romania's and Hungary's reliability vis-à-vis the Reich given the massive bombardments carried out by the Anglo-American airforce.[61] Two days following the invasion of Normandy, on June 8, 1944, a report notes rumors that American bombers were used in Romania and Bulgaria.[62] Finally, on July 13, it was reported that in Bremen and elsewhere there was "great concern over the Romanian oilfields."[63]

In view of the sensitivity of Germany's public opinion regarding the possibility of Romania's defection and, especially, the loss of petroleum, which such an act would represent, it was very difficult to inform the Germans that their fears had been realized. The psychological preparations for receipt of the shocking news was perceivable in the military communiques issued by the Wehrmacht. On August 23 mention is made of the joint German-Romanian actions designed to stop the advances achieved by the Soviet army during the Iași-Chișinău offensive;[64] on August 24

mention is made of the violent fighting on the lower Prut and the middle
Siret, as well as at Roman, however, without mentioning the actual com-
battants;[65] on August 25 it was announced that "certain Romanian units
have ceased their resistance against the Bolsheviks."[66] During the night of
August 26, at 12:45 a.m., Berlin radio announced that "no statements
regarding the measures which have been taken and will be taken against
Romania" have been issued from the Wilhelmstrasse. It was stated, nevertheless, that the Reich would not take these events "lying down."[67] Only
on August 26 was it announced that "the isolated resistance of the partisans of the royal clique had been crushed. In the surroundings of Bucharest and in the city itself the traitors' repeated attacks have been repelled."[68] The communique reports also common actions of German troops
and Romanian forces which remained loyal to the Reich which existed
only in the imagination of the authors of the communique. Henceforth,
the insurrection is no longer mentioned in the communiques of the Wehrmacht and German public opinion is kept informed only about the advance of Soviet troops into Romania and the fierce resistance of German
units and, as of August 28, Hungarian forces fighting alongside the Germans are mentioned also for the first time.[69] In the evening of August 24,
at 8:45, the broadcast in Portugese transmitted by radio Berlin stated
that "a group of Romanian patriots has started the epuration of the
camarilla" and that in Bucharest there was "heavy street fighting."[70]

Significant too are the indications given the German press by the Ministry of Propaganda on August 24. Newsmen were asked to "condemn"
the uprising as a "heinous crime," characteristically, however, also with
the admonition that "nothing should be said about the Romanian forces'
treason. Nor must there be given, for the time being, any information
about German countermeasures."[71] Indeed, the communiques issued by
the Wehrmacht in no way mention the attack staged by Gen. Gerstenberg
or the aerial bombing of Bucharest. The insurrection was presented as a
palace putsch, devoid of popular support and, as such, doomed to failure.

Only when the magnitude of the insurrection caused the failure of German countermeasures and the collapse of the totality of the German forces
located between the Carpathians and the Danube was the status of the
"South Ukraine" Army Group brought to the public's attention but, even
then, in terms which masked the true dimensions of the catastrophe and,
most noteworthy, without any mention of the contribution of Romania's

insurrection to the débacle, even though that contribution had been acknowledged by Hitler in confidential discussions.

At the Romanian level, German propaganda could not fail to take into account the reality of the situation, the common action of the Romanian people and army directed to the regaining of national independence and to chasing the German troops from Romanian soil. Yet, illusions in the power of "magic of words" still persisted. The German radio station Ilse II, located near Bucharest, broadcast from the evening of August 24th until the evening of the 27th the appeal of the "Romanian national government" according to which the insurrection had been put down throughout the country except in Bucharest where "weak resistance," without any chance of success, still persisted. As stated, retrospectively, by a German eyewitness, "At no time could there by found a Popescu or Ionescu, or as we would say a Heinz or Kunz, who would have lent his name to the appeal for reconstituting a pro-Axis Romania."[72] The propaganda activity of the aforementioned radio station, in fact, backfired. Because of its otpimistic presentation, so contrary to the reality of the situation, broadcasts contributed to the "total disinformation" of scattered units such as night aircraft intercepters and others, which had lost contact with the upper echelons."[73] The *Obergruppenführer* Artur Phleps issued a manifesto calling on the Romanians to fight alongside the Wehrmacht;[74] Andreas Schmidt asked that proclamations signed by Horia Sima be broadcast as well as distributed as printed manifestos.[75] Both men became aware of the futility of their hopes as there were no defections with the insurrectionary forces. On September 6 Werkmeister reported, inter alia, that "Phleps was surprised that no Romanian general joined him."[76] The Nazi propaganda measures were doomed to failure a priori as they could not dent the moral and political unity of the Romanian people.

Conclusions

The German measures designed to liquidate the Romanian insurrection of August 1944 were based on an accurate perception of Romania's political, economic, and strategic significance as the Romanian territory was vital for the maintenance of the German military forces in South-East Europe and for the continuous functioning of the German wartime economy. Hitler himself, in a conversation with Gen. Gerstenberg, in August 1944, stated, with reference to the significance of the Romanian oilfields, that "We risk everything. If we lose the oil region we can no longer win the war."[77] At the crossroads of two main strategic coordinates—toward South-Eastern and Central Europe—Romania was of fundamental importance in the general war strategy of the Reich. Her staying in the German camp insured Nazi control of the Balkan Peninsula and cut off access toward the Panonian Plain, Austria, and southern Germany. The military events that followed the Romanian insurrection confirmed the accuracy of the German High Command's assessment of the political and strategic importance of the Romanian territory. Shortly after the success of the insurrection the German military establishment in South-Eastern Europe disintegrated and the strategic route toward Hungary and southern Germany was made good use of by Soviet forces, then allied with the Romanian army.

The element of surprise, so integral a component of the Romanian insurrection created confusion within both the German High Command and the German forces in Romania. This resulted in an improvised German response to the insurrection. The rapid sequel of directives from the OKW reveals the inability of the upper German echelons to work out a set of unitary and coherent measures to keep Romania under German control.

The improvised character of the German reaction was determined, from the beginning to the end of the insurrection, by the Romanian forces of the insurrection. The realities of the battleground invariably negated the effectiveness of the countermeasures ordered by the German commanders who were out of step with the evolution of events in Romania.

If the "defection" of Italy, on September 8, 1943, was thwarted, in part, by German countermeasures which allowed the reestablishment of Nazi control over more than half of the Italian peninsula and if the possible defection of Hungary was prevented through the occupation of the country, the Romanian insurrection was the first action from within the Axis camp, directed against Germany, which fully attained its goals. The inability of the German High Command to reestablish control over Romania was yet another manifestation of the crisis faced by Hitler's Reich in the conduct of the war, a crisis made irreversible by the Romanian insurrection.

The success of the Romanian insurrection was possible through the intertwining of political-military preparedness, carefully organized and led by the Romanian Communist Party, with conditions specific to the Romanian tradition of the entire people's war. [78]

CHAPTER IV

THE MILITARY-STRATEGIC CONSEQUENCES OF
THE ROMANIAN REVOLUTION ON THE
DEVELOPMENT OF WORLD WAR II

A. Romania's Strategic Importance in the War
as a Whole in the Summer of 1944

The as truthful as possible assessment of Romania's strategic importance in the development of the war in Europe in the summer of 1944 requires, first of all, a general survey of the military situation for the two conflicting sides on the continent.

To begin with, what was the dynamics on the main land front of World War II, namely where were, starting June 1941, the military forces of the Soviet Union and of Hitler's Germany that were facing each other?

Following the failure sustained by the Luftwaffe in the air battle for England, the counteroffensive of Moscow in the winter of 1941 had forever debunked the myth of German military invincibility, built up in Poland and Western Europe during a previous period. The "Blitzkrieg," on which the "Barbarossa" had relied, was utterly compromised and the German-Soviet war was to change into a prolonged conflict. Stalingrad (winter 1942-1943) and Kursk (1943) had led, through the decisive victories of the Red Army, to the latter's definitively having the strategic initiative.

The Soviet-German front was the main theater of operations of World War II, with the Soviet Union making the greatest contribution to the defeat of Nazi Germany; the former boasted the broadest resistance movement (some one million men) in the occupied territory and sustained the most painful human and material losses.

In 1944, the Soviet Supreme Command dealt a number of extremely heavy offensive blows at the enemy along a considerably vast front—some 4,500 km—from the Barents Sea to the Black Sea.[1] First, in the north. Starting with mid-January until late February, three Soviet strategic groups relieved Leningrad and advanced 200-220 km westwards, crushing the bulk of the German Army Group "North." Triggered off as early as late 1943, the offensive operation carried on by five Soviet fronts west of the Dnieper grew, in April 1944, into a huge advance of the Red Army, which freed most of the Ukraine and the Crimea, penetrating into the north-east of Romania in late March. In the area of Leningrad and Novogrod the Soviet troops penetrated some 300 km into the enemy disposition, while in the southern sectors of the front 600 km on the average. Starting June 23, 1944,the Soviet Command planned and carried through a powerful offensive operation against the German Army Group "Center" in the central sector of the Soviet-German alignment. In late July as a result of the successful development of the offensive, the front alignment in that sector was pushed to the Vistula and the eastern frontier of Eastern Prussia. The next broad-scope Soviet offensive was mounted in the southern sector of the Soviet-German front, between the northernmost end of the Romanian Eastern Carpathians and the estuary of the Dniester. Known in Soviet historiography as the "Jassy-Kishinev" operation, it was launched on August 20, 1944. Through a strategic directive of the Soviet High Command, the 2nd and 3rd Ukrainian Fronts were assigned the mission to reach the towns of Focşani and Galaţi,[2] which meant an indepth advance of 150-200 km. On August 23, 1944, the moment the Romanian insurrection was triggered off, the Soviet forces were deployed along the following alignment: west of the Pruth—north of Tîrgu Neamţ, north-east of Roman, north of Bîrlad, north-west of Huşi; east of the Pruth—north-west of Bujoru, north of Kishinev, south-east of Rezina, east of Leovo, Taraclia, north of Tatar-Bunar.

In the summer of 1944 in Western and Southern Europe there were some other fronts of continental strategic importance. In Italy, where it was opened as early as in autumn 1943, the Allies had scored a number of successes among which most notable were clearing the south of the peninsula of German troops, the liberation of Rome (June 4, 1944) and the offensive mounted against the German transpeninsular defensive disposition called the "Gothic Line" (starting July 21, 1944), between Pisa and Rimini.[3] On August 4, the Allies planned a new attack on the "Gothic Line"—"Olive" plan—with the main blow to be dealt at the left wing of the enemy defenses. The decisive attack was to be delivered on August 25, 1944, by the American Fifth Army—its rear on the Arno river—on an 8 mile-long front between Florence and Pontassieve; the British Eighth Army, meant to bear the brunt of the whole operation, was supposed to attack with three army corps in the Adriatic sector (its starting base on the Meturo river). After minute preparations, the Allied offensive against the "Gothic Line" started at the scheduled date.

The front in north-western Europe, in France, had been opened on June 6, 1944, through the greatest landing operation ever known—"Overlord." By setting a firm "foot" in North-Western France, the Allies enlarged the bridgehead established in Normandy with every passing day, eliminated a large German group in the Falaise-Argentan "pocket," whose reduction started on August 17, 1944. On August 21, 1944, leaving behind enough troops for the annihilation of the "pocket", the Allied troops continued the pursuit of the enemy eastwards, toward the Seine. On August 23, 1944, the French 2nd Armored Division began to move, heading for Paris with the mission to assist the anti-Hitler resistance forces in the Capital of France in freeing the city. On August 25, 1944, the line of the main Allied front in Western Europe was the following: north of Le Havre—Elbeuf—the course of the Seine up to Montereau—the course of the Yonne,—south of Nogent sur Seine—Troyes—St. Florentin —south of Joigny—Gien—the course of the Loire.[4]

On August 19, 1944, the Supreme Command of the Allied expeditionary forces in the west of the continent decided to force the Seine and continue the pursuit of the enemy to the German border. Another, less important, front had been opened in the south of France on August 15, 1944. Carrying through the plan of the "Anvil" Allied operation, the American Seventh Army, with the French "B" Army of General de Lattre de Tassigny under its command, quickly established a powerful bridgehead in the Marseille-Toulon area, by August 23, 1944, having engaged in combat against the German garrisons on the southern coast of France.

To the situation of the fronts in Europe in August 1944 one should necessarily add two components of utmost importance. First, there was the anti-Hitler resistance movement of the subjugated European peoples, which in 1944 knew its acme by the triggering off of national insurrections. On June 15, 1944, the insurrection of Vercors broke out, the French patriots fighting for more than a month (until July 23) to set up the "Vercors Republic" on that mountainous plateau, an embryo of free France. In Warsaw, the capital of Poland, which the Soviet commanding officers could easily see through their binoculars, the insurrection broke out on August 1, 1944; the Polish insurgents had not informed the Allies about their decision, as they considered it an act of sovereignty.[5] The Romanian insurrection would be followed—in a temporal and causal succession—by similar people's risings in arms against the occupants in Slovakia and in Sofia, the capital city of Bulgaria. Alongside the front armies of the Allies, the resistance movement as a whole dealt heavy blows at the Hitlerite occupants; in some countries—particularly in Yugoslavia, but also in occupied Albania, Greece, France, Italy, etc.—vast territories got out of the Wehrmacht's control, while considerable forces of the latter would be pinned down.

The second component of the military background in Europe was the air war. Powerfully mounted in June 1944, the Anglo-American "oil offensive" was solely aimed at the oil-fields and oil processing facilities—the plants for synthetic fuel included—in the European territories under Hitler's control (Romania, Austria, Hungary) and in the Reich; the Western Allied strategy also envisaged the bombing of Hitlerite communications of any kind throughout Europe, particularly those in the rear of the future offensive directions, of the main economic areas of the Reich, and also of the major German towns (with the purpose of wearing down the German resistance capacity and of stirring the civilian population to revolt).[6]

On the other fronts of World War II—in Asia, on the Pacific and Atlantic oceans—the military forces of the Anti-Hitler coalition and of the resistance movement of the subjugated peoples were dealing deadly blows at the occupants. The naval forces of the anti-Hitler powers—particularly those of the USA—had the strategic upper hand in the confrontation with the Nipponese enemy, gradually restraining the "sphere of co-prosperity in South-East Asia," built up through aggression by the Japanese Empire in the previous years. The Chinese liberation army, the patriotic forces in the other Asian occupied countries were successfully fighting for winning back national independence and sovereignty.

What was the military-strategic importance of Romania within that wide military context?

Due to her geographical location, to her natural resources (oil and cereals in particular) and to the railway tracks and the roads crisscrossing her national territory, Romania held first rate attributes in the war in Europe in the summer of 1944. There were the Romanian Carpathians there, a true barrier in the way of military movements from the east toward the center of Europe and vice-versa.

The geo-strategic importance of the Carpathians had been many a time attested to in the history of the Romanian people. Alongside the Danube, the Carpathians belong to the geographical coordinates of the Romanians' past and, as noticed, they have been the "element polarizing the Romanians."[7] From time immemorial, the Carpathians were a true stronghold under the shelter of which the power and civilization of the Geto-Dacians developed. Their link with the Carpathians was so strong that it would strike even their contemporaries, among whom Florus, who said concisely: "daci inhaerent montibus" (the Dacians stick to the mountains). It was in the mountainous areas that the Geto-Dacians put up the most stubborn resistance to the Roman invaders. During the epoch of the migrations, the stronghold of the Carpathians proved impenetrable the waves of steppe populations being compelled into taking roundabout ways or just vanishing following the impact with its walls. As it has been observed, if the Romanian people "have managed to survive in these places it is precisely because this stronghold itself [the Carpathians—a.n.] where it was born also defended it, protected it and enabled it to preserve its own being afterwards."[8] While for the Romanians, the people of the land, the Carpathians have never been a barrier, for the foreign invaders they have always been an obstacle, their crossing requiring long efforts and a heavy toll in human lives. In World War I, the Romanian army crossed the mountains, enthusiastically welcomed by the Romanian population in Transylvania; when the Austro-Hungarian and German troops launched the offensive trying to break through the Romanian defense in the mountains, it took them almost two months to penetrate into the Jiu Valley, the other passes being "locked up" by the Romanian forces, which carried on extremely bitter fighting. The same firm resistance would be put up by the Romanian soldiers in the pass of Oituz (the Trotuş Valley) and in the curvature of the Carpathians during the the grim fighting in the summer of 1917. Despite the repeated attempts of the enemy to force his way through the mountainous area and to penetrate into Moldavia, the Romanian defensive held on successfully. A conclusion attested to by the entire historical development of the Romanians is that the natural barrier of the Romanian Carpathians, arranged militarily and steadfastly defended, is an obstacle of utmost strategic importance, its crossing by the attackers requiring huge efforts and a considerably long period of time.

Anyone trying to penetrate from the north or east toward South-East Europe, into the Balkan Peninsula, had necessarily to cross the Romanian territory or pass through it close proximity. Joining two big natural obstacles with great military bearings—the Carpathians and the maritime Danube—by a permanent fortification in the Focşani-Galaţi area was a serious obstacle in the way of such an attempt. To quote the pertinent remarks of a specialist, this line: "is potentially one of the strongest positions for the strategic defense of Europe." With one flank defended by the Black Sea and by the swamps, and the other one by the Siret and by the Carpathian Mountains, the opening inbetween could be attacked but directly from the Danube, an almost impossible operation unless the strongholds of Galaţi and Ismail are carried first."[9] And that the more so as the Romanian Plain and Dobrudja lent considerable depth to the defensive in that direction. Under the concrete circumstances in the summer of 1944, the Romanian Plain presented a twofold importance for the strategic balance of the two conflicting coalitions. First, it allowed for passing around the Carpathian arch, easily defendable but difficult to cross, through an offensive from the east; second, the plain was a vast flank of the German disposition in the Balkan Peninsula, offering good opportunities for successfully carrying on military actions against the latter north-southwards (the Craiova-Bechet-Sofia-Istanbul or Craiova-Sofia-Salonica variants) or north-east—south-westwards (the Craiova-Belgrade-Trieste variant). The mastery of the Romanian Plain by an allied Romanian acquired paramount importance in the summer of 1944; it held the Soviet forces join hands with the people's liberation army in Yugoslavia, organized and led by Josip Broz Tito, and actually disintegrated the flank and rear of the Hitlerite disposition in the Balkan Peninsula.

Dobrudja, with Romania's seacoast, was important not only as a safe territory for a possible defense on the Eastern Carpathians and the maritime Danube. Under the circumstances of Romania's changeover, it not only opened the strategic coastline route (used in the previous centuries too for penetrating in-depth the Balkan Peninsula), but also deprived the Reich of its land bases, essential to a German maritime presence in the basin of the Black Sea.

As it has been mentioned, the Romanian Carpathian chain was a natural barrage of utmost importance in front of military progress from the east toward Central Europe. Its being under Romanian authority not only denied the Wehrmacht the chance of prolonged defensive action but the possession of the Transylvanian Plateau and of the plain lying west of the mountains also allowed for their turning into a huge bridgehead to be used for mounting a decisive offensive toward the southern borders of the Reich on the routes Vatra Dornei-Sighet-Budapest-Vienna or Timişoara-Arad-Budapest-Vienna. Therefore, not only was the Reich denied the chance of prolonged resistance—as a Germany military analyst would maintain even before the war was over—but, what counted more, some wide "locks" would be opened to the subsequent offensive carried on, across Romania's western plans and the vast Hungarian steppe, toward Vienna.

The Carpathians, the Danube and the Black Sea, the geographical coordinates of the making of the Romanian people, proved of remarkable consequence on the European strategic chess-board in the international circumstances in the summer of 1944. Their inclusion in the strategic "dowry" of the United Nations—sanctioned by the Romanian insurrection—was expected to have and actually had a paramount impact on the development of the war, speeding up its issue.

As it is known, time is a cardinal factor in the development of military operations. The length of a military operation closely depends on the number of forces engaged in the defensive or the offensive, on the strength and complexity of the engineer works done on various alignments and, last but not least, on the geo-climatic conditions in which the confrontation takes place. Thus, a defensive operation carried on in a rough terrain

allowing the turning to good account of its features for efficiently organiz-
ing successive alignments is obviously more likely to succeed than in a flat
area, lacking natural irregularities, therefore favoring the offensive. The
stronger and more efficiently used, form the military point of view, the
natural obstacles, the longer such a defensive operation.

In the history of World War II, like, as a matter of fact, in all military
conflicts, time had an utmost strategic importance. The length of the
military operations depended on the number and quality of the forces
committed to battle by either side, and also on the political developments
which entailed fundamental changes in the military situation. Both camps
involved in the 1939-1945 conflagration attached paramount importance
to time. For instance, during the last stage of the conflict the political-
military leaders of the Nazi Reich banked on a prolongation of the war
with a view to turning operational the new weapons, at the time in an
advanced stage of the research-design-serial production cycle. Within the
anti-Hitler coalition, American long-term planning, for example, took into
account the time needed for gearing the huge economic potential of the
USA to wartime requirements, and such decisions as would suit the carrying on of combined military operations in both hemispheres. Time was
attached equal importance by the Soviet Union during the first stage of
the war against Hitler's Germany, when the huge transfer of industrial
output and facilities from the west to the east of the country was a top
priority of the Soviet military-strategic planning.

B. "When Germany's Defeat Was Not Yet Clear"

One salient feature makes Romania's resolute action of August 1944,
by which she turned her weapons on Nazi Germany and joined with her
entire military and economic potential the coalition of the United Nations, stand out in bold relief. The Romanian changeover—an instance
of exemplarily asserting the attributes of State sovereignty—achieved without an initial understanding with the allied partners as for the timing
and the ways of its implementation—occurred at a moment when the
developments on the theaters of war were not indicative that the victory
of the United Nations was a certain fact yet. In other words, Romania,
an independent State, joined the war against the Hitlerite coalition
through a national option that suited her highest interests at a time when

the lot of the world conflict had not been decided yet, while Germany was far from being defeated.

Contemporary highly authorized people would emphasize that defining characteristic of Romania's action. In the Decree issued by the Presidium of the Supreme Soviet of the USSR on July 6, 1945, by which the head of the Romanian State at the time was awarded the "Victory" Order, the Soviet's highest war honor—it should be mentioned here that only six other foreign personalities have been awarded the highest Soviet war decoration—it was pointed out that Romania had effected a resolute change in her policy "at a time when Germany's defeat was not yet clear." At the Peace Conference in Paris, V. M. Molotov, the representative of the Soviet Union, reasserted that appreciation in even clearer terms: "On August 23 [1944], when the prospects of the future development of military events were not obvious yet, while Germany's lot was far from being decided, Romania's foreign policy took a decisive turn."[10]

The analysis of facts fully corroborate such appreciations. In the summer of 1944, Germany had 9,365,000 soldiers and officers, 124,000 artillery muzzles, 12,400 armor, 5,700 combat aircraft, 474 ships (of which 411 were submarines).[11] The other combat partners of the Wehrmacht —the Romanian army included—totalled 2,700,000 manpower, 22,000 artillery muzzles, over 600 armor and 2,000 combat aircraft.

In the summer of 1944, the world conflict generally indicated a ratio of forces that helped, in some respects and in classic terms, a long defensive of the coalition opposing the United Nations.[12]

The manpower and war materiel Nazi Germany possessed were considerable resources for carrying on a flexible defensive on the European continent. And that was not all: there were availabilities enabling her to mount offensive operations, even wide-scope ones, likely to shatter the Allied fronts.

The development of events subsequent to August 1944 rendered evident the defensive and offensive capabilities of the Wehrmacht's military power. In September 1944, less than a month after the successful Romanian insurrection, the largest airborne operation ever known, combined with a bold advance on land—both bearing the code name of "Market Place"—would be quickly thwarted by the German forces in Holland. The Western Allies' attempt to cross the Rhine by one blow was thus baffled, and Germany's natural western border would be crossed only

Manpower and materiel	The antifascist coalition (the USSR, the USA and Great Britain)	Hitler's coalition (Germany and Japan)	Ratio of forces
Manpower (thousands of people)	25,610	13,822	1.8:1
Cannon and throwers (thousands of pieces)	223.6	140.0	1.6:1
Armor (thousands of pieces)	28.9	15.7	1.8:1
Modern battleships	1,295	653	2.0:1

later (March 7, 1945),[13] over the bridge at Remagen, the only bridge left undamaged by some miracle. A wide-scope offensive response would be staged and carried through by the Wehrmacht High Command in the Ardennes in December 1944. Its aim was "to win a decisive victory in the West,"[14] and during an earlier stage of the operation, as a result of a successful breakthrough of the American front, "The Allies were on the verge of disaster [. . .] due to a neglect of their defensive flank."[15] The psychological impact of the German offensive "spasm" was so high that one of the American military leaders, General George Patton, commander of the American Third Army, would note down in his diary on January 4, 1945: "We can still lose this war."[16] The combination of the Western Allies' exemplary defensive in the Ardennes with a new Soviet offensive —launched upon the Anglo-American's request starting January 12, 1945— turned the operation in the Ardennes into a "second Stalingrad," to quote the German Division General Hasso von Manteuffell.[17]

On March 6, 1945, the Wehrmacht mounted a new offensive, this time on the Soviet front, whose success was expected to bring Hitler as a present for his birthday (April 20), among other things, nothing but the Romanian oil![18] The operation—its code name "Frühlingserwachen" started successfully, the German armor managing to penetrate some 25 km in depth the Soviet defense in two days. However, the Soviet counter-offensive launched on March 16 put an end to that last German offensive of the war.

The defensive capabilities of the Wehrmacht were no less striking through their performances during the months subsequent to Romania's joining the war alongside the United Nations. Suffice it to say in this respect that while Berlin was falling under the Soviet offensive blows, which actually marked the end of the war in Europe, there still were powerful Hilterite forces in Czechoslovakia, Austria, Holland, Denmark and Norway.

May 9, 1945, saw the surrender of the German forces in the Channel Islands and of the garrisons at Dunkirk, Lorient and St. Nazaire (on the coast of Brittany, France). Resistance to the last man of the German forces in the redoubt of the Austrian Alps had also been taken into account, a fact that greatly worried the Western Allies.

The Wehrmacht's military availabilities in 1944-1945 would be strongly increased through an industrial effort that in some fields reached over that period the highest figures throughout the entire world war. In 1944 the German war industry yielded 149,000 artillery muzzles, 18,300 armor, 37,900 aircraft. Quite relevant for the growing vitality of the German armament industry is that in the latter half of that year the output of the first semester was topped by 39.9 percent with cannon, by 19.8 percent with armor and by 36.9 percent with aircraft.[19] The monthly armor output would attain the highest figures in December 1944, when 1,799 tanks and motor cannon were sent to the front. The monthly armor output kept up at 1,600 pieces all throughout November 1944-February 1945. In November 1944 the number of Luftwaffe aircraft was the greatest since the beginning of the war in September 1939: 8,103 aircraft (exclusive of carriers), out of which 5,317 were operational.[20]

Starting in the summer of 1944, the Germans produced new weapons, credited, not without success, in the ranks of their own troops, as a result of Goebbels' propaganda, with a decisive impact on the development of war, conducive to the Wehrmacht's victory. On June 13, 1944, the first V-1 (Vergeltungswaffe—the weapon of revenge) missiles hit England, launched from pads on the western coast of France, and then dropped from bombers. In September 1944, V-2, a supersonic missile, became

operational and the towns of England would almost daily be the target
of such weapons. Between June 13, 1944, and March 29, 1945, 5,900
V-1 rockets were launched on England, and more than 1,000 V-2's between September 8, 1944 and March 27, 1945, resulting in considerable
damages.[21]

When assessing the military consequences of the Romanian insurrection in August 1944 one has also to take into account the chances of
enriching—quantitatively and qualitatively—the Wehrmacht's arsenal by
a number of highly efficient weapons.

The discoveries made after the downfall of the Third Reich highlighted
the advanced stage of research on and production of new types of armament—particularly in the field of aircraft and missiles—which, given their
exceptional performances, might have had—had they been massively
employed—a strong impact upon the development of military operations.

A brief presentation of some of those achievements show the prospects
opened to Hitler's Germany by progress in the field of combat technology. In the field of the navy, for instance, two submarines—the "electric
submarine" XXI and its smaller variant XXIII—had such technical-tactical
qualities that made them almost invulnerable. Their capacity for avoiding
detection and attacks, of launching a sheaf of six torpedoes from a depth
of 50 m, the latter themselves provided with almost unfailing mechan-
isms, turned them into a redoubtable weapon. In May 1945 the Kriegsmarine had 80 submarines of the XXI type and 40 of the XXIII type.

The achievements made in the field of aviation were even more spectacular. Germany had built the first jet plane in the world as far back as 1939.
Five years later, in autumn 1944, the first squadron of jet-fighters Messer-
schmitt Me262 (speed: 980 km/h; armament: four 30 mm guns and 24
R4M rockets) was created. Their efficiency was proved already in their
first battle mission: during an air combat six Me 262 shot down 15 Allied
four-engine bombers in only a few minutes. In February 1945, Heinkel
He-162, known as "Volksjäger" (popular fighter) became operational, a
plane that at an altitude of 6,000 m reached a speed of 840 km/h. The
Luftwaffe had in Arado-234, the first jet reconnaisance bomber: its speed
was of 800-880 km/h, its range of flight 1,500 km, and its transport
capacity of two tons of bombs; the Junkers Ju-287 was the first jet heavy
bomber, with a speed of 965 km/h, a range of flight of 1,500 km, and a
transport capacity of four tons of bombs. For the bombing of the United

States, the two-stage A9/A10 intercontinental missile had been designed, with the first stage meant for the take-off, afterwards A9 being able to continue its flight independently, reaching while descending on the target the speed of 7,850 km/h. Finally, it should be mentioned that in the field of air-to-air missiles, the R4M type built by the Germans proved remarkably efficient in April 1945, when 24 German fighters provided with a type of missile succeeded in shooting down 40 Boeing heavy bombers in just a few minutes. As pointed out with good reason by Ph. Masson, from whom we have taken the above data, "in 1945, Germany was about to introduce a series of new weapons in battle, meant to bring about a true tactical revolution. As a matter of fact, with the exception of the nuclear arms, those new types are even today the essential arms of the conventional forces of all the countries of the world. The introduction of the XXI type submarine called for a reappraisal of the entire doctrine of convoy defense; the missiles meant the end of the heavy, slow strategic bomber. Finally, the missiles announced the obsolescence of heavy artillery, ushering in the era of intercontinental bombings."[22]

Such prospects were to a great extent annulled by the Romanian insurrection, which deprived the Nazi Reich of the time and fuel it needed for the production and use of those weapons. Speeding up the end of the war by 200 days, Romania's action contributed to those redoubtable achievements of German combat technology remaining in the design stage or at a small-scale production level. The massive use of those weapons—the specialists have agreed on it—would have prolonged the war and would have raised considerable obstacles in the way of the anti-Hitler coalition's victory.

In addition to the redoubtable military power of Nazi Germany in the latter half of 1944, one should not forget the generally high morale of the Werhmacht troops.[23] In February 1945, a decree providing for recruitment up to the age of 45 allowed for the setting up of eight new divisions.[24] Looking back at the epoch, it is indeed hardly understandable that in 1945 Hitler's Germany and the Wehrmacht still hoped for victory, a hope that explains, among other things, their desperate resistance to the end of the war. North Africa, France, Belgium, Luxemburg, Crete, most of the Balkan Peninsula, Italy and Poland, parts of Holland, Czechoslovakia and Yugoslavia, Eastern Prussia had been freed from German occupation. The territory of the Reich—towns, communications, industrial areas—were the target of continuous Allied bombing. And despite all those facts spelling defeat, the Wehrmacht continued to fight, and Hitler's Germany tried hard, desperately, to hold on.

Therefore, Romania's joining the war alongside the anti-Hitler coalition on August 23, 1944, was not dictated by some calculations of opportunism, with the certitude of the Hitlerite Reich's defeat as a fundamental element, but it was an act of resolute will to influence the course of the world war. The immediate alliance with the United Nations through the insurrectional act also meant Romania's resuming her natural foreign policy, abruptly interrupted in the autumn of 1940 as a result of some developments in the political-military European arena that had imposed the Reich's domination over the greatest part of the continent. Four years later, the Reich continued stubbornly to hold on and was far from being defeated.

Under those complex strategic-political circumstances, dominated by a paroxistic confrontation between the belligerents, whose issue had not been decided yet, the Romanian insurrection of August 1944 sensibly tipped the scales in favor of the anti-Hitler coalition, speeding up the latter's victory.

C. The Collapse of the German Defensive at the Southern Wing
of the Soviet-German Front

The Soviet offensive of Jassy-Kishinev launched on August 20, 1944, scored significant results already in its first day. It aimed at encircling and smashing the main forces of the "South Ukraine" Army Group through two powerful blows converging on Huşi, and at reaching, during an earlier stage, the Bacău-Leovo-Tarutino alignment. The subsequent task of the 2nd Ukrainian Front was to pursue the offensive toward Focşani, while the 3rd Ukrainian Front toward Ismail-Galaţi, that is up to the Focşani-Nămoloasa-Brăila fortified line.[25] Already in early August 1944, General Hans Friessner, the commander of the German strategic group in Romania, had anticipated that, in the event of a wide-scope Soviet offensive, the need would arise of a rapid reshuffling on the Danube-Siret-the Carpathian line.[26] Approval for such an action was given on the night of August 22, 1944 (at about 10 p.m.), after Marshal Antonescu, Romania's dictator, visiting the front, had established with Hans Friessner (August 22, 3:00-3:30 p.m.) the details of the reshuffling.

According to Hans Friessner's reminiscences and to some Soviet or German historiographic works, the encirclement of the bulk of the "South Ukraine" Army Group was carried through by the Soviet forces on the morning of August 25,[27] therefore more than 40 hours after the triggering off of the Romanian insurrection, which had lent a new course to the military developments at the southern wing of the Soviet-German front. Was the new course, the exclusive outcome of the Romanian insurrection?

On the evening of August 22, the left wing of the German-Romanian disposition between the Eastern Carpathians and the Black Sea, consisting of the Romanian Fourth Army and the German Eighth Army, fully preserving their combat strength, had started reshuffling. The final target of the reshuffling was the F.N.B. line but the action was supposed to be carried out in stages.

Details should be given here on the importance attached to the Focşani-Nămoloasa-Brăila line by Marshal Ion Antonescu. In order to check the Soviet offensive on that alignment, he had ordered that three fortifications detachments (the 106th, 115th and 121st), totalling nine battalions, the 8th Motorborne Cavalry Division, a detachment of which had arrived south-east of Tecuci on August 23, 1944, and the 6th, 15th and 21st Training Infantry Divisions be brought over, alongside a great number of AAA pieces shifted from the Bucharest and Ploieşti areas to be used against armor. Likewise, the plans for the defense of the fortified line also contemplated the participation of other Romanian and German units withdrawn from the Jassy-Kishinev front: the Romanian 1st Cavalry Division and the III and VI Army Corps, the German XXIX Army Crops, and others.

Here is how Ion Antonescu conceived, only two hours before his being arrested, the reshuffling of forces from Moldavia with the purpose of setting up a new defensive alignment on the Eastern Carpathians and the Focşani-Nămoloasa-Brăila fortified line: "Yesterday, I dictated the order for the withdrawal of the Fourth Army by successive echelons toward the back position [F.N.B line], with the exception of the [Romanian] VII Army Corps and the [Romanian] 20th [Infantry] Division, which have been entrusted with the mission of covering communications toward Pipirig and Piatra Neamţ [therefore, meant for the defensive on the Eastern Carpathians]. This measure was taken in agreement with

General [Erik] Wöhler [commander of the German Eighth Army] yesterday, August 22, at 11:00 a.m. The order also provides, in broad outline,
for the modality of withdrawal of the German troops [. . .] now east
of the Siret [. . .]. The withdrawal operation has to take place on the
night of [August] 22 to 23. For the second stage, the order stipulates
the movement of the troops south of the Moldova [river] [. . .]. The
subsequent successive stages of the operations are to be decided today
depending on the development of the events."[28]

The same day, at 11:20 a.m., Hans Friessner would inform the Chief
of the General Staff of the German land forces that *"The Brăila-Focşani
line can be maintained without difficulty* [our italics]."[29] Simultaneously
ready to head for the F.N.B. area were four Romanian divisions, a detachment belonging to one of them having reached as far as beyond Rîmnicu
Sărat on August 23, 1944 (quite interesting, upon the start of the insurrection the forces of those divisions were directed toward Bucharest-
Ploieşti zone and took part in the fighting carried on against the German
troops there).

On the evening of August 24 (at 7:35 p.m.), as a result of the state of
war instituted between Romania and Germany and of the hostile attitude
of the Romanian troops, the command of the "South Ukraine" Army
Group inevitably reached the conclusion that the "defense of the Brăila-
Focşani line was no longer possible."[30] An opinion Hans Friessner com-
municated to his superior at the OKH, General Heinz Guderian, one day
later: "The Galaţti-Focşani line cannot be maintained unless big decisions are taken."[31] By big decisions he probably meant the need for
quickly suppressing the Romanian insurrection, the only chance to ensure
the contemplated resistance front a safe rear, and, no less important, to
win back the "loyalty" of the Romanian troops on the front. The strategic directive Hans Friessner received the following day (August 26), at
9:05 a.m. (a second one, the first being transmitted at 3:05 a.m.) from
the OKH read: "[. . .] the army group had the mission to establish a
new defensive front on the Galaşi-Focşani the slopes of the Carpathian
line and to get back control over the Danube course between its mouth
and Galaţi [. . .] Likewise, all German forces in the Romanian territory
would have to be organized into combat groups and clear off, by force,
the Galaţi—the Danube (south of Buchaest)—Bucharest-Ploieşti-Braşov-
Focşani area."[32]

Actually, that strategic directive of the German supreme leadership was utterly unrealistic from the moment of its very issuing. On the evening of August 23, the interior Romanian troops meant for the F.N.B. line had been assigned different missions, being engaged in battle against the German forces. The divisions of the Romanian Fourth Army moving southward on August 23, according to Ion Antonescu's plan, were assigned by the insurrection leaders, the same evening, the task to establish defenses "facing the north," between the sources of the Putna river and Brăila, on what was intended to be an "armistice alignment" with the Soviet forces. The fluidity of the military situation in Romania, the need not to hinder the rapid advance of the Soviet forces, which did not know about the understanding reached regarding an "armistice alignment," led the Romanian General Staff into taking the decision—on the night of August 25-26, 1944—of opening up the "Focșani gate," by dismantling the Focșani-Nămoloasa-Brăila fortified line.[33] The nine Romanian battalions specialized in fighting in the fortified zone left the casemates, also dismantling the heavy armament, and joined the forces of the Romanian Third and Fourth Armies in their shifting toward the new concentration zone which was the Bucharest-Ploiești area. The F.N.B. fortified line practically ceased to exist, a fact that enabled the Soviet troops freely to advance in-depth the Romanian Plain starting on August 27.

The OKH directive was a dead letter the very moment it was issued. In this respect, one cannot fail to notice a strange historical coincidence: at one and the same time (on the night of August 25-26, 1944) two adverse supreme commands issued orders pertaining to the same target—the F.N.B. line: while one of them—the German one—required that resistance should be put up against the Soviet offensive, the other—the Romanian one—provided for the dismantling of the fortified alignment in order not to impede the progress of the Red Army.

There is one relevant detail for understanding the "dispute" over the Focșani-Nămoloasa-Brăila fortified line that should be mentioned here.

During the talks carried on by the plenipotentiaries of Ion Antonescu and the Romanian opposition with representatives of the Soviet government in Stockholm prior to August 23, 1944, the former had insisted upon the inclusion among the terms of the armistice of April 12, 1944 of some demands expressed by the officialdom in Bucharest starting from the complex situation in Romania. In the mandates give to the Romanian representatives in Cairo, Barbu Ştirbey and Constantin Vişoianu, on August 24, the insurrectional government had insisted upon the agreement of the Soviet government—conveyed through the agency of the latter's ambassador in Stockholm, Alexandra Kollontai—on the inclusion among the armistice terms, of the following: "1. The Romanian government shall allow the German army a fifteen-day delay for leaving the country. Only in case of refusal shall the Romanian army fight side by side with the Soviet Army and other Allied armies for driving the Germans out of Romania. 2. On setting the war damages, Romania's difficult economic situation shall tave to be taken into account. 3. The Romanian government shall be allowed a free zone, which the Soviet troops shall not cross, if military operations are necessary for driving the Germans out of Romania."[34] Applying for information on those clauses, which they did not know about, the ambassadors of the United States of America and Great Britian to Moscow would be given the following answer by V. M. Molotov, on August 26, at 5:40 a.m.: "in order to keep up the prestige of the new Romanian government, the Soviet government has suggested that the following three clauses should be added to the armistice terms forwarded in April [in Stockholm—a.n.]:

a) a reduction of the war damages;

b) the setting up of a free zone as a seat of the Romanian government;

c) guaranteeing the German forces a fifteen-day delay for leaving the country.

With reference to point c), he [Molotov—a.n.] said smilingly that twelve German divisions had been encircled at Kishinev."[35]

It is obvious, therefore, that, in a first stage, the insurrectional government required the national military leadership to adapt its plans to that previous understanding reached with the Soviet government, and the Romanian General Staff acted accordingly, seeing the F.N.B. line and the maritime Danube as a presumptive armistic alignment between the Romanian and the Soviet forces.[36] It was only the news that elements of the Red Army had crossed the Danube line that made the Romanian General Staff renounce that presumptive armistice line[37] —and the absence of any communication made to the Romanian government in this respect—and consider the Bucharest-Ploieşti area as the negotiated "free zone" for the Romanian government.

The new course lent to the military developments in Romania by the insurrection resulted in a major change on the strategic chess-board: the defensive on the F.N.B. fortified line intended by the Wehrmacht was thwarted, and the Romanians opened the "gates of Moldavia" to the free advance of the Soviet troops onto the Romanian Plain.

There is one fundamental question arising here, the answer to which may (in)validate the above assertion. Was resistance against the Soviet offensive on the F.N.B. line possible?

The answer can be reached by taking into consideration the following elements of the military situation:

1) The depth of the Soviet Jassy-Kishinev strategic offensive was, according to the strategic directive (cf. ante) 150-200 km, therefore close to the characteristic of other Soviet offensive operations in 1944 (see the table below:

No.	Name of Operation	Length of operation	Depth (in km)
1	Byelorussia[38]	June 23-July 23, 1944	185-650
2	Petsamo-Kirkenes[39]	October 7-25, 1944	150
3	Debreczen	October 5-29	130-275
4	Budapest	October 29, 1944- February 14, 1945	120-150
5	Vienna[40]	March 16-April 15, 1944	170-230

The F.N.B. line was the natural terminal point of a strategic operation. Its crossing required the mounting of another operation. On August 27, 1944, the Soviet Supreme Command issued a new strategic directive, whose coordinates relied precisely on the dismantling of the F.N.B. line by the Romanians. The 2nd and 3rd Ukrainian Fronts had to deploy their troops all over the Romanian Plain and in Dobrudja and to force the Eastern Carpathians.[41]

2) On August 23, 1944, the left wing of the Romanian-German disposition in Moldavia preserved its combat strength almost untouched "having a knitted together front on the Moldova and Siret rivers, up to Bacău.'"[42] On August 22, 1944, in the afternoon, Hans Friessner and Ion Antonescu

had agreed upon the successive stages of the reshuffling of forces from that "knitted together front" to the F.N.B. line. The first stage was carried through on the night of August 22 to 23, while the second one was to take place the following night.

3) The F.N.B. line was provided with nine fortifications battalions, and three inland divisions were ready to move to that zone (a fourth one had already sent part of its forces).

The fortified line consisted of some 1,600 concrete casemates with a density of 10 casemates per one front kilometer. More than 60 km of anti-tank ditches had been arranged in the probable directions of enemy armor attack. Another 1,800 emplacements for automatic and antitank armament had also been built of concrete and wood all along that 150 km-long fortified position. The planning of a possible defense on the line had included the assigning of each sector up to regiment level.[43]

4) In the interior of Romania there were considerable Romanian military forces (see the table on p. 69), while important German effectives were deployed in Romania and in the vicinity of her territory. Those forces could have been brought over to reinforce a possible defensive on the F.N.B. line.

5) By an order of the insurrectional government on the evening of August 23, 1944, the Romanian Fourth Army, at the time on the Moldavian front, managed—elements of the Romanian Third Army too were reshuffled south of the maritime Danube—to withdraw on the F.N.B. line, the presumptive armistice line, taking up defensive positions "facing the north."

Through the rapid action of the entire army, the Romanian insurrection prevented the virtual resistance on the Eastern Carpathians—the F.N.B.— the maritime Danube alignment from turning into reality. It practically made needless a new Soviet strategic operation meant to smash that possible defensive line set up on the above-mentioned alignment.

It is hard to make a close calculation of how much would the preparation and carrying through of that new Soviet strategic operation, which the Romanian insurrection made needless, have taken. Reference can be made only to the average preparation time (staff planning, concentration of forces, logistic arrangements, and the like) and the average fulfillment time needed by other strategic operations carried out in 1944. If we consider 25-30 days the average time needed for the preparation of a strategic operation, and 20-25 days for carrying it through, then we get an average total of 45-55 days that would have been necessary to cross by force the above mentioned alignment. Seen against the background of World War II as a whole, that figure was far from being insignificant in terms of casualties and materiel destruction. By completely annihilating the probability of such a Soviet strategic operation, the Romanian insurrection shortened the war and brought closer the defeat of Hitler's Reich.

D. "The Widest Open Flank That Had Ever Been Known in Modern War"

In the outlook of the German supreme military leadership "mastering the Balkans, as a component of the European stronghold, is *decisive* [our italics] out of strategic, political-military and economic reasons"[44] for the defensive in Europe. In 1943-1944, the Balkan countries were supplying 50% of the overall European oil output, 100% of the chromium, 60% of the bauxite, 29% of the antimony and 21% of the copper continental production. Those were indispensable raw materials to the smooth working of a modern war machine,[45] and Germany did not have rubber, bauxite, mercury, mica, while her resources of iron ore, copper, chromium, antimony, charcoal, nickel and oil were utterly insufficient. In a petition drawn up on February 18, 1944, Albert Speer, the minister of the Reich's armament, analyzed the development of war in this light and concluded that the war would be over "in some ten months' time or so after the loss of the Balkans,[46] taking into account particularly the chromium in that area.

In the outlook of the German strategists control over the Balkans was indispensable not only economically, but militarily also. On July 9, 1943, the Wehrmacht High Command analyzed the political and military repercussions of an Allied landing in the Balkans. Such an event—it was then assessed—would have entailed unfavorable consequences for the Reich: it might have led Turkey into renouncing her neutrality; and Bulgaria, Romania and Hungary into leaving the Axis; it would have brought the Allies dangerously close to the oil-fields at Ploieşti; finally, it would have deprived Germany of indispensable raw materials (chromium, bauxite, and others).[47] Consequently, the strengthening of the military defense of the Balkans was decided upon. Over July 15-October 15, 1944, the Wehrmacht forces in the area would be increased by six divisions, their total number rising to 16.

According to the German situation maps, the German South-East Command (Oberbefehlshaber Südost), which had been assigned the Balkan area (the occupied islands in the Aegean Sea included), had, in June 1944, twenty infantry, two armored and three mixed divisions (in the Balkans there also were 11 Bulgarian infantry divisions).[48] On the Balkan theater of operations proper there were also some 20% of the armored ones Germany had besides those committed to the huge confrontation with the Red Army on the Eastern Europe theater of war. In the summer of 1944, the German effectives in the Balkans were raised to more than 900,000 men.[49] There, the 39 divisions of Yugoslavia's national liberation army waged a vigorous partisan war.

Berlin saw the maintenance of the Balkans in its own military sphere as decisively important for the continuation of the war. The occupation of Hungary by the German troops in March 1944 was meant, among other things, for that very purpose. In early August 1944, during a talk he had with General A. Jodl, Chief of the General Staff of the OKW, Hitler had said: "to us the preservation of the Hungarian territory is also vitally important as regards the communications as a premise for the preservation of the [European—a.n.] South-East as a whole."[50]

Equal importance would be attached to the Balkan area by the Western Allies in their military plans. British Prime Minister Winston Churchill was a resolute supporter of a military operation in the Balkans, considering the "soft underbelly" of German defense in Europe. A decision on whether the landing was to take place in the Balkans ("an attack from the Adriatic towards the Danube in order to join hands with the Russian forces that were about to penetrate into Romania")[51] or in north-western Europe ("Overlord") was taken at the Three Great Powers' Conference held in Teheran (November 28-December 1, 1943). Despite British insistence, the American side decided for the latter alternative, thereby putting an end to a hot dispute between the two shores of the Atlantic.[52] Churchill would continue to insist—though in vain—until in early June 1944 on an "invasion" in the Balkans, this time as an alternative to a landing in southern France. The Anglo-American disputes over a military "opening" in the Balkans point to the utmost importance attached to that area for launching a decisive attack against the Reich. The Balkan alternative appears as a Western attempt to find an easier approach to Germany, the other alternatives being materialized through the "Overlord" and "Anvil" operations.

Immediately after the news about Romania's "front change" by an insurrection had reached the world press agencies, political and military
commentators in the countries belonging to the anti-Hitler coalition
pointed out that that meant the end of Hitlerite political-military domination in the Balkans.

Historiographic research attests to the utterly remarkable military impact of the Romanian insurrection upon the development of World War
II. First, a crude historical fact. On September 6, 1944, Romanian navy
subunits belonging to the Fluvial Forces Command cooperated with a
Soviet detachment under the command of Lieutenant-Colonel Volokov
in an assault crossing the Danube in the Kladovo area (Yugoslavia). Therefore, the Soviet forces resumed military operations 620 km away from
where they had been on August 23 (Bîrlad), actually engaging after only
14 days the German disposition (its eastern flank) in the Balkans. Six
hundred and twenty kilometers covered without practically coming
across any significant German resistance, through a territory that had
been already freed by the Romanian insurrectional forces. On the average,
the Soviet forces had covered 45 km a day, an advance rate by far bigger
than the one commonly attained during wide-scope military operations,
characteristic of a march and not at all of combat. For comparison, here
is a table with the daily advance rates attained during some strategic
operations carried on in 1944:

No.	Name of operation	Number of days	Daily advance rate
1	The offensive in Byelorussia	35	12.3 km
2	Petsamo-Kirkenes	18	8.3 km
3	Debreczen	23	9 km
4	Budapest	108	2.5 km
5	Vienna	31	12.8 km
6	Jassy-Kishinev	8	18.6 km
7	Seine-Rhine	21	12.4 km

General M. V. Zaharov, Chief of Staff of the 2nd Ukrainian Front, would recall with respect to the high advance rate of his motorized troops through the Romanian Plain: "they advanced more than 50 km a day, while the infantry 35-38 km. Such rates were by far higher than those in a number of other operations."[53]

The rapid advance of the Soviet troops across the Romanian Plain was possible because the Romanian insurrectional forces had cleared that territory of enemy troops before, and because, given the swiftness with which that action was carried out, all communications in the area were left undamaged. On August 23, the Soviet troops were at Bîrlad, the following day at Bacău, Roman, Tîrgu Neamţ and Periprava (the Danube mouths), and on August 25 at Tecuci, that is 25 km away from the starting point. On August 26 they reached Mărășești, and passed through the Focșani gates the following day. On August 28 they were at Buzău, that is at a 60 km distance from where they had been a day before, keeping that advance rate up to Bucharest (they had a last clash with German troops north of Ploiești, where they cooperated with the Romanian forces, which had previously pinned the enemy, to the latter's smashing). From Ploiești toward the Romanian-Yugoslav and Romanian-Bulgarian borders and also northwards beyond the Carpathians the advance of the Soviet forces would not be hindered by any obstacle whatsoever, benefiting from the enthusiastic assistance of the Romanian population. Troops belonging to the Soviet Fifty-Third Army and Sixth Armored Army arrived east of Bucharest on August 29, 1944. At Sinești, near the Capital, their advanced forces were welcomed by a delegation of the Communist Party, which informed them of the fact that the insurrectional forces had freed the city and its surroundings. On August 30 and 31 Soviet large units were welcomed with acclamations by the inhabitants of Bucharest. During the following days the Soviets continued their strategic march through southern Romania, heading for central Transylvania and Romania's western border.

A military operation across the Romanian Plain, crossed by rivers running lengthwise able to be turned into serious resistance alignments, would have undoubtedly taken a long time which again is hard to calculate accurately. However, if we take the average daily advance rate attained in reference military operations—10.1 km per day—covering the straight distance from Focșani to Turnu Severin would have required, according to this index, some 45 days of fighting. Given the particular military situation in Romania, the fact that a defense line might have been set up all along the Southern Carpathians, therefore a new almost 400 km-long front, and that resistance might have been put up on the rivers crossing the Romanian Plain—the assault crossing of the Argeş and Olt rivers would have required long and heavy fighting—the time needed for the crossing of that territory through fighting should be at least doubled when compared to the average time during the reference military operations. To conclude with, crossing through fighting the Romanian Plain, after storming the F.N.B. fortified line, would have meant about 90 days of bitter fighting, huge material destruction and painful casualties. Those were days by which World War II in Europe was shortened as a result of Romania's resolute initiative of August 23 of turning weapons on Hilter's Germany and of joining with her entire military and human potential the United Nations.

A first notable effect of the Wehrmacht's removal from the southern part of Romania by the Romanian insurrectional forces, an event of utmost significance for the military situation in the Balkan Peninsula, was Bulgaria's leaving the alliance with Hitler's Reich. If in the months of July and August 1944—according to the Bulgarian historiography—there were "favorable internal and home circumstances for a decisive change in the Bulgarian foreign policy, for breaking off the alliance with Germany and for leaving the war," a fact "highly important for Bulgaria and for the development of the world war." No sooner had Romania's changeover occurred that the situation of her southern neighbor immediately and seriously worsened. On August 26, a communique of the Bulgarian government announced Bulgarian neutrality, on September 5 the Soviet Union declared war on Bulgaria and on September 9, the anti-fascist people's insurrection broke out. That rapid succession of events had its starting point on August 23, 1944, and was an instance of the impact the Romanian insurrection had upon the situation in the Balkan countries. Bulgarian historian I. Dimitrov says that "The steps taken by the Bulgarian leading circles after August 23 [1944] actually marked the beginning of a reorientation in the Bulgarian foreign policy, expressed in breaking off the military alliance with Germany, though not of diplomatic relations, in the attempts to quickly conclude an armistice with Great Britain and to normalize relations with the USSR."[54]

The German side would immediately realize the negative impact exerted by the Romanian insurrection on the friendly military disposition in the Balkans. Documents belonging to the enemy attest to the effect had by the "front change" rapidly and surprisingly carried out by Romania. The strategic area of the Romanian Plain suddenly turned unfriendly was a matter of utmost importance for the solidity of the Hitlerite disposition in the Balkans. On August 31, in Belgrade, the file of orders of the German Army Group "F", deployed in Yugoslavia and Greece, recorded that the "road from Bucharest to Belgrade, via Craiova, is practically opened to the enemy."[55] Consequently, steps were immediately taken for preventing a true military disaster. The opening of the left flank through Romania's initiative was aggravated by the state of war arising between the USSR and Bulgaria on September 5, 1944, which made of the latter's leaving the Axis a certain fact.

On August 26, 1944, Oberbefehlshaber Südost ordered the reshuffling of a mountain division (the Army Group "E" deployed in the interior of Greece and in the islands, totalled 300,000 men). Three days later, Berlin issued an "Order for the defense of the South-East," which provided for the concentration of all reserves belonging to the Oberbefehlshaber Sudost in the Belgrade-Nish-Salonica area and for effecting preliminary preparations for a withdrawal from Greece. On September 20, Field Marshal Maximilian Von Weichs, commander of the "South-Eastern Theater of Operations," suggested the complete evacuation of Greece (the islands in the Aegean had been evacuated on Hitler's order five days earlier). His suggestion also took into account the fact that the Soviet and the Romanian troops were massed, after having baffled the offensive attempted in the Banat starting September 13, at Romania's south-western border. The final decision would be made on October 10, when the evacuation of all German troops from Greece, Albania and southern Macedonia was ordered. On October 14, Belgrade was liberated by the forces of the People's Army for national liberation in Yugoslavia, led by Marshal Tito, in cooperation with Soviet troops, with which the former had joined hands on October 5, 1944.

Only 44 days after the breaking out of the Romanian insurrection the Soviet troops had therefore effected the junction with the troops of the liberating army of Yugoslavia, actually making the final collapse of the German military system in South-East Europe. That fact was also made possible by the military exploitation of the Romanian Plain, freed by the Romanian insurrectional forces and instantly turned to the strategic benefit of the United Nations.

The truth of the above assertion has been highlighted by foreign military historians and experts. We here first quote the well-known British military theoretician B. H. Liddell-Hart, in whose suggestive and synthetic opinion the Soviet troops were thus enabled to capitalize on the "widest open flank that had ever been known in modern warfare."[56] In the opinion of another historian of World War II, "to the Soviet troops the Romanian campaign was just a movement for the occupation of Romania's east and south, and of the Carpathians, an exercise in rapid movement [. . .]."[57] Analyzing the swiftness with which the Soviet troops had crossed the Romanian territory after August 23, 1944, rapidly reaching the new front opened by the Romanian forces in Transylvania and the Banat, another historian shows that "their [the Soviet troops'] advance had a twofold purpose: on the one hand, of isolating the German forces spread over the Balkan countries, while on the other hand of maneuvering on the Danube in order to encircle Hungary."[58] The insurrection in Romania, which directly entailed Bulgaria's leaving Germany's camp faced the Wehrmacht with a huge uncovered front—a front therefore opened to being exploited militarily by the forces of the United Nations— which was, to quote another military analyst, "425 miles long [. . .] from the Hungarian border to the Aegean Sea."[59]

Such appreciation by military experts who have analyzed after the war the decisive impact of the Romanian insurrection on the Balkan Peninsula could go on only to reveal the same truth considered even at that time of paramount importance: the Romanian changeover also entailed the collapse of the Balkan military system built up by the Wehrmacht in 1940-1941 and carefully preserved in the ensuing years. Undoubtedly, further research will not be late in highlighting, on a scientific basis, the even greater military impact of the event of August 23, 1944 upon the Balkan front, in order to emphasize even more thoroughly and convincingly the continental importance of the Romanian people's rising in arms for the liberation and independence of its homeland.

E. A Huge Front Translation

We have briefly outlined the remarkable importance of the Romanian Carpathian range for the whole of the military developments on the eastern front in the summer of 1944. One cannot insist enough on the strategic opportunities offered by the Romanian Carpathians as a whole to a German defensive. The southern range was—after a possible crossing of the F.N.B. fortified line and a breaking through the defense alignments in the Romanian Plain, those too taken into consideration by the German military planners—a considerable natural obstacle which favored a long resistance. It was necessary to close the passes in those mountains in order to deny penetration into the Transylvanian Plateau and farther into the Hungarian steppe. As a matter of fact, this was what the Wehrmacht High Command tried to do in early September, when it would mount an offensive from the Transylvanian Plateau toward the mountains against the alignment of the new "classic" front established by the Romanians during the insurrection through the covering operation.

On August 29, 1944, the "South Ukraine" Army Group received a new strategic directive from the OKW by which it was assigned the mission "to secure by advancing and preserve an unbroken defensive front moving from the Romanian-Bulgarian border onto the peaks of the Carpathians [that is to say the southern part of the western range, the southern and eastern Carpathians] until junction will be effected with the right wing of the XVII Army Corps [deployed in Bukovina]."[60] The goal of the offensive was firmly to set the defense on the eastern and southern Carpathians and to re-establish a continuous link with the Western Balkans, in eastern Yugoslavia, with a view to prolonging domination in South-East Europe. The offensive failed as a result of the powerful resistance put up by the Romanian troops and the Germans were left no chance —Hans Friessner would write in his memoirs—to win the "passes in the Southern Carpathians—the Predeal, Turnu Roșu and Vulcan passes [. . .], *This proved fatal, because the mountains were our best allies* [our italics]. The enemy [the Soviets and the Romanians—a.n.] could have been stopped here with relatively few special troops far better than in the area lying north of these passes [. . .]."[61]

There is one more sui-generis peculiarity of the importance of the Romanian Carpathians in the strategic context of the summer of 1944. The

Romanian army controlled the entire western Carpathian range, the covering actually implying the establishing of a front on either side of the Bihor massif. But, as it is known, the Western Carpathians are the last barrier toward the vast plain of the Tisza. Through the firm control the Romanian forces set by the insurrection over the western Carpathian range not only was a possible German resistance alignment in front of the pouring of the United Nations' forces into the free space of the Tisza Plain eliminated, but the Hitlerite attempt to re-establish a virtual defense disposition relying on the mountains in sub-Carpathian Ukraine and reaching Greece, through eastern Yugoslavia, was likewise thwarted.

Both Hitler and Ion Antonescu's plans had taken into account the setting up of several resistance lines in the Romanian Carpathians. Antonescu's government had contemplated, after a possible ceding of the Romanian Plain, that a first defensive line be constituted in the massifs of the Southern Carpathians. The following large units had been already destined to close the passes: 6th Cavalry Division (the Buzău Valley), the 8th Cavalry-Training Division (the Teleajen Valley), the 1st Guard Division—the sedentary part (the Doftana Valley), the 1st Mountain, 13th and 15th Infantry Divisions (the Prahova and Ialomița Valleys), the 21st Infantry Division—the sedentary part (the Dîmbovița Valley), the 3rd Mountain Division and the 14th Infantry Division—the sedentary part (the Olt river), the 2nd and 4th Mountain Divisions (the Jiu Valley), the 5th Cavalry and 1st Infantry Divisions (the eastern slope of the Mehedinți Mountains), the 9th Cavalry Division—the sedentary part (the Iron Gates), the 19th Infantry Division (Orșova). Such a defensive line established on hard-to-climb massifs, their passes denied by considerable forces—15 divisions—would have enabled the delay of any offensive.

The second defensive line envisaged by Antonescu's government—which wold have become operational had the one organized on the Southern Carpathians collapsed—passed through the Deva-Hunedoara-Hațeg-Petro-șani depression, relying on the Apuseni Mountains in the north.[62]

Following the victorious Romanian insurrection, the whole mountainous area of Romania definitively ranged with the strategic losses of the Third Reich. The setting up of Romanian control over the mountainous area was the result of the insurrectional actions, and the Romanian troops also won the plains (tableland) lying beyond the mountains. They would thus establish a vast strategic bridgehead of some 50,000 sq km on the

other side of the Southern and Western Carpathians, likely to allow the
concentration of large military forces for the subsequent offensives. The
contact area of that bridgehead crossed the Transylvanian Plateau on the
Romanian-Hungarian demarcation line established through the Vienna
Diktat of August 30, 1940, the Bihor massif and farther on following the
Romanian-Hungarian and Romanian-Yugoslav borders. In the file of
orders of the Wehrmacht High Command the very maintenance of that
alignment after the Romanian insurrection appeared as a contingency
undertaking: "from the point of view of this war's history, it is quite
a miracle that afterwards [after Romania's leaving the Hitlerite war—a.n.]
the establishment of a defensive front, no matter how frail the latter,
was still possible at the Hungarian border [the Romanian-Hungarian
demarcation line in Transylvania—a.n.] and at the Serbian one."[63]

The "jump" of the Soviet forces over the Romanian Carpathians (in
their western and southern parts) was therfore effected instantly, through
the very Romanian insurrection, which made wide-scope military operations, implying a great waste of human lives and war materiel, as well
as an unavoidable prolongation of the war, needless.

On September 7, 1944, only 15 days after the outbreak of the Romanian insurrection, the Soviet forces were able to mount a limited offensive from the inside of the Carpathian arch, where they had been previously concentrated, in cooperation with the Romanian forces. From
Bîrlad, where they had been on August 23, 1944, the troops of the Red
Army resumed the offensive north of Brașov, that is 300 km westwards
(a distance measured following the outside line of the Carpathian curvature). Moreover, the wide-scope offensive that Soviet and Romanian
forces mounted from the inside of the Carpathian arch and from west of
it on October 5, 1944—the Debreczen operation—would take place 44
days after the event of August 23, 1944, and at a 900 km distance from
the place the Soviet forces had been the same day of August 23. Consequently, a huge front translation had been effected during a extremely
short span of time, a considerable drive back of the southern wing of the
German defensive disposition in Europe, unparalleled in the history of
World War II.

That "huge front translation" has a characteristic feature which makes
it differ from other similar instances recorded through history. Thus, while
the Soviet troops were fighting in the Moldavian Plateau, the Romanian

insurrectional forces opened, consolidated and defended the new front in Transylvania and the Banat, through their own forces, for almost 20 days. Therefore, the Romanian army, assited by the entire people, opened by itself the new front and, moreover, it mopped up the enemy operational rear up to the slopes of the mountains, thereby establishing a vast bridge-head for the safe concentration of the Soviet troops, necessary for mounting subsequent offensives: a new front and a vast bridgehead which the Romanian army achieved by devotedly and heroically fighting the numerous, battle-scarred military forces of a great imperialist power and of the latter's satellite.

On September 5, 1944, the German and Hungarian forces embarked upon an offensive in the center of the Transylvanian Plateau, aiming mainly at reaching the Carpathians for taking hold of the passes and denying the access of the Soviet troops. The Romanian Fourth Army needed four days to thwart that enemy attempt, the passes in the Southern Carpathians being ensured full safety, some 110-140 km behind the front line. West of the western Carpathians, the enemy launched a series of attacks that would assume the nature of a wide-scope offensive on September 13, 1944. There too, the Romanian troops belonging to the First Army—which had to stop the attack of nine German and Hungarian divisions—made the enemy attempt to get control over the mountains end in failure.

Driving back the enemy divisions aiming at taking hold of the Carpathians through bitter fighting by the Romanian forces stood out as a valuable contribution of Romania to the anti-Hitler war in Europe as a whole. As underlined in a previous chapter, this would be acknowledged by the Soviet General I. M. Managarov, who in an order of the day of September 23, 1944 said that "by checking the onrush of the German and Hungarian troops, the Romanian troops covered the movement of the Red troops toward the Hungarian Plain."[64]

By this, not only was the Wehrmacht deprived of the Southern Carpathians' barrier, but the Romanian new front in the Transylvanian Plateau also upset the German defensive system established in the Eastern Carpathians. The south-eastern part of Transylvania, then under Hungarian occupation, where German forces regrouped from the Moldavian front had been concentrated, was the target of a joint offensive of Soviet and Romanian troops on September 7, and was to be liberated 21 days later, the Allies reaching the Mureș river. The passes in the southern part of the

Eastern Carpathians were thereby opened to the circulation of the Soviet forces, while the Romanian-Soviet offensive through the main passes (Prislop, Tihuţa) in the northern part of the same mountains was facilitated.

The front translation had been carried through in a very short span of time under the exclusive impact of the Romanian event of August 23, 1944. The calculation of the time it would have needed under ordinary circumstances—namely as planned by the Hitlerite military leadership which had counted on Romania's further siding with the Axis—again shows how the Romanian insurrection shortened the length of the world conflagration in Europe.

If we take into account that for the crossing through fighting of the Romanian Plain, from the F.N.B. line to Turnu Severin, some 90 days would have been necessary—according to the average daily advance rate of 10.1 km in reference to Allied operations and according to the concrete military situation in Romania—and if the average time needed by preparations for a new operation is added we reach a total figure of 115-120 days. That would have been the presumed time required for breaking through the Southern Carpathians and the southern part of the Western ones. Another 20-25 days would have been necessary for successfully carrying through the operation proper. Consequently, according to these calculations, the crossing of the Carpathian mountainous barrage would have required 135-145 days of bitter fighting against the German enemy who, at the subsequent operations were to prove, desperately fought for ever inch of land, for every natural obstacle. This makes almost five months which, we stress again, the Romanian insurrection was "snatching" from the war in this part of Europe, thereby ensuring the United Nations the control over and use of the Romanian Carpathians. If to the above figure one adds the 45-55 days needed by the presumed military operation for breaking through the F.N.B. fortified line, one gest a sum total of 180-200 days, which the historic events of August 23, 1944, namely Romania's immediate and unreserved joining the anti-Hitler coalition, "spared" World War II in Europe.

We insist upon the aleatory nature of the calculations we have made, given the presumptive nature of assessments pertaining to a "future in the past," because it is obvious that one cannot ascertain all the determinants of a fact that might have happened but actually did not. In our case, for instance, one cannot say for sure what would the next strategic options

of the Soviet Supreme Command had been, had the front been stabilized
—again a possible, probable but not certain fact—on the alignment planned
by Antonescu-Friessner and approved by the OKW. Would operations
have immediately been prepared as we have presumed? Or would there
have been an "operational break" dictated by some other strategic options? Only a counter-factual historical approach might find an answer
to these questions, but anyone would admit that the path it follows
might prove dangerously slippery.

The presumed dynamics of operations in Romania subsequent to
August 23, 1944, on which our calculation is grounded, has been intended to make the strategic results of the Romanian insurrection, its considerable military impact on World War II as a whole, particularly in terms
of speeding up its issue—so eulogistically commented upon abroad—more
striking, and to provide them a factual and critical groundwork. As any
"scenario," this one has extracted all its fundamentals from reality.

The military commentators of the time were not late in realizing the
paramount importance of depriving the Reich of the Romanian Carpathian barrage. A commentary broadcast by a British broadcasting station
on August 24, referred to earlier in this book, pointed out that *"Through
the gate of the Carpathians opened by the Romanians* [our italics], the
Russians will be able to reach Munich and advance to Berlin."[65] "Romania has not laid down arms, but she now continues the fight alongside
the Allies"—B.B.C. broadcast in German three hours later. "By Romania's
joining the fight alongside the Allies, the Danube is now open."[66] Editorials carried by Swedish newspapers issued on the afternoon of August 24,
1944, characterized Romania's changeover as a "terrible blow dealt at
the German war leadership."[67] In Latin America, the Argentinian newspaper "La Prensa" of August 25, 1944, carried the following commentary
on the consequences of the Romanian insurrection: " [. . .] The difficult
barrier of the Carpathians practically disappears, and the vast plain of the
Danube leading to Belgrade, Budapest and Vienna, and ever further, to
Germany, is now open to the Russians [. . .] The threat is less impending
for Hungary than it is for the Balkans, but no less dangerous for that
reason. The armies may delay the invasion of her territory but they will
not be late in air bombing her capital. As far as Austria and Czechoslovakia
are concerned, Germany cannot harbor the least illusion either."[68] The
German side was forced to admit the highly damaging impact of the Romanian action on its own defensive.

On August 25, 1944, the Nazi "Transocean" Press Agency considered that the front change effected by Romania would have "some bearings upon the southern front."[69] In a report submitted to Hitler, the Hitlerite military chiefs, headed by Keitel, assessed the "immediate military consequences" of Romania's action by that it entailed an "extremely dangerous overturn of fronts," which "jeopardizes the entire German Army in the Balkans," and "as a result of which the Russian armies will be able to reach Budapest in a few weeks' time."[70]

The historiographic retrospect, too, was not late in highlighting the importance of the Carpathian barrage "siding," through Romania's action, with the United Nations. The Belgian historian Henri Bernard would write in 1968 that the "Romanian insurrection is of cardinal importance. By it, the whole country and its resources that are indispensable to the Reich instantly joined the [former] enemy, without any significant battle. *The gate toward Central Europe is opened* [our italics]."[71] And in the opinion of Sir B. H. Liddell-Hart, "The outflanking [of the German disposition in the Balkans, and implicitly, of the southern wing of the eastern front— a.n.] was mainly a matter of logistic entailed by movement and supplying rather than by enemy opposition."[72]

F. A Change in the Balance of Forces Between the Conflicting Coalitions

That exact understanding of the impact the Romanian insurrection had upon the balance of forces between the two conflicting coalitions calls for a brief survey of their combat readiness in 1944. This aim in view, let us see first, as it is but natural, what were the military forces of the United Nations commited to battle against the Wehrmacht in the summer of 1944?

In early 1944, on the Soviet-German front, the main theater of operations on land of World War II, the Red Army had 6,736,000 men. Out of that number 571,000 made up the reserve of the Soviet High Command (408,000 men belonged to the Air Force, 266,000 to the Navy, while 75,000 were airborne troops), which is a total combat strength of 6,165, 000 Soviet troops.[73] On the same front, the Nazi Reich (together with its satellites) had by the same time 236 divisions and 18 brigades (38 divisions and 12 brigades of which belonged to the satellite armies). The reserve of the Wehrmacht High Command cosisted of 15 divisions and one brigade (another 102 divisions and three brigades were fighting on the fronts in Western and Southern Europe).[74]

In 1944, in Western Europe the Allies of the United Nations had the following combat strength: the USA (August 1944)—1,904,709 men (838,108 in land troops, 365,429 in the Air Force, and 374,054 in the logistic services); Great Britain (October 1944)—771,267 men; Canada (October 1944)—124,645 men;[75] Poland—in the West (August 1944)—129,000 men; in the East (August 1944)—149,695 men, therefore a total strength of 278,695 men;[76] France (August 15-September 15, 1944)—200,000 men.[77]

Consequently, the armies of the United Nations fighting on various European fronts boasted a combat strength of 10 million men.

According to German command maps, on June 6, 1944, the Wehrmacht forces deployed on the various European fronts and in the interior of Germany were the following: 226 infantry divisions and two infantry brigades, 47 armored divisions and 5 armored brigades, and 37 mixed divisions and three mixed brigades, which makes a total of 310 divisions and ten brigades.[78] However, many of those divisions were just "paper units," that is commands without troops. An accurate assessment of the German military forces on the European front in early September 1944, shows: 252 divisions and 15-20 brigades, whose combat strength varied. The overall combat strength of the Wehrmacht at the same date was 10,165,503 men (out of which 207,000 belonged to the Waffen SS).[79]

Romania's resolute joining the coalition of the United Nations, through the changeover effected on August 23, 1944, shattered the balance of human forces involved in the gigantic conflict taking place in Europe. At the time, the importance of the impact the Romanian action had upon the "assets" of the Wehrmacht were seen at once, a fact that has been dwelt upon at large in a previous chapter. With respect to the matter under discussion, an article carried by the "New York Times" of August 28, 1944, pointed out: "By *not means* will Hitler's Reich be able to replace the 30 Romanian divisions [our italics]."[80]

On August 23, 1944, the day the Romanian insurrection broke out, Romania's military forces numbered 975,947 men (781,264 belonged to the land troops, 37,196 to the aeronautical forces, 21,016 to the Navy and 36,471 to the anti-aircraft artillery). If the strength of the military schools, depots, and so on (that is all Romanian military forces on August 23, 1944) are added to the above figure, one gets a total figure of some 1,100,000 men.[81] Consequently, about 1.1 million military joined the ranks of the anti-Hitler coalition. The change occurred in the balance of forces was therefore substantial, the ratio of forces suddenly becomng, through Romania's bold action, more advantageous for the United Nations and disadvantageous for Germany than in the period previous to August 23, 1944.

Indeed, through the Romanian changeover of August 23, 1944, Hitler's Reich lost: the strength of some 40 Romanian divisions (20 of which were on the front line); some 24 divisions "fighting on the Romanian front, which, under the pressure of the Soviet army, their retreat lines cut off through Romania's action, were captured or smashed by the Soviet forces;"[82] the German military made prisoners or killed by the insurrectional forces, that is the equivalent of approximately six Wehrmacht divisions. Right after the success of the insurrection, Romanian military experts assessed that the "total combat strength lost by the Germans following the action carried out by Romania amounts to 40 + 24 + 6 = 70 divisions."[83]

In an indirect way, the Reich lost, under the impact of the Romanian insurrection, the "equivalent of 17 German divisions in the Balkans, which were led to destruction;" the "equivalent of 23 Bulgarian divisions, because in August 1944 Bulgaria strategically depended on the circumstances in Romania."[84] Such calculations regarding the divisions directly or indirectly lost by the Wehrmacht would lead the Romanian military experts of the time to the right conclusion that the Romanian insurrection entailed "such a reversal in the ratio of forces in South-East Europe in favor of the United Nations, that if the moment when and the area in which it occurred are taken into account, may be considered as catastrophic to Germany."[85]

Through the very military forces Romania added to the coalition of the United Nations on August 23, 1944, she ranged the third in the "hierarchy" of the Allied armies fighting in Europe in terms of available combat strength (975-947 men), right below the Soviet Union and the United States of America and before Great Britain (in October 1944 she had an expeditionary force of over 771,000 men in Europe), which however fought the enemy on other theaters of operations besides the Eastern one, Poland (over 278,000 men) and France (200,000 men).

G. A Defeat Greater Than . . . the Victory Won in Poland

The human loss sustained by the Wehrmacht as the exclusive result of the insurrectional fights in Romania were no less relevant for the development of World War II as a whole. More than 61,500 German military were made prisoners or killed during the fighting against the Romanian troops between August 23-31, 1944. That year the ceiling of a German infantry division (Volksgrenadieredivision) had been cut down to 10,000 men,[86] and therefore the enemy combat strength annihilated by the Romanian insurrectional forces is equal to some six Wehrmacht large units. That equivalence becomes the more credible if one takes into account the great number of German senior officers and generals captured during the Romanian insurrection (14 generals and 1,421 officers).

What was the "objective" amount of the losses sustained by the Wehrmacht during the fights against the Romanian insurrectional forces? To answer this question, reference should be made to similar campaigns and battles in which the German army participated in World War II.

During the first "Blitzkrieg," the one in Poland, waged between September 1-October 6, 1939 (when the Polish combat group "Polesie" surrendered in the Kock area) the Wehrmacht sustained 44,303 casualties (16,343 killed, 27,640 wounded and 320 missing),[87] that is a daily average of some 1,230 men. That daily casulty average was by far smaller than the one recorded by the Wehrmacht during the Romanian insurrection (some 7,600 military).

The casualties inflicted upon the Wehrmacht over September 1, 1939-June 22, 1941—when the attack against the Soviet Union began—rose to 97,136 men, that is to say only 1.5 times larger over some 400 days than the ones sustained during the eight days of insurrectional fighting in Romania.

Over June 6-September 1, 1944, the casualties inflicted upon the German land forces during the fighting carried on in Western Europe rose to 293,802 killed, wounded and missing,[88] which means a daily average of 3,400 casualties, a figure again smaller than the one characteristic of the Romanian insurrection.

During five years of world war (since September 1, 1939), the Wehrmacht had sustained 3,744,489 casualties (killed, wounded and missing) on all fronts. That would mean a daily casualty average of 1,950 men, therefore by far smaller than the one recorded during the fighting in the Romanian insurrection.

The blow dealt by the Romanian revolution at the Wehrmacht combat strength is also rendered evident by the fact that, starting early July 1944, Hitler had ordered the setting up of 15 new divisions meant to reinforce the German front against the Red Army. The divisions were to consist of recoverable wounded (by lowering the recoverability level), and of auxiliary forces transferred from the Luftwaffe and the Kriegsmarine to the land troops. In early September 1944 those fifteen new divisions were hastily shifted to the eastern front (another two in the West and one in Norway).[89] They were also intended—which was impossible, though—to fill the gap created by the six German divisions smashed by the Romanians, and by the 40 Romanian divisions that were fighting alongside the United Nations starting August 23, 1944.

H. A Daily Average of 19,000 sq km Cleared of German Occupation

During the eight days of fighting against the Wehrmacht, the Romanian insurrection had driven away the occupant throughout the territory under Romanian state authority (therefore, with the exception of the territory wrenched through the fascist Vienna Diktat of August 30, 1940, and the central and northern parts of Moldavia, where the Jassy-Kishinev operation was under way)—an area of 150,000 sq km that was equal to the area covered by Belgium, Denmark, Holland and Switzerland taken together.

The removal of German forces from a vast area in such a short span of time (whose strategic importance has been emphasized earlier), achieved through the insurrection, appears as an event of European import, when compared to other Allied strategic operations.

All throughout 1943, the Soviet forces had freed through bitter fighting an area of 1,020,000 sq km, which means a daily average of 2,800 sq km, six times smaller than the one attained during the Romanian insurrectional operation.[90] During the strategic operation in Karelia (mounted on June 21, 1944) the Soviet forces freed a territory of some 60,000 sq km in 30 days (on July 21, 1944 they reached the Soviet-Finnish border).[91] The Polish military forces fighting against the Wehrmacht on the western front liberated during the fighting carried on in 1944-1945 a territory of some

16,000 sq km, while on the eastern front an area of 131,000 sq km in 287 days of fighting (July 28, 1944- May 9, 1945).[92]

The table on the following page shows how the Romanian insurrection stands out, through this index too, among some Allied strategic operations.

A "scenario" of the days the forces of the United Nations would have needed to free the Romanian territory, cleared of Wehrmacht troops by the Romanian insurrection, becomes superfluous in the light of the figures in the above table. And this the more so as it should have to refer to parameters such as: the geographical pecularities of the terrain, the forces available for being committed by the belligerents to the "dispute" over the Romanian territory liberation through the insurrection, the possible "operational breaks" and, especially, some presumed contingency political developments.

Beyond the possibility of working out such a "scenario" and of its "historicity," there is the striking fact that during the Romanian strategic operation of August 1944, the insurrectional forces freed the national territory at a daily average of 19,000 sq km.

* * * * *

The military characteristics of the Romanian insurrection and their remarkable ompact on the development of World War II in Europe lead to one conclusion alone. Through the insurrection the length of the world conflict was considerably shortened by some 200 days according to the strategic "scenario" we have worked out, with inevitable consequences in terms of sparing human lives and material assets. Such a conclusion is also justified by appreciations made by authorized political or military commentators. The British historian Hugh Seton-Watson was of the opinion that *"[Romania's] action of August 23 [1944] was one of the decisive events of the Second World War* [our italics]."[96] To John Erickson, the reputed British historian, "23 August 1944 proved to be one of the decisive days of the entire war." He pointed out: "The Romanian defection of 23 August turned Germany's military defeat into a telling catastrophe which made itself felt far beyond the bounds of a single army group . . . the whole of southern Bessarabia, the Danube delta and the passes through the Carpathians lay wide open to the Red Army. Neither the Danube nor the Carpathians could bar the Russian advance. Ahead of the Soviet armies

No.	Operation	Length	The freed area in sq km	The daily average in sq km
1	The Romanian Insurrection operation	August 23-31, 1944	150,000	19,000
2	Liberation of southern Karelia	June 21-July 21, 1944	60,000	2,000
3	The operation carried out by the Polish forces in the West (Italy, France, Germany)[93]	54 days in all	16,000	300
4	Operations carried out by the Polish forces in the East	287 days in all	131,000	450
5	The offensive of the 2nd and 3rd Ukrainian Fronts in the Ukraine	December 23, 1943-April 17, 1944	300,000	2,600
6	The offensive in Byelorussia	June 23-July 28, 1944	200,000	6,000
7	The operation carried out by the American Third Army in Lorraine[94]	September 1-December 18, 1944	7,000	70
8	Budapest[95]	October 29, 1944-February 14, 1945	some 60,000	550
9	Debreczen[96]	October 5-29, 1944	some 160,000	7,000
10	Vienna	March 16-April 15, 1944	58,000	1,900

lay the route to the Hungarian plains, the gateway to Czechoslovakia and Austria, as well as the road to Bulgaria and Yugoslavia, the collapse of the entire German defensive system in the south-eastern theater. All this was precipitated by the Bucharest coup."[97] Paris broadcast on January 12, 1946, a commentary by Pierre Durant who, making a survey of the "admirable act of August 23, 1944" and of the subsequent Romanian contribution to the defeat of the Third Reich, showed that *"through her contribution Romania determined a shortening of the war by at least six months* [our italics]."[98] A conclusion fully supported by the reconstitution of events and the comparisons made on the basis of the data and facts supplied by documentary sources.

Through a resolute act of national self-determination carried out on August 23, 1944, Romania shortened by some **200** days the second world conflagration of the 20th century. **200** days of great casulties and losses of material assets whose exact calculation is impossible to make. **200** days during which the progress of human civilization would have had to suffer the vicissidtudes of a world conflict. **200** days which Romania and the Romanian people bestowed on world peace.

CHAPTER V

LOGISTIC CONSEQUENCES OF THE ROMANIAN REVOLUTION

Romania, or to be more precise some of her natural resources, held a significant place in the war economy of the Third Reich. Already during World War I, after the conclusion of the Peace of Bucharest,[1] Germany and Austria-Hungary's access—through the means of force they had as occupying powers—to great quantities of cereals[2] and as a matter of fact to other products in Romania enabled the former to put up prolonged resistance. "In the summer of 1918"—the well-known British military historian and theoretician J. F. C. Fuller writes—"had the Central Empires not profited by the cereals in Romania and the Ukraine, they would have been forced into surrendering by hunger."[3]

While preparing for revenge, the Nazi regime was determined to prevent the situation in 1914-1918, which had led to the collapse of William II's Germany, from happening again. Counteracting the effects of a new blockade, which—this was most certain—would have been set the very first day of the war, was a priority need. That need was the more so stringently felt as the future war was foreseen, given the essential role of the tank-plan binomial, as a war of engines. The development of combat technology implied a great consumption of iron, non-ferrous metals and of other raw materials. B. H. Liddell Hart shows with good reason: "There were some twenty basic products essential for war. Coal for general production. Petroleum for motive power. Cotton for explosives. Wood, iron, rubber

143

for transport. Copper for the general armament and all electric equipment. Nickel for steel-making and ammunition. Lead for ammunition. Glycerine for dynamite. Cellulose for smokeless powders. Mercury for detonators. Aluminium for aircraft. Platinum for chemical apparatus. Antimony, manganese, and others for steel-making and metallurgy in general. Asbestoes for munitions and machinery, Mica as an insulator. Nitric acid and sulphur for explosives."[4]

As shown by the same author, Germany did not have cotton, rubber, tin, platinum, bauxite, mercury and mica, while the quantities of iron ore, copper, antimony, manganese, nickel, sulphur, wool and oil supplied by the national economy were not sufficient. "Here lay the greatest weakness of all in the war-making capacity of the Axis"—nor had Gemany's partners, Italy and Japan, such raw materials and substances—"in times when armies had come increasingly to depend on motor-movement and air forces had become a vital element in military power."[5]

The Nazi decision-making factors understood that in the absence of those raw materials and substances, of oil in the first place, their chances to win the war, on which they counted in order to get continental and then world hegemony, were practically nil. Ensuring the petrol needed to make the engines of the tanks, planes and ships work—called upon to play a decisive part in the war—thus became quite an obsession to those in chareg of the German war production. The achievement of a true oil autarchy through the exploitation of home resources and large-scale development of the synthetic fuel output[6] was seen as the ideal solution to all problems generated by the disproportion between Germany's wartime fuel needs and her availabilities. According to estimations made on June 30, 1939, the Reich needed over 13 million tons of fuel in the event of a war as against 7 million tons in times of peace (the 1939-1943 plan provided for an increase ranging from 11.68 million tons in 1939 to 13.83 million tons in 1943).[7] Failing to obtain the much-coveted oil autarchy, the Reich attempted to achieve at least a partial one, expressed in the plan worked out by Minister C. Krauch in July 1938, containing the percentages to be provided by the national output,[8] as follows in the table on the following page.

The Krauch plan reveals, therefore, the Reich's dependence, particularly in the earlier stage of the war, on foreign oil sources. At the time the plan was drawn up, Germany was securing the bulk of the oil she needed

	1939	1940	1941	1942	1943
Plane petrol	21%	47%	57%	77%	77%
Automobile petrol	34%	45%	62%	75%	88%
Diesel oil	12%	30%	63%	67%	97%
Tar	23%	28%	60%	46%	60%
Lubricants	31%	63%	87%	100%	100%
Total	26%	45%	62%	72%	79%

from Mexico and the Dutch West Indies (42%) and the United States of America (23%), while the European producers—Romania and the USSR—supplied her with an altogether small quota: 12% and 7% respectively. The impossibility of securing oil from the traditional suppliers in case of war, as they were on the other side of the Atlantic, necessarily called for their replacing by the national output and by imports from Europe. Romania, which ranked fifth in the world in oil production,[9] appeared as the ideal supplier of the badly needed oil. Taling into account the Romanian output and the expected increase in the Reich's own production, the Krauch plan established, on the basis of Romania's oil export figures, the following percentages for meeting Germany's oil needs:[10]

1939	1940	1941	1942	1943 and the ensuing years
98%	83%	65%	52%	39%

The mere presentation of these figures instantly shows to what extent Germany was interested in Romanian oil and in its flowing toward the Reich's military potential. Recent research has shown that starting in 1938, when the Krauch plan pointed to the Reich's dependence—in case of war—on Romania's oil sources, Romanian-German relations entered a new stage.[11] Fully aware of the fact that without that oil the war against Great Britain had no chance of success, the Reich would intensify pressures

on Romania in order to make the latter change her foreign policy in favor
of Germany's interests; within this context, it started to exploit the Ro-
manian-Magyar antagonism, generated by the revisionist policy of the
government in Budapest, resolved to denounce, as soon as an opportunity
arose, the Trianon Treaty (June 4, 1920), which had acknowledged the
union of Transylvania to Romania (December 1, 1918).

A memorandum of April 1939 on *Germany's provisioning with mineral
oil in wartime* outrightly and brutally set Romania's role in ensuring the
provisioning. "Here [in Romania—a.n.] lies the solution to Germany's
provisioning with mineral oil in wartime. She actually represents the sole
possible solution, wherefrom the necessary acknowledgement of mastering the Romanian oil-fields and, consequently, the Danubian areas as a
prerequisite for a plentiful provisioning of Germany with mineral oil
during a long war."[12] The means for the attainment of that goal were,
according to the memorandum, of an economic, political and military
nature, aiming—in the listed order—at setting up a German monopoly
on Romanian oil, the conclusion of an unconditional military alliance
(ein bedingungslos Bündnisvertrag) and at absolute control over the
country. As the efforts of the Reich's diplomacy to secure control over
the oil deposits in Romania through economic and political means yielded
no results,[13] the military means, the author of the memorandum showed,
were the only ones able to ensure the Reich's control over the Romanian
oil-fields in the event of a war.

The economic interest of the Reich did not confine itself to fuel alone.
In August 1939, another German document made a general analysis of the
Romanian availabilities for the Reich's war economy if—as the document
suggested—a "large economic space" had been created, with a view to
turning the Allies' blockade inoperative: "As regards the war economy,
Romania's strong point is the mineral oil output, which represents 40%
of the overall needs. Likewise, some profit for the synthetic rubber output
can be derived from the methane deposits. In addition to this, the rich
bauxite deposits play an essential role in building one's own aluminium
production (2.2%) as well as in the chromium output (15%)."[14]

German fears of a possible break in fuel imports from Romania in case
of a war proved justified by the substantial decrease in Romania's oil supplies in the winter of 1939-1940[15] —following shipment difficulties and the
blocking of some traditional communications as a result of the war and
the territorical changes that had taken place in Eastern Europe.[16]

The military victories won by the Wehrmacht in the spring of 1940 enabled the Reich to exert fresh pressure on Romania, which, after the conclusion of the German-Soviet Non-Aggression Pact of August 23, 1939, the surrneder of France and the retreat of the British troops from the continent, found herself completely isolated from the diplomatic point of view. The outcome of those tragic circumstances was—as shown above—the territorial amputation in the summer of 1940, followed by King Carol II's abdication and the replacement of the royal dictatorship by a military-fascist one. After the Vienna Diktat (August 30, 1940), which wrenched northern Transylvania from Romania to cede it to Hungary, Berlin was provided with a further instrument for blackmailing Bucharest, as the hope of regaining the lost territory—and that was a constant aim of Ion Antonescu's policy—was linked to answering the Reich's economic demands.

With the setting up of the military-fascist dictatorship and the German troops' entering the territory of Romania, the Romanian oil-field area became a part of the envisaged "great economic space."

A regime of economic exploitation would be imposed on Romania, which even a constant promoter of the alliance with the Reich such as Ion Antonescu attempted to oppose when it assumed excessive forms.

According to data coming from a reliable source,[17] the mineral oil supplies to the Reich and the Wehrmacht units on the front amounted to:

1939	1,272,000 tons
1940	1,177,000 tons
1941	2,963,000 tons
1942	2,192,000 tons
1943	2,406,000 tons
1944	1,043,000 tons

When detailed per specific products, the figures are the following:[19]

Year	Petrol	Plane fuel	Petroleum	Black oil
1939	506,000 t	–	58,000 t	64,000 t
1940	528,000 t	12,600 t	58,200 t	99,700 t
1941	1,489,000 t	91,200 t	75,500 t	146,500 t
1942	1,184,000 t	103,800 t	225,300 t	125,200 t
1943	1,117,400 t	120,500 t	295,300 t	244,000 t
1944	383,000 t	59,600 t	254,800 t	66,400 t

In addition, mineral oil was supplied to the Protectorate of Bohemia and Moravia as follows:[20]

1939	284,000 t
1940	127,800 t
1941	210,700 t
1942	110,400 t
1943	66,700 t
1944	35,900 t

According to statistical tables, the Wehrmacht's consumption of 1,058, 147 tons of fuel for military transports on the territory of Romania was also ensured by the Romanian output.[21]

The strategic-economic weight of the Romanian oil-field area considerably increased after the failure of the 1942 summer campaign in the East, a major goal of which had been to secure control over the "oil-fields in the Caucasus area."[22]

Consequently, Germany relied solely on the oil-fields in Romania, Galicia, Hungary and Austria, but Galicia and Hungary's outputs were low: 340,000 tons and 150,000 tons had been extracted in Galicia and Hungary respectively in 1942. Two years later, German efforts would lead to an increase in the Hungarian output to 800,000 tons and in the Austrian one to 1,337,000 tons.[23]

Starting in 1943, Romania herself witnessed a reduction in her oil output. The German representatives would complain about the Romanian authorities' looking for pretexts or raising difficulties in order to spare oil. Quite true, as early as June 1942, Mihai Antonescu warned A. Clodius, the German representative: "At present Romania is exhausing her oil resources: It is obvious that she is not in the least interested in doing that, and if oil output is spurred, this is done for the exclusive benefit of the Reich."[24] Antonescu's government started to show reticence if not utter unwillingness to answering the German demands for an "utmost increase in the oil supplies,"[25] which threatened the national oil industry with a true bankruptcy. Consequently, in 1943, only 43% of the extraction plan would be fulfilled.[26] An investigation made in Romania by the OSS—the American intelligence office—in September 1944 reached the conclusion that, actually, "The general behavior of the Romanians—officials and businessmen included—seems to have followed the policy of answering the German demands to the least possible extent. Even the Romanians who collaborated with the Germans gave considerably less than they had been expected to. The outcome was that the Romanians succeeded in saving a substantial part of the country's two most important resources: foodstuffs and oil."

During the period under analysis, fuel was undoubtedly the most important thought not the sole item imported by Germany from Romania. The Romanian agrarian economy was seen in Berlin—as shown before— as complementary to the industrial economy in Germany. The Reich secured large foodstuff supplies from Romania as shown below:[27]

1940	979,866 t
1941	305,389 t
1942	173,064 t
1943	107,145 t

Over 1940-1944 (August), Germany would import 1,378,450 tons of cereals and seeds, and 75,147 tons of cattle and meat products from Romania, to say nothing of the food packages sent by the German soldiers home from Romania and the food consumed by the German units on Romanian territory.[28]

Moreover, during the same period Germany was also supplied with 428,522 tons of wood and other materials, whereas some other 3,640,000 tons of raw materials were delivered to states in the Reich's orbit.[29]

Consequently, to Hitler's Germany, Romania was a highly important supplier of fuel, raw materials, and foodstuffs. These supplies were imposed on Romania by her forceful integration in the Reich's sphere of hegemony, as a result of the ratio of forces in East and South-East Europe over August 1939-September 1940. The Romanian people's hostile attitude to Nazi Germany would compel Ion Antonescu's government into attempting to set some limits or restrictions on exports in order to save the country from bankruptcy.[30] The Reich's decision-making factors fully realized the essential strategic-logistic role of Romania's natural resources for the functioning of the German war economy. Addressing the gauleiters in Munich on November 7, 1943, General Alfred Jodl said that "no enemy success there [in the East—a.n.] can be more terrible to us than the occupation of Romania's oil-fields."[31] In consonance with that viewpoint, steps were taken to ensure the defense of the Romanian oil-field area against Anglo-American air attacks.[32] In the Prahova Valley oil-field area the German anti-aircraft artillery had emplaced 250 heavy and 400 light cannon. The 88 mm cannon were disposed on a 16 km diameter belt, the 105 mm ones on a 17 km diameter belt, while the 128 mm ones on a 13 km diameter circular railway track. The fighter air forces in the area consisted of 300 aircraft. In addition to anti-aircraft artillery and fighters, an important means for defending the area was the artificial fog. While on May 5, 1944, Ploieşti ranked the second, after Berchtesgaden (Hitler's residence) and Salzburg (both holding first place),[33] on priority delivery lists of artificial fog-producing substance, on May 27 a new order ranked Ploieşti as first, together with the hydrogenation and synthesis plants.[34] There were 2,000 artificial fog generators, with a 180 liter-capacity each, spread over an area of 34 sq km.

Hitler himself would unequivocally express the importance he attached to preserving the Romanian oil. In August 1944 he told General Gerstenberg, who was in charge of the Ploieşti area defense: "We are staking all we've got. If we lose the oil regions, we cannot win the war."[35]

When, as a result of the Romanian insurrection of August 1944 those apprehensions were about to turn into reality, Hitler would react violently trying to hold the oil-field area at all costs: by Hitler's first directive on

the evening of August 23, 1944, concerning the suppression of the Romanian insurrection, the German commander of the oil-field area in the
Prahova Valley was ordered to see that the routes for the transportation
of the oil products, so vital for the functioning of the German war
machine, to the Reich—on the Danube and through the Predeal pass—
were safe; on August 27, 1944, after an abortive attempt to occupy
Bucharest, the OKW consented to the retreat of the Stahel-Gerstenberg
group that had fought north of Romania's capital city; at 11:15 p.m. the
German "South Ukraine" Army Group agreed on the retreat, however
stressing that the Ploieşti area had to remain under German control "at
all costs."[36]

The loss of the Romanian oil dealt a heavy blow to the war economy
of the Reich. The apprehensions Hitler evinced during the talk he had
with General Gerstenberg proved justified: with the oil deposits in Hungary and Austria alone—even if the oil output were considerably increased
due to intensified extraction—the Germans could no longer win the war.

Romanian oil supplies ceased right when the Anglo-American strategic
bombing of the synthetic fuel plants proved most efficient. Started in May
1944, the air raids were mainly directed against fuel, synthetic rubber and
nitrogen facilities, succeeding in bringing about a real crisis.[37]

The synthetic fuel output would see a catastrophic drop: synthetic
plane fuel alone decreased from 175,000 tons in April to 30,000 tons in
July, and to only 5,000 tons in September.[38]

Under such circumstances, the idea of winning back the Romanian oil
—however abberant—would obsess Hitler—who was ever more losing control of his sense of reality and, therefore, of what was still possible and
what was not—to the end of the war.[39] Banking on a synchronization of
the subversive activities carried on by the Iron Guard and the German
ethnic group in Romania with an offensive mounted from Hungary, he
hoped to win Romania back.

What made this country particularly "appealing" to him follows from
the orders given to the soldiers participating in what was to be the last
German offensive of World War II—the one at Balaton—triggered off on
March 6, 1945: Hitler had to be given the oil of Ploieşti as a present for
his birthday (April 20).[40] That was yet another telling proof of the mo-
mentus impact the Romanian insurrection had on the Reich's war economy and, thereby, on the Wehrmacht's strategy and logistics.

Yet, the loss of the resources in the Carpathian-Danubian area was not the only loss. The Romanian insurrection of August 1944 entailed the disintegration of the entire German disposition in South-East Europe.[41] General A. Jodl's earlier referred to report of November 7, 1943, reads: "the maintenance of the Balkans as a constituent part of the European 'fortress' (Festung) is decisively important from the operational, political-militayr and economic points of view." That area, he pointed out, provided 50% of the oil, 60% of the bauxite, 29% of the antimony, and 100% of the chromium European outputs.[42] These were vitally important raw materials for the Reich to keep up its war effort, and Hitler would not reconcile with the idea of losing them. Through the "Waldteufel" operation" (the offensive in Hungary in March 1945) the German aims at occupying the Sava-Danube triangle, and then advance south-eastwards. Looking at the map, Hitler—"full of hopes," as an eye-witness would recall—told those present, in an address meant to explain the goals of the offensive: "In all probability, we'll see the inhabitants of these regions rise all in one so that with their support we may regain the Balkans through a life-and-death struggle. Because, dear Sirs, I've always been resolved to go on the offensive in the East.'"[43] Beyond the fanatism of such plans, one can see the importance Hitler attached to an area he had lost as the result of the Romanian insurrection of August 1944. In his moments of lucidity —such as during his talk with General A. Jodl in March 1945—he admitted that he should have had to commit suicide ever since November 1944.[44] The bankruptcy of the Third Reich—in the autumn an obvious thing even to its founder—had been hastened—as shown by the above analysis—by Romania's action of August 1944.

This conclusion is fully substantiated by the opinions of Albert Speer, former minister of the armament of the Third Reich, expressed in an interview granted in 1975: recalling that on June 30, 1944, he had submitted a petition to Hitler in which he warned against the catastrophic reduction of fuel supplies, he added: "Starting June 1944, we could ensure less than 50,000 tons of petrol monthly, while from August onwards, when our troops had to leave Romania, the figure fell below 20,000 tons. It was obvious that we were heading towards disaster. That was the cause of our defeat. It was brought about not by the strategic bombing carried through by the British and Americans, since the output of the Western oil wells kept on growing, but by the loss, after August 23, 1944, of the supply sources in Romania [. . .]. Undoubtedly, that day of August 23, 1944, led to a decisive turning point in the history of war output and economy, therefore in the history of the conflagration itself."[45]

CHAPTER VI

POLITICAL CONSEQUENCES OF THE ROMANIAN REVOLUTION

If, according to Clausewitz's famous definition, war is the further promoting of policy by other means, it stands to reason that the changes occurred in the military field during a war have direct bearings on politics. The Romanian insurrection of August 1944, which led to the disintegration of the German military system in South-East Europe—an area of outstanding strategic, economic and political importance—comparable, in the opinion of Hitler himself, to the Anglo-American landing in France and the collapse of the "Center" Army Group in Byelorussia,[1] also had political repercussions of utmost significance.

Taking into account the critical situation of Germany, now faced with the strategic logistical and political consequences of Romania's change-over, Foreign Minister J. von Ribbentrop submitted a petition to Hitler in which he was asking for approval to make peace soundings. "It is infantile and naive to look for a favorable political initiative at a moment of grave military defeats," Hitler irritatedly replied, thus hinting once more at the serious situation the Reich was faced with as a result of the act of August 23, 1944.[2]

Domination over South-East Europe had been a major purpose pursued by the expansionist policy of the Third Reich, and what might be called *Drang nach Süd-Osten* had started to take shape already during the first months after the setting up of the Nazi regime. In the spring of 1941, after

154

the occupation of Yugoslavia and Greece, this part of the continent was trampled under the German boot. Maintenance of the Danubian-Balkan area under German control was seen by the OKW as a prerequisite for continuing the war, which accounts for the presence of considerable forces in the Balkan Peninsula despite the critical situation on various other fronts, and, primarily, on the Soviet-German one.

The Romanian insurrection had the effect of a true earthquate in this part of Europe, whose shock wave would rapidly propagate, entailing or just hastening political crises in the states belonging to Berlin's orbit: Hungary, Bulgaria and Croatia.

The Political Crisis in Hungary. Solidary with Hitler's Germany in the latter's revisionist policy of undermining the European status quo after World War I, and benefiting from the territorial changes resulting from the Reich's hegemony in Central and Eastern Europe between 1938-1940—the Vienna Diktat is an example—Horthy's Hungary hurried—as soon as there were signs indicative of a Nazi defeat—to reach an understanding with Great Britain and the United States, able to save her socio-political structures[3] and, equally important, the territories she had gained with German support. Faced with a possible Hungarian defection, Hitler reacted violently, and, after a dramatic meeting with Horthy, he occupied Hungary on March 19, 1944. The presence of the Wehrmacht units encouraged the right-wing and fascist circles to intensify their activity and sharpened the dispute between the partisans and the opposers of collaboration with Germany. The replacement of Döme Sztójay's government by another one, presided over by General Géza Lakatos, had been suggested to Horthy before by Count Istvan Bethlen, the regent's closest councillor, in a secret memorandum forwarded in late June,[4] however, informed in time of those intentions, the Germans—they themselves prey to the disputes between the Ministry of Foreign Affairs and the Intelligence Service (R.S.H.A.— Reichssicherheits—Hauptamt) over the composition of the government— compelled Horthy to postpone his plans.

Therefore, the news about the outbreak of the Romanian insurrection arrived in an atmosphere of internal crisis and of utter suspicion in the German-Hungarian relations. The struggle of the Romanian people, led by the Romanian Communist Party, for overthrowing Antonescu's dictatorship and for driving the Hitlerite troops away from the national territory had

known its acme and, by its reverberation in the international arena, it
brought the Horthyist regime to the verge of collapse.

Capitalizing on the confusion in Berlin as a result of the events in Romania, Horthy succeeded in obtaining the removal of Döme Sztójay and
in appointing, as suggested by Istvan Bethlen—after a few days of long
and heated disputes—a new cabinet chaired by Géza Lakatos. However,
Béla Jurcsek and Lajos Reményi-Schneller, the "eyes and ears" of Veesenmayer, the German plenipotentiary in Hungary,[5] would be also included
in the government upon German insistence, after the Reich's representative had had to cope with the insistent demands of Szálasi, the leader of
the Hungarian fascists, to be entrusted the power, as, according to him,
"Horthy no longer believed in a German victory and was in the hands of
Bethlen and of the Anglo-Jewish gang."[6]

The main problem, however, was of a military nature: what were the
steps to be taken in order to counterbalance the consequences of the Romanian insurrection inside the Carpathian arch? The meeting of the Council of Ministers on August 25 revealed the lack of unity of the Magyar
cabinet, mirroring itself the political crisis brought about in Hungary's
political life by the Romanian insurrection: a government minority upheld that the Hungarian Second Army, commanded by General Lajos
Verres and deployed in northern Transylvania at the time, should immediately engage in action and take hold of southern Transylvania; in that way
the Soviet Army would have been denied the possibility to advance
through the Carpathian passes, while the old goal of Magyar interwar revisionism, that of possessing Transylvania in her entirety, would have been
attained.[7] The majority of the government members considered, however,
that a military action was risky both from the military point of view—
due to insufficient combat strength and armament—and from the political
one, as offensive operations carried on outside Hungary's frontiers might
have spoiled her otherwise limited chance of political manuevering in the
international arena.

The contradiction between strategic and political reasons—the former
called for a blocking of the passes in the Carpathians, while the latter
for avoiding that such a decision be made—faced the Hungarian government with a dilemma and delayed military steps. The dilemma would be
aggravated by the secret negotiations opened in Bern on August 29, between Hungary's representatives—György Bessenyei, plenipotentiary

minister, and Colonel László Rakolczay, the military attaché—on the one hand, and those of the USA, Allan Dulles and General Legge, on the other, concerning the occupation of Hungary by Anglo-American troops alone. On September 1, Colonel Rakolczay cabled home that, according to his American interlocutors, "An offensive action against the Russians or the Romanians, that is going beyond the present Hungarian border, should be avoided at any costs."[8]

Faced with two contradictory options, its activity attentively watched by the Reich's political and military representatives, and by their fascist instruments in that country, the Hungarian government finally decided—after much postponing—to pass on to offensive action in southern Transylvania, which, however, came up against the stubborn resistance of the Romanian troops, and eventually failed.[9]

On September 7, the Hungarian Crown Council faced Germany with the following alternative: either she sent, within 24 hours, five divisions—armored to the extent that was possible—in order to reinforce the Hungarian frontier, or Hungary was compelled to cease fighting and sue for an armistice.[10] The assurances given by Weesenmayer, even when accompanied by threats, could not shatter the conviction harbored by the greatest part of the Hungarian political circles that the war was lost. On September 10, during a meeting of Hungarian political personalities held at Horthy's residence, the conclusion was reached that Hungary had to sue for an armistice.

Yet, no practical steps followed: on the contrary, after the visit of General Janos Vörös, Chief of the Hungarian General Staff, made to Hitler's headquarters, Hungarian-German military collaboration would be further promoted. "Every step we take should aim at winning the confidence of our ally,"[11] General Janos Vörös declared at the meeting of the High Defense Council of September 14, 1944.

Such a policy was deeply detrimental to the Hungarian people. "Soon after the Romanian insurrection"—a report of the Budapest Police Department showed on August 31—"the wide circles of the Magyar public opinion realized that they were faced with the alternative of following the Romanian example."[12] In early September, "Szabad nép," the newspaper of the Hungarian communists, warned: "Hungary's reactionary leaders do not want to know about what has happened in Romania, Bulgaria, Finland. There has been too much talking about these states so far,

and now they are referred to as traitors. Why? Because they have had the
power and the courage to give the people back its freedom. Because they
will not sacrifice what has been left of their peoples for Hitler's war. When
will he who does not agree to bleed for Hitler cease being branded a
traitor?"[13]

The worsening of the political crisis in Hungary as a result of her catastrophic military situation forced Horthy into overtly breaking with Germany. As it is known, his announcing on October 15, 1944, the conclusion
of the armistice aroused a quick German reaction, to the effect that
Szalasi's fascist regime was set up. The Hungarian army would continue
to fight alongside its Hitlerite ally. Hungary was to be liberated through
the joint fight of the Soviet and Romanian armies, and of the Hungarian
patriotic forces.

It clearly stands out that the Romanian insurrection of August 1944
had decisively contributed to shattering Horthy's regime and to speeding
up Hungary's liberation from German occupation.

The political crisis in Bulgaria. During the last talk Hitler had with
Antonescu (Rastenburg, August 5-6, 1944), when the Romanian dictator
raised the question of a possible defection of Bulgaria, Hitler allegedly
answered—P. Schmidt, the interpreter records—that he could not "give
any guarantees as to Bulgaria's stand. It goes without saying that Germany
will defend herself against any breach in Bulgaria's loyalty; one doesn't
know who will assume the regency in the future. Ever since the assassination of Boris by the Secret Service,[14] he [Hitler] has not been able to get
rid of a feeling of uncertainty about Bulgaria, and, therefore, other sur-
prises may crop up."[15]

Hitler's doubts regarding the Bulgarian ally were engendered by the progress of events in that country. While the Third Reich was gradually getting control over South-East Europe, Bulgaria joined the Tripartite Pact
(March 1941), followed by her increasing integration in the Reich's political and military orbit. Although a base of operations against Greece and
Yugoslavia, Bulgaria found herself in the odd situation of being at war
with Great Britain and the United States (December 13, 1944), but of
not taking part in the Wehrmacht's campaign against the Soviet Union.
"Prompted by military-strategic and political reasons, Berlin would not
necessarily look for an unconditional break with the USSR, because in
this way she could be freely used as a supply base for the campaign in

Russia, the Bulgarian army kept as a reserve against Turkey and for fighting the partisans, while the Bulgarian government could still represent Germany's interests in the Soviet Union."[16] Bulgarian troops would be used by the German command to keep territories in Greece and Yugoslavia under control.

The defeats sustained by the Wehrmacht on the German-Soviet front gradually eroded the groundwork of collaboration between the Nazi Reich and Bulgaria, making the latter look for a way to conclude a separate peace with the Western Allies. Tsar Boris III's death, shortly followed by the official announcement of the Italian armistice, would increase the action of destabilizing forces. The antifascist forces in Bulgaria, led by the Bulgarian Workers' Party, intensified their activities, finding a political and organizational framework in the Homeland Front, the program of which, broadcast as early as July 17, 1942, by "Hristo Botev" Broadcasting Station, was a platform rallying all the socio-political forces of the country, resolved to put an end to the royal-fascist regime and to collaboration with Germany. The insurrectional people's liberation army, set up in the spring of 1943, intensified its actions throughout the country, and in the autumn of 1943 as well as in the winter of 1943-1944 thwarted the offensive of the government's army aiming at suppressing the partisan movement. Following the guidelines set by the Bulgarian Workers' Party, the insurrectional army assumed the offensive, carrying through over 500 actions between January-May 1944.[17]

The considerable worsening of the Third Reich's military situation led to the aggravation of the political crisis in Bulgaria as a result of the confusion of the ruling circles. Faced with the impending collapse of the German front in the East and the advance of the Soviet Army towards the Balkan Peninsula, the Bulgarian governmental circles tried to save the bourgeois structures by concluding peace with Great Britain and the United States and by suppressing the partisan movement.

In order to show a credible face to the governments in London, Washington and Moscow, the official circles in Sofia resorted to a political "make up" operation: on June 1, 1944, D. Bojilov's cabinet would resign in favor of a government presided over by I. Bagrianov. The change had been precipitated by the summoning of the Soviet minister from Sofia and by the notes of the Soviet government (April 17 and 26, May 9 and 18) which pointed to the incompatibility between the Bulgarian neutrality and the use of Bulgarian harbors and airports by the Wehrmacht; the note demanded that Soviet consulates were reopened in Varna, Burgas and Ruse, in order to watch the activities of the German navy, which rendered illusory Bulgaria's neutrality. On June 3, the new cabinet hurried to announce a series of steps meant to attenuate the dictatorial regime, such as amnesty for political detainees, abolishment of concentration camps, and the like, but they were never carried into effect; instead, a true offensive was initiated against the resistance movement with a view to smashing it. In point of foreign policy, though not meeting the Soviet demand of opening the consulates, Bagrianov's government nevertheless promised to permit the utilization of the Bulgarian ports by the German fleet no longer.

In the meantime, in London, the European Advisory Commission was busy with working on the clauses of the armistice with Bulgaria;[18] on July 21, Balabanov, the Bulgarian minister to Ankara, contacted the American representative to inform him of the efforts made by the new cabinet in Sofia to break away from a both compromising and detrimental alliance, and of the promises—whether wishful or real—of the German government to no longer transit troops across Bulgarian territory and to withdraw its troops from that country.

The attempt of the cabinets in London and Washington to make the Soviet Union join the debates of the European Advisory Commission (not being at war with Bulgaria, she only attended the proceedings as an observer) ended in failure. The Soviet stand was expressed by V. M. Molotov, who on August 11 stated that "we have reached no conclusion as regards Bulgaria."[19]

In London, Bulgaria's situation was considered in close connection with that of her neighbor Greece, the latter being highly important for preserving Great Britain's strategic and political positions in the Eastern Mediterranean, first and foremost for securing the safety of the imperial road connecting the British metropolis to its possessions in the Near, Middle and Far East, with Gibraltar and Suez as its main landmarks. Keeping Greece in Great Britain's sphere of influence had been a central goal of Churchill's efforts since spring (May) that year in order to reach an agreement with J. V. Stalin as regarded the division of South-East Europe into spheres of interest.[20] Bordering on Greece, Bulgaria, which had taken part alongside Germany in the occupation of some Greek territories and was harboring herself annexionist intentions as regarded northern Greece in order to secure an outing to the Aegean Sea, aroused more interest in London than Romania. Logically, the contact with the Bulgarian government was a need for the British Cabinet. Consequently, the latter showed a willingness to recieve a Bulgarian emissary—obviously informing the Soviet ally—in order to discuss Sofia's armistice proposals. On August 14, 1944, Stoychjo Moshanov, a former president of the Bulgarian Sobranja (the Parliament), had a first meeting with a British representative, and on August 16 he was received by Sir Hughes Knatchbull-Hugessen, the British ambassador to Turkey, whom he informed of his country's wish to leave the war. According to the Bulgarian emissary, the implementation of Bulgaria's decision was being delayed by two factors: the need for gathering as much as possible of that year's crop before the expected German retaliation, and the effort to unite the political forces inside the country, which, in the opinion of Moshanov, would have taken a couple of weeks. On August 23, Moshanov and the other Bulgarian representative, Gheorghi Kiseliov, an industrialist, submitted their credentials for the negotiations, during which they hoped to secure Anglo-American support in order to preserve the socio-political structures of the kingdom.[21] Actually, on the eve of the Romanian insurrection, Great Britain and the United States were still discussing the terms of the Bulgarian armistice in London, the Soviet Union showed a reserved attitude, while Bulgaria asked, through her emissaries, to be informed of the armistice terms.

The events of August 23, 1944 in Romania completely altered the situation, with immediate and obvious repercussions in the area. On August 24, Ambassador F. T. Gusev, the representative of the Soviet Union in the European Advisory Commission, was instructed to take part in the working out of the text of the armistice with Bulgaria; the following day the Foreign Office ordered Knatchbull-Hugessen to inform Moshanov that talks with the representatives of Great Britain and the USA for the conclusion of the armistice were to be held in Cairo, and that he was supposed to leave immediately. On August 26, V. M. Molotov informed Sir Archibald Clark-Kerr and Averell Harriman, the British and American ambassadors to Moscow, that, according to the last hours news, the Bulgarian government had demanded from Germany the day before to withdraw her troops from Bulgaria unless she wanted them disarmed, expressing its resolve to adopt a "totally neutral stand."[22]

The Bulgarian antifascist forces, led by the communists, welcomed the Romanian insurrection, pointing out that the "Romanian workers and peasants have chosen the right path of struggle and are about to free themselves from the German spoilers and occupants." The leadership of the Bulgarian Workers' Party and of the Homeland's Front shared the opinion that "Romania's changeover to the Allied side has led to the complete isolation of our country [Bulgaria—a.n.]," that "the recent events [. . .], particularly in Romania, aroused commotion and panic with the fascist circles," concluding that "we must also do"[23] what the Romanian people had done under the leadership of the communists.

The victory of the Romanian insurrection "unlocked" the Gates of Focșani, opening the way towards South-East Europe to the Red Army. The new military circumstances offered the Soviet Union new opportunities for political action. On August 29, the Soviet chargé d'affaires left Sofia, while Ambassador F. T. Gusev was instructed to stop attending the proceedings of the European Advisory Commission. As early as August 26, the Central Committee of the Bulgarian Workers' Party had set the goal of triggering off the armed insurrection and the steps to be taken for its carrying through.[24]

All throughout that period, Bagrianov's government had actually not taken any measure to impede, in one way or another, the movements of the German troops. The ending of the state of war with Great Britain and the United States and the declaration of neutrality (August 26)—turned down by the Soviet Union on August 30—had not been accompanied by any act of hostility toward the Wehrmacht units, apart from the disarming of some German military who had crossed over to Bulgaria, being driven away from Romania. Quite relevant, the remnants of the German units smashed by the Soviet army and the Romanian insurrectional forces on Romania's territory tried to find an escape by crossing over to Bulgaria.

The German High Command was able to attain the goals set as a result of the large gap the Romanian insurrection had effected in its disposition, namely to reorganize its military system in South-East Europe, not in the least hindered by a Bulgarian action. It is easy to see what catastrophic consequences a Romanian insurrection conjoined with a similar action in Bulgaria would have had for the German troops in the Balkans; the OKW did not want to have in Bulgaria the sad experience it had in Romania: as a matter of fact, the scarce forces it had there as well as the total political isolation of the pro-German circles left a possible attempt of getting complete military control no chance of success. The withdrawal of the German troops to the northwest of the Balkan Peninsula appeared to the OKW as the best solution under the new circumstances.[25]

On September 2, a new government, led by K. Muraviev, was set up in Sofia after an abortive attempt of the governmental circles to split the Homeland's Front by suggesting the setting up of a government of that coalition, though presided over by Bagrianov. Consisting of representatives of the "legal opposition," the new cabinet did not hurry to take action against Germany, and, despite the absolute neutrality it had proclaimed, it continued to adopt a tolerant attitude toward the German units. "At the time, the Soviet press abounded in data showing that crushed German military units that had managed to escape from Romania with their armament, through north-western Bulgaria and Yugoslavia were returning to Romania or to other sectors of the Soviet-German front."[26] In keeping with the TASS News Agency corresponding reporting from Constanţa, "in the harbor of Ruse alone 112 German ships of various types had found shelter, among them 12 large naval ships. The Bulgarian government did not confine the crews of 74 ships, scuttled by the Hitlerites themselves on August 26-30, and sent them over to Germany."[27]

Faced with such a situation, the Soviet government sent a note to Muraviev's government on September 5, showing that for three years it had accepted Bulgaria's alleged neutrality, taking into account the disproportion of forces between Germany and Bulgaria; however, now that the Nazi Reich was on the verge of collapsing and Bulgaria, under the guise of neutrality, continued to collaborate with Germany, the Soviet Union was compelled to consider herself in a state of war with Bulgaria, which had for a long time been engaged in war against the Soviet Union.

While on September 8, Muraviev's government finally decided to declare war upon Germany (the declaration came into force at 6 p.m.), the popular forces, led by the Bulgarian Workers' Party, were preparing the insurrection in keeping with the plans worked out by the Political Bureau of the Bulgarian Workers' Party on September 5. The revolutionary turmoil in the country was drawing to its acme. On September 8, the Soviet army crossed the Romanian-Bulgarian frontier, and on September 9, the successful antifascist and anti-imperialist revolution in Bulgaria ushered in a new era in the history of the Bulgarian people.

As seen before, the Romanian insurrection played an essential role in bringing about the favorable conditions for that issue and it was the Romanian revolution again which, through its strategic-military impact, entailed a change in the policy of the Great Powers in the anti-Hitler coalition toward Bulgaria.

The Political Crisis in Croatia. The Reich's aggression against Yugoslavia in April 1941 led to the latter's splitting. Under the circumstances an independent Croatian State was set up—a kingdom whose crown had been offered to the Duke of Spoleto, who, in his turn, showed no hurry to take it, and in which political power was wielded by Ante Pavelich, one of the gloomiest figures in the gallery of fascist dictators, the "poglavnik" (leader) of the Ustash terrorist movement. A scene described by Curzio Malaparte in his book entitled *Kaputt* is relevant in itself for the atrocities, associated, with good reason, with the name of that bloodthirsty tyrant: when recieved by Ante Pavelich, the well-known Italian writer saw a vase with eyes of killed partisans on the dictator's bureau!

The terrorist regime set up by the Ustash leader in Croatia was nevertheless corrupt and inefficient. In a report of February 27, 1943, Colonel-General Löhr, commander of the South-East theater of operations, suggested the overthrow of Ante Pavelich, the setting up of a new government and the abolution of the Ustash movement.[28] Faced with the impetuous development of the Yugoslavian peoples' resistance movement, which found in partisan warfare its best-organized, most vigorous and efficient form, on October 29, 1943, Hitler issued a directive for the "unitary conduct of the struggle against communism" in Yugoslavia.[29] The directive ordered—among other things—that Siegfried Kasche, the German plenipotentiary to Croatia, the plenipotentiary German general for Croatia (der Bevollmächtigte Deutsche General in Kroatien) and the Reichsführer SS' chargé with the Croatian government better coordinate their activities (in this respect, the Ustash militia was to be backed as part of the Croatian army).

However, the relations between the authorities in Berlin and the puppet government in Zagreb was far from conducive to that unity of action Hitler hoped for. The German troops in Croatia were involved in political and national conflicts in the area. On the one hand, the German units came into conflict with the Ustashes—as a result of the atrocities perpetuated by the latter against the Serbian and Muslim population in

Montenegro and Dalmatia, which entailed an increase in the resistance spirit; on the other hand, in order to step up the fight against the partisan movement led by I. B. Tito, they started collaborating with Pavel Djurishich's Chetniks, a fact that deeply upset the authorities in Zagreb. The setting up (upon Himmler's initiative) of a Muslim division, also called "Handzar," in Bosnia-Hercegovina, would worsen the already strained relations between the ruling circles in Berlin and Zagreb.

The Reich's military failures would put Germany's chances to win the war under a big question mark; the collapse of the Third Reich seemed impending. Breaking off with the Reich appeared as necessary at least to some quarters of the Zagreb political establishment. As a result, on July 5-6, 1944, Ante Vokich, the War Minister in the puppet-government, organized in Sarajevo a secret meeting of the chief commanding officers, who decided that in case the German troops retreated from Croatia, they were to be attacked, while their ammunition and equipment depots were to be taken hold of; likewise, provisions were made for training the Croatian troops in underground warfare; for integrating the local militia in the Ustash movement or in the local military units (Domobrane).[30]

In that atmosphere of tension and suspicion, the news of the insurrection in Romania spread to Zagreb, too. In the opinion of Ante Pavelich himself, expressed during a meeting he had with Hitler on September 18, 1944, the Romanian insurrection had brought about a political crisis in Zagreb: "Croatian intellectuals, among whom members of the Croatian cabinet as well, lost faith in victory, advocating that something had to be done before the war was lost, so that the British might reach Croatia before the Russians."[31] Among those blamed by Ante Pavelich were Ante Vokich, the War Minister, and Mladen Lorkovich, a minister without portfolio. Those favoring a rapid break with the Reich had been in touch with the Peasant Party (Radich-Machek) and demanded the suppression of the Ustash movement and the maintenance of local units (Domobrane) alone. The reaction of the "poglavnik" would be prompt and resolute. The ministers were removed from the government, court-martialled or put in jail along with all those who had evinced pro-British feelings (they were not executed because, as Pavelich himself declared, he did not want to make martyrs out of them).

The events in Romania triggered off a true chain reaction: Bulgaria's leaving the Axis entailed, in its turn, a second, even more serious crisis in Zagreb. As Pavelich told Hitler, an important feature of the second crisis was the increase of acts of sabotage, which paralyzed the entire system of communications (in some places, there would be 90 mines laid on but one kilometer of railway tracks).

The Domobrane units witnessed serious breaches of discipline: desertions, changeovers to the partisans and the like. The public opinion was seized with a true defeatist psychosis, expressed in fanciful rumors about the fall of Zagreb and the leader's arrest.[32]

Resorting to retalitory steps, the government of Pavelich managed to survive that crisis, too. Pavelich's Croatia ranged alongside Szalasi's Hungary, with the last allies of the dying Reich. After the fall of Zagreb (May 4), the puppet government took refuge in Austria and was captured in Reutte (Tyrol). Pavelich succeeded in escaping the punishment he fully deserved.[33]

While not engendering the fall of the Pavelich regime, the shattering impact of the Romanian insurrection weakened its position and revealed its frailty.

Finland. Though located at a great distance from Romania, Finland, too, felt the impact of the Romanian insurrection of August 23, 1944. As early as 1943, as a result of a gradual worsening in the military situation, the decision-making circles in Finland started to probe the possibilities of leaving the war, benefiting in this respect by the discrete support of the United States and the overt assistance of Sweden. Secret negotiations began in Stockholm, in February 1944, to be later moved to Moscow. However, the terms put forward by the Soviet government were deemed as excessive in Helsinki, and negotiations were broken off.[34]

The Soviet offensive in June 1944 and the victories won by the Red Army made the resuming of the Soviet-Finnish dialogue appear as a stringent need to the government in Helsinki. Finnish demands for economic and military assistance would be met, Hitler said, provided that Finland pledged not to conclude a separate peace. Following a visit of Ribbentrop to Helsinki, Risto Ryti, the then President of Finland, initialled a declaration to this effect, but as it was not passed by the Parliament, it involved but his person and his ministers. However, the Reich was no longer able to send his hesitating ally either cereals, or ammunition, or troops. The political-military realities were therefore to have their say. On August 1,

President Risto Ryti resigned in order to render null and void the pledge he had toaken to Germany. Marshal Mannerheim, who took over the office, resumed secret negotiations with the Soviet Union. Talks were underway when the news arrived about the overthrow of Antonescu's government in Bucharest.

The OKW quickly realized that what happened in Bucharest was to make a strong impression on Helsinki. During the first hours after the outbreak of the Romanian insurrection, the Chief of the Amtsgruppe Ausland (the Department for Foreign Countries) at the Wehrmacht General Staff, asked that a stand were taken as to what had happened in Romania, "primarily intended for General Talvela [the Finnish military attaché in Berlin—a.n.] with a view to informing Mashal Mannerheim." The same German source points out: "the developments in Romania and the German reaction towards the latter's attitude are followed with peculiar interest in Finland, as the Finns may find there, among other things, a stimulus for a similar attitude."[35] The following day, August 25, at 4 p.m., the Amtsgrupped Ausland informed a series of German high military bodies that the events in Romania had apparently made a "strong impression in Finland," where the political circles had keenly perceived the "difference in the Soviet Union's position toward Finland as compared to that toward Romania (see the declaration for the observance of Romania's independence made by Molotov some time ago)."[36]

While the German authorities were not capable of assessing "if and to what extent have peace tendencies been favored by the events in Romania,"[37] the facts were to give an outright answer: on August 25, Alexandra Kollontai, the Soviet ambassador in Stockholm, was conveyed a message from the Finnish government, whereby the latter asked to be informed on the conditions for a resumption of the armistice negotiations. The Soviet answer, which "reached Helsinki in a record time,"[38] contained but two conditions: a) to break off diplomatic relations with Germany; b) to evacuate all Wehrmacht units from the territory of Finland until September 14, a deadline after which the Finnish authorities were supposed to confine the German military who had not left the country. On these grounds, a cease-fire was reached on September 5, and two weeks later, on September 19, the armistice was signed.

Therefore, the Romanian insurrection had been a true political catalyst for Finland's leaving the anti-Soviet war.

The impact of the Romanian insurrection of August 1944 on Germany's sphere of domination in Central and South-East Europe had a major weight in breaking up the Nazi Reich's hegemony and military system in this part of the continent, as well as in speeding up the end of World War II. Opening the Focşani Gate, and thereby enabling the Soviet Army to advance in two strategic directions—South-East and Central Europe—the insurrection contributed to shaping the political configuration of post-war Europe. Assessing, from his point of view, the political consequences of the Romanian insurrection, Winston Churchill noted, even before such consequences were discernible, that "Romania's joining the Allies has meant an extremely great advantage to the Russians, as they would reach Belgrade, Budapest and probably Vienna before the Western Powers broke through the Siegfried Line."[39]

The crumbling of the German military system in South-East Europe and the rapid advance of the Red Army across that area as a result of the Romanian insurrection entailed significant changes in the relations between the members of the anti-Hitler coalition. If, as shown before, their stand toward Bulgaria was powerfully influenced by Romania's turning her weapons against Hitler's Germany, Great Britian's policy in South-East Europe would be deeply affected by the strategic-political changes brought about by the Romanian insurrection in that area. In her concern with ensuring safe passage through the Suez Canal—a vital part of the imperial road connecting the British metropolis to its Asian colonies— Great Britain endeavored to find a political formula able to elude the political consequences of the Soviet troops' presence—then in the Balkan Peninsula—in the vicinity of Cyprus—the outpost of Suez—and of Suez itself. W. Churchill's talks in Moscow between October 9-17, 1944, and the percentages agreement were aimed at dividing South-East Europe into spheres of influence, and at ensuring thereby that British interests in the Eastern Mediterranean would remain intact.[40]

The comments made during the days of the Romanian insurrection as well as the results of a thorough-going analysis of sources rbought to light after 1945 are converging on showing that the insurrection of August 23, 1944, in Romania, ranks, through its strategic, economic and political consequences, with the greatest events of World War II.

CHAPTER VII

AUGUST 23, 1944—THE START OF A NEW ERA

The antifascist and anti-imperialist revolution for social and national liberties marked the beginning of a revolutionary process in the course of which the Romanian society would know deep-going changes in all its fundamental structures, passing from the capitalist system onto the socialist one.

The very first decrees issued by the insurrectional government showed that the removal of Antonescu's dictatorship did not mean a return to the old bourgeois order, but paved the way for the changes that were to be wrought within a long comprehensive revolutionary process, with social freedom and the building up of a new system as its main goals.

The socio-political events in Romania were part of the wide post-war renewing trend in Central, East and South-East Europe, whose essential characteristic was the transition from capitalism to socialism; however, in Romania it would bear the stamp of the reality specific to the Romanian society, a fact that would lend a specific physiognomy to the building of socialism in this country.

The event of August 23, 1944, was—as shown—the result of the joint action of all socio-political forces in the Romanian society, interested in restoring national independence and sovereignty, in taking Romania out of the war she was waging against the United Nations, and in winning back northern Transylvania. Those forces found in the Romanian Communist

Party a dynamic resolute organizer and leader, which prepared and ensured the victory of the revolution of August 1944.

Solidary in the attainment of the national goals, the parties making up the National Democratic Bloc nevertheless shared differing views as to Romania's subsequent development as soon as she would have left the orbit of the Nazi Reich. The National Peasant Party members and the national-liberals expected the event of August 23, 1944, to lead to a restoration of a bourgeois-democratic regime of the type that had functioned until 1938. The left-wing parties and groups felt the need of embarking upon a new road which, in the communists' outlook, could be but the socialist one. The Romanian Communist Party was the only political party to have worked out a comprehensive, all-embracing program for turning Romania from a capitalist country with a poorly and unevenly developed economy into a socialist country with a great industrial-agrarian potential. That program was not a mere list of desiderata, but the result of a multilateral analysis of the historical circumstances in which the Romanian society had developed, an analysis that yielded adequate, realistic and practical solutions.

Already during the first days after August 23, 1944, the symptoms cropped up of a confrontation between the political parties and groups that had participated in the overthrow of Antonescu's regime. During the struggle for power that followed, the democratic forces, rallied under the leadership of the Romanian Communist Party, within the National Democratic Front, benefited by wide steady assistance from the part of the people's masses, expressed through such wide-scope demonstrations that had no precedents in the political life of the country. The struggle for setting up the revolutionary-democratic power would be carried on at both the local and the national levels. Led by the communists, the people's masses started wide-scope activities for taking over State power at the local level (they would remove prefects and mayors), a fact that gradually sapped the political authority of the bourgeoisie exerted through the State apparatus. Actually, starting in August 1944 until early March 1945 there was a true power duality in Romania, as the bourgeois parties formed the majority in the three cabinets succeeding one another at the helm of the country (two cabinets presided over by General Constantin Sănătescu and one by General Nicolae Rădescu).

The revolutionary trend, backed by the majority of the population, which had been won over to the idea of the setting up of a regime able to ensure social equity and economic prosperity in Romania, asserted itself with increased vigor in the winter of 1944-1945, both at the local and at the national power levels. Thanks to the policy of alliance promoted with remarkable suppleness by the Romanian Communist Party, the Peasant and Liberal Parties would see themselves ever more isolated in the political arena. The unbroken original nature of the alliance policy promoted by the communists enabled the Romanian Communist Party to rally under its leadership all the political forces interested in a renovation of the structures of the Romanian society. Relying on the United Workers' Front—the alliance between communists and social-democrats— that wide coalition, directly supported by the people's masses, won the battle for power: on March 6, 1945 under the immediate pressure of the masses, expressed by ample meetings and demonstrations throughout the country, the helm would be taken by the democratic revolutionary government presided by Dr. Petru Groza, which was preponderantly a worker-peasant government. Therefore, what happened on March 6, 1945 was not a mere change of government, but a change of the political regime itself, through the setting up of the revolutionary-democratic power of the workers and peasants.

With reference to that battle for power ended in the victory of the progressive forces on March 6, 1945, President Nicolae Ceaușescu underlined: "In all these class struggles and large revolutionary mass movements the Romanian Communist Party gave living proof of the fact that it had become in that period the principal force in Romania."

"In these circumstances, by strengthening the unity of the working class, of the Workers' United Front, by developing cooperation with the other democratic forces, the Romanian Communist Party worked for the carrying into effect of deep-going revolutionary social reforms, for widening the democratic freedoms and defending the interests of the working class, of the whole people. Priority was given to the remaking of the national economy, to the independent economic and social development of the country. An important role in this process was played by the installation, on March 6, 1945, of the first genuinely democratic Government in the history of the country with a pronounced worker-peasant character. That was an essential event in the successful development of the people's democratic revolution, in the revolutionary transformation of the Romanian society."[1]

The passing of the land reform on March 23, 1945—actions for dispossessing the landowners of their land had spontaneously started earlier that year—solved in a democratic spirit one of the problems that had deeply and for a long time hindered the progress of Romanian society: the agrarian question. That reform was the first one in a train of steps that would be taken over 1945-1947, that is during the period when the bourgeois-democratic revolution was completed.

The victory of the left-wing forces during the first postwar elections (1946),[2] an expression of the Romanian people's adhesion to the democratic-revolutionary transformation of the Romanian society, envisaged and promoted by the Romanian Communist Party, created the prerequisites for the consolidation of the democratic regime, allowing for the implementation of the program contemplated by the Romanian Communist Party: the nationalization of the National Bank (1946), the monetary reform (1947), the setting up of industrial offices that paved the way for the nationalization of industry.[3] With the advance and deepening of the revolutionary process, there came the political and organizational breaking up of the Peasant and Liberal Parties, which, overtly opposing the democratic renovation of the country, gradually lost its ties with the public opinion and finally went bankrupt, politically, disappearing from the Romanian social life.[4]

A component of utmost importance of the revolution for social and national liberation of August 23, 1944, was Romania's participation, with all her forces, in the war waged against the Nazi Reich. If as far as the shaping of life at home revealed that the stands taken by the political forces which had prepared and carried through the changeover of August 23, 1944 were irreconciliable in terms of program-platforms one could notice that all the extant parties at the time held converging views as to the armed struggle for driving the occupants away from the national territory and for defeating Hitlerite Germany.

The governing program of the National Democratic Front, a body rallying the progressive political and democratic organizations under the leadership of the RCP, published on January 29, 1945 pointed to a major goal meant for the "salvation and prosperity of the Romanian nation": "[Romania's] participation, with an utmost effort, in the war alongside the

United Nations, for the speediest smashing of Hitlerism and for the liberation of the peoples. The increase of our war potential will be achieved through the strengthening and democratization of the army, through cementing brotherhood-in-arms between the Red Army and our army as well as through increasing production and plentifully supplying the front with war materiel, food, clothing, and so forth."[5] On October 16, 1944, the National-Peasant Party published in its turn its program, stipulating Romania's participation in the anti-Hitler war, fulfillment of the armistice terms, the punishment of those guilty of the country's foreign stand over 1941-1944, a.o.[6] A similar attitude as to Romania's participation in the war against Hitler's Reich, would be adopted by the National-Liberal Party (Gh. Tătărescu) which in its program-manifesto published on December 14, 1944, stipulated: "Continuation of the war alongside the glorious army of the Soviet Union, up to the complete defeat of our and the United Nations' enemies. The exemplary implementation of the armistice of September 12, to which should contribute not only the State bodies, but also the entire population, aware of the fact that it is on the accomplishment of this act that both the country's safety at present and the fulfillment of her expectations for tomorrow depend."[7]

That national political consensus created the best prerequisites for embarking upon a wide-scope military effort, whose impact upon the development of the war against the Reich in general would prove substantial.

The strategic conception of carrying out the offensive for the liberation of the occupied Transylvanian territory was laid down by the Romanian General Staff at the end of the first stage, in its directive of August 30, 1944. According to the latter, the First Army—which had carried out the covering of the entire contact alignment in Transylvania and the Banat— and the Fourth Army—whose large units had completed the reshuffling from Moldavia—were assigned clear missions regarding "some major offensive actions for conquering northern Transylvania."[8] For minutely preparing those actions, they had to take resolute steps in order to check any enemy offensive that might attempt to reach the Carpathians, and to carry on soundings in the enemy disposition with a view to taking hold of such places and areas that would be needed during the final offensive.

The initial plan of the Romanian general staff for completing the liberation of the national territory would be subsequently changed under the incidence of several factors. The most important among them was the pouring, over the first ten days of September 1944, of the Soviet large units in the bridgehead in southern Transylvania and the Banat and the subordination of the two Romanian armies to the 2nd Ukrainian Front. The Armistice Convention concluded between Romania and the United Nations on September 12, 1944, expressly stipulated the Romanian-Soviet military collaboration in the fights for the liberation of northern Transylvania, as well as other domestic and international obligations for Romania.

In September 1944, the military actions for the liberation of northern Transylvania showed the dynamic picture of concomitant strategic offensive and defensive, though in areas remote from each other. Between the Western and the Eastern Carpathians, therefore in the Transylvanian Plateau, the Romanian and Soviet troops concomitantly carried on an offensive for the reduction of the "Szeckler salient," and a defensive for thwarting the offensive mounted by the "South Ukraine" Army Group on September 5, 1944. West of the Western Carpathians, in the Banat and Crişana, the Romanian and Soviet large units first baffled the enemy offensive meant to take hold of the entire western Carpathian range and then carried out an impetuous advance south-northwards toward Salonta and Oradea.

In early October 1944 the Romanian-Soviet troops embarked upon the final liberating offensive. Inside the Carpathian arch and west of the Western Carpathians the Romanian and Soviet large units engaged in an energetic pursuit of the enemy, rapidly driving him beyond the homeland's natural borders. Between October 10-25, 1944, the Romanian troops gradually entered Hungarian territory.

During the battle for the liberation of northern Transylvania, the Romanian troops and commands, irrespective of arm, evinced high soldierly virtues, managing to overwhelm, alongside the Soviet allies, a stubborn and battle-scarred enemy.

The offensive battle for reducing the "Szeckler salient" (September 5-14, 1944) demonstrated, for the first time during the war, the efficiency of operational and tactical cooperation between the Romanian and Soviet troops and commands. Eliminating the salient which the enemy from had driven into the Romanian disposition north of Braşov was called for by the need to remove the danger threatening the Braşov industrial area and the right flank of the Romanian troops in the Transylvanian Plateau. The crushing of the enemy followed a "classic" military scheme: an extremely powerful frontal attack—delivered by the Romanian Mountain Corps (the 1st Mountain and 3rd Infantry Divisions) in cooperation, in its earlier stage, with the "Tudor Vladimirescu" Division and a Soviet large unit—combined with a blow at the left flank and rear of the enemy disposition. That outflanking maneuver was carried through from Moldavia across the Eastern Carpathians, by crossing the massifs at altitudes of some 1500 m, by the 103rd Mountain Division, the 7th Heavy Artillery Regiment and by the armored detachment of Lieutenant-Colonel Gheorghe Matei, in cooperation with Soviet forces from the Seventh Guard Army.

Significant fights took place north of Brașov, around the towns of Sf. Gheorghe, Odorhei, Reghin, Aita Mare, Baraolt, Rupea and in the Niraj Valley, in the Tarcău Mountains and in the Berzunt massif; the troops of the Mountain Corps carried out in the move the assault crossing of the Tîrnava Mare and the Tîrnava Mică rivers pushing their way towards Tîrgu-Mureș.

The Romanian army committed 26,500 men to that battle (to which one should also add the combat strength of the "Tudor Vladimirescu" Division which took part in the fighting between September 7-9, 1944) sustaining 1500 casualties. The enemy disposition was destroyed, the mountain troops penetrating 120 km in that area, a highly important fact for the subsequent offensive toward Tîrgu Mureș and Cluj.

The defensive battle in the Transylvanian Plateau started on September 5, 1944, and it would be carried out with exemplary bravery by the Romanian Fourth Army for three days (after September 7, 1944 Soviet large units began to arrive in the intra-Carpathian area and immediately engaged in battle). The enemy had intended quickly to break through the Romanian disposition and to reach in no time the peaks of the Southern Carpathians, 100-120 km behind its rear. For three days on end, the Fourth Army carried on hard defensive fighting in the area delimitated by the Arieș, the Mureș and the Tîrnava Mică rivers, succeeding in checking the enemy attacks. On September 9, 1944, it initiated offensive actions in cooperation with the Soviet troops for repelling the enemy north of the Mureș and the Arieș rivers (September 9-October 4, 1944).

Concommitantly, grim fighting took place at Turda and in the Mureș and Arieș valleys. During the fights in the Mureș Valley highly conspicuous for their bravery were the 8th Motorborne Cavalry Division (the

Sîngeorgiu Hill) and the 11th Infantry Division (at Oarba de Mureş), while the 18th Infantry Division covered itself with glory during the fighting in the Arieş Valley.

The defensive battle in the Banat and Crişana (west of the Western Carpathians) actually implied the checking of the enemy advance started on September 13, 1944 on a broad front, its main effort in the Mureş Valley. Important fighting took place in the valleys of the Crişul Alb, Crişul Negru and Mureş rivers, and in the Banat. The Romanian troops succeeded in stopping the enemy advance (forces belonging to the Hungarian Second and Third armies and to the German Army Group "F") at the entrance to the defile sof the Crişul Alb, Crişul Negru and Mureş rivers, while in Banat—west of Timişoara, Reşiţa and Orşova.

During the defensive actions carried on west of the Apuseni Mountains until September 20, 1944, the Romanian First Army engaged almost 56,000 men in action, sustaining 4,483 casualties. Worth mentioning are, for their remarkable contribution to checking and repelling the enemy, the units belonging to the 3rd Mountain Division, 19th Infantry Division, 13th Călăraşi Regiment (the latter's commander heroically fell while leading his troops during the defense of the city of Timişoara) a.o.

The outstanding results of the success scored during the defensive battle carried on west of the Western Carpathians was that the pouring and concentration of the Soviet troops in the bridgehead in southern Transylvania and Crişana as well as in the Banat were ensured absolute safety. General I. M. Managarov, commander of the Soviet 53rd Army, who deployed his troops in Crişana and the Banat showed in an order of the day of September 23, 1944: "The units of the Romanian First Army have stopped the German-Magyar onrush, covering the movement of the Red troops toward Hungary . . . [they] have proved resoluteness and daring, creditably fulfilling the lofty mission they had been assigned."[9]

The battle for assault crossing the Mureş river and for reaching the western border started during the last ten days of September and ended on October 25, 1944. It was part of the comprehensive strategic plan for the preparation and carrying through of the Debreczen operation (mounted west of the Western Carpathians, on October 5, and east of the same mountains on October 9) by the forces of the 2nd Ukrainian Front.

The Romanian Fourth Army, flanked first by the Soviet Seventh Guard Army and then by the Soviet Fortieth Army (on the right) and by the Soviet Twenty-Seventh Army (on the left), secured bridgeheads north of the Mureş river, liberated the town of Tîrgu Mureş, broke the enemy front in the Turda area, rapdily mounting the offensive toward Cluj (liberated on October 11, 1944), and continued the pursuit of the enemy in the direction of Zalău–Careii Mari until the western border of Romania was reached.

Momentous fighting took place during the assault crossing of the Mureş, for securing the bridgeheads needed in order to develop the offensive in the direction of Turda–Cluj, for liberating Tîrgu Mureş and Cluj, as well as during the resolute pursuit of the enemy precipitantly withdrawing through the Someş gate toward Hungary. A great many units and large units cut a conspicuous figure during those fights: the 9th Infantry Division, in the Sîngeorgiu on Mureş bridgehead (between Cipău and Iernut) and at Carei (the last Romanian locality freed on October 25, 1944), the 2nd Mountain Division in the Cluj area, the 21st Infantry Division at Corpadea, the 20th Infantry Division at Bonţida and Răscruci, the 1st Mountain Division at Tîrgu Mureş and elsewhere.

During the interval (September 20-October 25, 1944) the Romanian Fourth Army committed to battle an effective strength of 93,789 men, sustaining a high percentage of casualties: 22%. While crossing Romania's western border, Army Crops General Gheorghe Avramescu, commander of the Fourth Army, addressed the Romanian fighters by the following touching words: "You have enthusiastically answered the call of the country to freeing Transylvania wrenched through the Vienna Diktat, never losing faith in the victory of the Romanian people's right cause . . . Smashed by the killing fire of your artillery and by your repeated attacks, the enemy has been driven away from our dear Transylvania."[10]

The final battle carried on west of the Western Carpathians, included the fighting for the liberation of the towns of Oradea and Salonta as part of the wide-scope offensive assumed by the Romanian and Soviet forces during the first ten days of October, 1944. Committed to those fights were three divisions of the Romanian First Army and the "Tudor Vladimirescu" Division of Romanian volunteers (the latter subordinated to the Soviet XXXIII Army Corps). On October 6, the 3rd Mountain and "Tudor Vladimirescu" Divisions as well as the Romanian Cavalry Corps passed on to the offensive, in cooperation with Soviet forces, in the direction of Arad-Debreczen-Csap. On October 12, the town of Oradea was liberated, and the following day subunits of the 3rd Mountain Division continued the fight beyond the border in Hungary. There was bitter fighting in that area too, the 3rd Mountain Division and the Cavalry Corps sustaining casualties amounting to 7% of the total combat strength.

The contribution of the air force, navy, engineer and signal units to the fighting was part of the effort made by the entire Romanian military establishment for freeing the national territory. Here are some relevant figures:

—Between September 20 and October 25, 1944 alone, the *Air Force* carried out 527 missions, meaning 1,200 flgihts and 1,745 flight hours as well as 164 tons of bombs launched in support of the Romanian and Soviet troops' advance.

—During August 23-September 20, 1944, the *Navy* committed to battle 70 ships, 28 naval artillery batteries and 6 battalions of marines (21,016 men). They cleared the Danube of enemy ships between Brălia and Turnu Măgurele, supported the crossing of Soviet forces to Bulgaria and Yugoslavia, sent 60 enemy ships to the bottom.

—The *Engineer Corps* (between September 20-October 25, 1944), the pontoneers enabled the friendly troops to cross 5 rivers, building up 10 bridges; over the same interval, the pioneers built 39 bridges, repaired some 25 other bridges, laying or lifting 10 minefields.

—the *signal troops.* During the final stage of the fighting fro the liberation of Transylvania (September 20-October 25, 1944), specialized troops built up, repaired and maintained some 30,000 km of permanent or field communication lines.

The summaries of the fighting carried on by the Romanian army for completing the liberation of the national territory are illustrative of the major war effort made by the Romanian nation in defense of its ideals, of freedom and unity. Between September 1-October 25, 1944, the Romanian army engaged in action 27 divisions, one air corps, and two anti-aircraft artillery brigades, that is an effective strength of 265,735 men (some 100,000 more than stipulated in the armistice convention). The casualties sustained by the Romanian troops attained 49,744 km men (killed wounded and missing). During the offensive, 872 localities were liberated, 8 towns included. The enemy was inflicted 11,434 casualties (prisoners and counted dead, the total figure being undoubtedly greater). On the whole, over August 23-October 25, 1944, the casualties sustained by the enemy throughout the Romanian territory reached 72,937 (among whom 66,275 were prisoners).

In *Hungary* the Romanian army actually started operations on October 6-7, 1944, when large units of the First Army penetrated through fighting on the territory of that neighboring country. However, the bulk of the field army entered Hungary after October 25, 1944, when the Fourth Army rapidly crossed the western border, in its northern sector.

On the whole, the operations of the Romanian army on the Magyar territory, carried through in keeping with the strategic conception of the 2nd Ukrainian Front, covered a vast area of the neighboring country, with three major centers of gravity in the zonal development of the fighting. The first one was the north-eastern part of Hungary, where large units of the Fourth Army fought starting October 25, until mid-December 1944; the second one was the middle course of the Tisza, where the enemy was attacked by the divisions of the First Army; finally, the third "major zone" was the fighting road covered by the VII Army Corps, form the Middle Tisza onto the heart of the Hungarian capital city, Budapest.

In the north-eastern sector of Hungary the Romanian divisions made an outstanding contribution to the battle of Debreczen (also in the Nyiregyháza area, north of that town), then to the fighting carried on in the Tokaj region (the encircling of the Hegyalja massif) and for carrying the Bükk and Matra massifs.

The first Romanian large units to penetrate into that area were the 1st Infantry-Training and 1st Cavalry-Training Divisions (October 9-10, 1944). Subsequently, the 2nd, 3rd Mountain Division, and the "Tudor Vladimirescu" Division also participated in the battle for Debreczen. By October 26, the eight divisions of the 4th Army had been already engaged in the offensive on the Hungarian territory.

The fighting in north-eastern Hungary was extremely dynamic. The Romanian cavalry and mountain divisions assumed the offensive on Debreczen in cooperation with Soviet large units. The cavalrymen denied the communications west of that large city, while the mountain troops belonging to the 3rd Mountain Division were committed to a frontal attack south-northwards against the enemy disposition, with the Romanian volunteers from the "Tudor Vladimirescu" Division by their side; the 2nd Mountain Division effected an ample outflanking maneuver east of the city, side by side a Soviet large unit. After bitter street fighting, on the night of October 19 to 20, 1944, the city was completely mopped up.

Meanwhile, east of Debreczen a mobile group of Soviet forces quickly passed by the city, forcing its way to the north. In broke the enemy front, liberated the town of Nyiregyháza, and reached the upper course of the Tisza, facing the enemy with the gloomy prospects of being cut off from the retreat from Romania. Under the circumstances, the enemy resorted to a desperate defensive on the TiszafüredHajduhadház alignment, his resistance being meant to offer a way of escape to the remnants that had managed to pass through the Someşgate and were pursued at a high pace by the Romanian forces of the Fourth Army a chance to escape.

Breaking that enemy alignment required the mustering of powerful forces, which were also joined by the five Romanian divisions that had fought at Debreczen. Starting October 21, 1944, the breaking of that alignment was tried on the move, a tactical scheme that seemed to end in a success after the 2nd Mountain Division had freed Hajduhadház by an assault. However, the enemy assumed the offensive, managing to encircle a group of Soviet forces in the Nyiregyháza area. He aimed at maintaining that defensive turn-table as long as possible, as it covered the corridor through which the Wöhler Army Group was withdrawing from Romania to the upper course of the Tisza.

Then, it was the turn of the large units belonging to the Romanian 4th Army to enter action which, impetuously developing the offensive, encircled the town of Nyiregyháza through the east. South of the town, the cavalry and mountain troops stubbornly withstood the enemy counter-attacks, keeping their offensive alive. On October 30, the offensive of the Romanian and Soviet troops in the Nyiregyháza zone generalized, and the enemy, hit from the south and from the east, started a precipitated retreat toward the Tisza.

On November 1, 1944, at dawn, the bulk of the Fourth Army and of the 2nd and 3rd Mountain Divisions reached the upper course of the Tisza, where they immediately started preparations for an assault crossing of the river, with a view to establishing a bridgehead north of it.

The well-prepared assault crossing and the fruitful cooperation with the Soviet forces led to a joint success in that sector. Starting November 7, 1944, the Soviets gained a bridgehead in the Tiszalök zone, where the river was also crossed by three Romanian divisions. From there, the Romanian and Soviet troops advanced in the direction of Tokaj, a town they freed on November 22, 1944.

At the same time, the 2nd and 3rd Mountain Divisions, which had been assigned the task of liberating the town of Miskole, got on the eastern slopes of the Bükk Mountains down into the Hernad Valley. The town had been freed by November 22. The Romanian troops immediately started the fighting for clearing the Hegyalja and Bükk massifs of enemy troops. The Romanian command decided to have the enemy disposition there encircled through the valleys of the Hernad and Bodrog rivers that are contiguous to the two massifs. Triggered off over the last ten days of November 1944, the action was crowned with success. The II and VI Army Corps (the Fourth Army) drove the enemy away from the Hernad Valley, dismantling his disposition in the Hegyalja massif and reached the Hungarian-Czechoslovak border on December 18, 1944. In the Bükk Mountains the mountain troops of the 2nd and 3rd Mountain Divisions assumed the offensive on November 23, 1944. Many heights would be climbed under brisk enemy fire and many towns and villages freed. By December 24-25, the Bükk Mountains had been pierced, and the mountain troops, too, reached the border between Hungary and Czechoslovakia.

In late 1944, the alignment of that frontier was reached in the Ipel river zone also by the "Tudor Vladimirescu" Division, which had fought the enemy west of the Bükk Mountains, in the Matra massif. The Romanian offensive for breaking through the enemy defense actually meant ten days of bitter fighting (December 20-30, 1944) carrying the highest peak in those mountains (1,010 m), the liberation of a large town—Salgotarján. By the new year of 1945, north-eastern Hungary had been completely liberated through the joint effort of the Romanian and Soviet troops.

Large units belonging to the Romanian First Army arrived on the Middle Tisza starting October 10-11, 1944, and were assigned the mission to replace the Soviet divisions operating in the bridgeheads west of the river, at Mindszent and Csongrád. At Mindszent, the 19th Infantry Division carried on heavy fighting starting on October 11, crossing the river under intense enemy artillery fire. On October 13, the 9th Cavalry Division crossed the Tisza north of Mindszent, at Csongrád, both Romanian divisions being assigned the mission to enlarge and strengthen the bridgehead in the area. On October 14, the two divisions effected the junction, following continuous fighting, carried on with an exemplary offensive spirit thereby creating a bridgehead west of the Tisza whose are totalled 250-300 sq km. That was a necessary outpost for the approaching planned offensive toward Budapest.

Other two divisions, the 2nd and 4th Infantry (subordinated to the IV Army Corps), engaged the enemy in the bridgehead at Szolnok (some 20 km north of Mindszent) on October 15-16, 1944. An enemy counter-blow carried on south-eastwards from a bridgehead which the enemy, in his turn, had secured on the eastern bank of the river, faced the Romanian-Soviet disposition on the middle course of the Tisza with an extremely dangerous situation. The shock of the enemy blow was felt by the Romanian 2nd and 4th Infantry Divisions. The 4th Division was forced to fight the encirclement starting October 19, 1944, and after a few days it was smashed as a result of the enemy's overwhelming superiority. By October 22, the 2nd Infantry Division cooperating with the Romanian large units in the Mindszent area and with other Soviet forces had managed to contain the south-eastwards advance of enemy armored spearheads. The latter had been entrusted the task of threatening the flank and rear of the Allied forces, and then of engaging in a rapid offensive toward Debreczen and north of the town.

After the containment of the enemy counter-offensive the Romanian forces, in collaboration with the Soviet ones, resumed the advance at an impetuous tempo. Important bridgeheads would be secured on the western bank of the Tisza. Through the joint action of the 4th and 19th Infantry Divisions and the 9th Cavalry Division, a bridgehead was gained in the Tiszáug zone, wherefrom the VII Army Corps would embark on the offensive toward Budapest.

There were two notable results pointing out the utmost importance of the victory won over the enemy in that sector of the threater of operations in Hungary: first, the operations carried out by the Romanian-Soviet troops in the north-east were ensured safe flanks and, second, favorable conditions were created for launching the decisive attack on Budapest.

During the grim battles fought in that area the Romanian artillery men would cover themselves with undying glory. The Romanian artillery played an important part in seriously hindering the advance of the German armor, particularly during the containment of the enemy counter-offensive at Szolnok. In an order of the day Army Corps General Victor Atanasiu, commander of the First Army, would record the bright feat of arms of the 1st Heavy Artillery Regiment which had efficiently engaged against 60 enemy armor on October 19, 1944: "The 1st Artillery

Regiment"—the order of the day shows—"has written down one of the most beautiful glorious pages in the history of the Romanian artillery."[11]

The Romanian VII Army Corps in Budapest. In the plans of the enemy command, the capital city of Hungary was a true turn-table of its defensive system in Hungary. Important enemy forces (some 55 divisions) had been massed inisde the city and on the approaches to it, while powerful defense centers had been built and successively arranged outside it, and piles of houses in the capital had been prepared for long circular defense.

The strategic operation for the liberation of Budapest was part of a wider framework of the war waged on Hungary's territory, being one of its central points. In the north-east, where, as shown, three Romanian army corps were fighting, the enemy had been pinned down since the latter half of October 1944, being prevented from exerting any pressure on the group of forces that was to mount the offensive on Budapest.

By January 1, 1945, the enemy had already been driven away from that sector beyond the Czechoslovak border, and forces of the 2nd Ukrainian Front would proceed to a strategic encircling of Budapest through the north. "Comfortable" bridgeheads had been secured on the Middle Tisza where all the forces needed by a head-on offensive against the defensive system of the Magyar capital could be massed. In the south, troops belonging to the 3rd Ukrainian Front collaborating with forces of the People's liberating army from Yugoslavia and with Bulgarian large units advanced northwards along the Middle Danube and effected the junction with the divisions of the 2nd Ukrainian Front, that had carried out the strategic encirclement, in the Vak-Esztergom gorge. In early January 1945 the turn-table of the enemy defensive in Hungary was powerfully squeezed in the Allied strategic "pincers."

Within that general context, the task of carrying out the head-on attack on the enemy defensive around Budapest devolved upon the Soviet 7th Guard Army, which passed on to the offensive from the bridgehads on the Middle Tisza, with the Romanian 7th Army Corps in its main offensive direction.

The latter large unit consisted of three divisions—the 19th Infantry, the 9th Cavalry and subsequently the 2nd Infantry—two heavy artillery regiments—the 1st and the 7th—and a Soviet antitank regiment.

On October 30, the VII Army Corps started on an 18-km wide offensive front strip its glorious fight road that would end eighty days later at two km's distance from the Danube, inside the Hungarian capital.

By fruitfully cooperating with the Soviet soldiers, the Romanian troops smashed the enemy defense kilometer by kilometer. On November 3, they reached the Ceglé-Abony railway sector 50 km away from the Tisza which they had conquered through fighting in only six days. On November 12, after breaking another enemy defensive alignment, the Romanian offensive forward elements reached within 40 km of Budapest. Five days later, they came into contact with the outer defensive belt of Budapest, built 30 km away from the city on three successive powerfully fortified lines.

December 5 was the day of the decisive attack. That day the first 3 km of the enemy defensive belt were conquered. The enemy counterattacks would not manage to wither the offensive spirit of the Romanian troops. On December 27, 1944, they initiated an attack on the Isaszeg-Cinkóta (a suburb of Budapest) direction and on December 30, 1944, the VII Army Corps reached the outskirts of the Hungarian capital.

That was the beginning of one of the most glorious pages written down by the Romanian army in the history of its participation in the anti-Hitler war: the offensive inside Budapest. The enemy desperately fought for every bit of ground, for every enemy block or quarter, for every crossroad. Efficiently using the artillery, making up combined (infantry and artillery) assault groups, or "manoeuvering groups" at the division echelon and benefiting by the valuable assistance of engineer teams, which opened the way by blowing up the enemy fortified support points, the Romanian soldiers would carry house after house, sustaining heavy casualties. By January 15, 1945—the last fighting day in Budapest—the VII Army Corps had carried more than 1,000 buildings stubbornly defended by the enemy and had opened wide approaches to the Danube through the great Hungarian, Rottenbiller and Rákoczy Boulevards.

Between October 30, 1944—January 15, 1945, the VII Army Corps penetrated through fighting 135 km into the enemy disposition; the toll of that brilliant feat raised to 11,000 killed and wounded, out of a total strength of 36,348 men committed to battle.

The airmen of the Romanian Air Corps also performed feats of valor in Hungary. They carried out daring strategic or tactical reconaissance for the benefit of the Allies troops, hit the enemy concentrations of forces or columns on the move and successfully fought against enemy aircraft, and the like. Of an utmost military importance was the successful bombing of the bridges over the Danube in Budapest with a view to cutting off military traffic between the two parts of the Hungarian capital.

The Romanian forces participating in the battles fought in Hungary consisted of: 2 army commands; 5 army corps commands (the II, IV, VI, VII and Cavarly Army Corps); 15 divisions with full strength and 2 training divisions (the latter would be withdrawn from action after the Debreczen operation), one air corps (15 squadrons and 174 aircraft) and 18 anti-aircraft batteries (122 muzzles). The total combat strength commited by the Romanian army to battle in Hungary rose to over 210,000 men, while the casualty figure to 42,266 (killed, wounded and missing). The enemy was inflicted with over 30,000 casualties (prisoners and killed) that is the equivalent of some four Wehrmacht divisions. In Hungary, the Romanian troops freed 1,237 localities, among them 14 towns, conquered three massifs and assult crossed four major rivers.

In Czechoslovakia. The campaign of the Romanian army in that country started on December 18, 1944, when the troops of the Fourth Army as a whole reached the Hungarian-Czechoslovak border. Gradually, the entire Romanian field army penetrated into Czechoslovakia either through fighting—the IV Army Corps (the 2nd and 3rd Mountain Divisions) on December 25, 1944, the "Tudor Vladimirescu-Debreczen" Division on December 31, 1944—or transferred from other theaters of operations— the VII Army Corps, on January 18, 1945.

In Czechoslovakia, the operations carried on by the Romanian forces took place mainly in mountainous areas, under extremely difficult weather conditions, fully put to test the endurance of the troops, the ingenuity and efficiency of the commands. Their fighting road was marked by some battles of utmost bitterness—at Rožňava, south of Košice, for the towns of Zvolen and Banska-Bystrica, for the assault crossing of the Hron river or for securing control over the Moravian region. Cooperation with the Soviet allies reached its acme, being an essential element for successfully working out and carrying through the operations for the liberation of the Czechoslovak territory.

Once in Czechoslovakia, the Fourth Army engaged the enemy disposition in two directions: Rožňava and Košice. Over December 19, 1944-January 12, 1945, large units belonging to that army carried on defensive actions in the Sena-Turna sector, seriously wearing down the enemy forces, thereby creating conditions for the subsequent offensives.

On Janary 4, 1945, after some wider restructuring of dispositions, it was ordered to assume the offensive toward Rožňava, in order to reach the upper course of the Hron river. Carrying through that mission implied the crossing of the Silička massif south-northwards during ten days of continuous fighting. On January 23, 1945, the town of Rožňava was liberated and the troops of the Fourth Army assumed the offensive west-wards, along the upper course of the Hron river, heading for Brezno. The two army corps making up the Fourth Army advanced toward Telgart and Tisovec and on January 31, 1945 Brezno was cleared of enemy troops. Thus, the bulk of the Fourth Army reached the upper course of the Hron. Here are a few characteristics of that operation (January 12-31, 1945): the width of the offensive strip: 20-60 km; the width of the breaking sector: 3 km; the depth of the advance: 70-80 km; the daily average advance rate: 3.7-4 km. The success of that operation also re-sulted from the well-worked out conception of the Romanian command. Thus, "comfortable" density of forces was achieved in the breaking sector: four infantry battalions per front kilometer (as compared to 1.3 of the enemy) and 70 artillery muzzles per front kilometer (as com-pared to 21 of the enemy); moreover, while the offensive was under way, a double maneuvering of the Silička massif (through the west and through the east) would be carried out in order to set the offensive up.

During that interval, the IV Army Corps (of the First Army), which had crossed the Hungarian-Czechoslovak border on December 29, devel-oped the offensive toward the town of Lučenec, which the Romanian mountain troops in cooperation with a Soviet army corps liberated after two weeks of bitter fighting.

Starting January 21, 1945, when the VII Army Corps arrived in Czecho-slovakia coming from Budapest, the Romanian First Army commited to battle its full strength, its immediate offensive task being that of mopping up the Javorina massif and of reaching the Hron river.

The offensive operation in the Javorina massif was triggered off on January 29, 1945. There, one had to pierce the four-five successive posi-tions built in by the enemy all along the mountain ridge (some 80 km) and to neutralize two powerful fortified zones that were the key to the defensive dispositions: Oremov Laz and Senohrad. The Javornia was defended by the 75th Infantry and 8th Mountain Divions of the Wehr-macht.

The offensive of the First Army, with each of its army corps concen-trating its efforts on one of those fortified zones, would be crowned with success in mid-February 1945. On February 18, the Oremov-Laz zone

come under the control of the Romanian troops, the same as the fortified
Senohrad a week later. The carrying of the Javorina massif was completed on March 6, 1945, when the offensive of the First Army was chan-
nelled in a different direction: northwards, towards Zvolen and the middle
course of the Hron. Again, here are some features of the offensive operation carried out in the Javorina massif that are relevant for the extremely
grim development of the fighting: the width of the offensive strip: 20-22
km; the width of the breaking sectors: 2-4 km; the depth of the operation:
42 km; the daily average advance rate: 1 km; the First Army engaged
71,050 men in the fighting to carry the Javorina massif and for reaching
the Hron, its casualties rising to over 21 percent, a telling percentage for
the enemy's steadfastness and the adverse weather conditions: terrible
snow storms, frost and heavy snowfalls.

The Romanian Fourth Army engaged in heavy fighting on the south-
western slopes of the Ore Mountains, was heading toward Zvolen also.
The conjoined efforts of the two Romanian armies, when at Zvolen
fought alongside important Soviet forces, led to the liberation of that
town on March 16, 1945.

The offensive toward the Hron river alignment continued to develop at
a high pace. The Fourth Army, cooperating with the Soviet Fortieth
Army, broke the enemy defenses north-east of Zvolen, rapidly advancing
toward Banska-Bystrica. On March 25, 1945, the 18th Infantry Division
entered that big town, an important strategic center and junction on the
upper course of the Hron. Through the offensive operation of Banska-
Bystrica—characteristics: depth—40-50 km; width of the offensive strip:
22-55 km; width of the breaking sector—3 km; length—43 days—the Romanian Fourth Army deprived the enemy of an important industrial
zone. "Notwithstanding the enemy's stubborn defense"—Army Corps
General Nicolae Dăscălescu, commander of the army, reported to the
General Staff at the end of the operation—"tens of factors and a lot of
raw materials for the heavy industry were left in the hands of our
troops."[12]

By the latter half of March 1945, the troops of the two Romanian
armies had reached the Hron alignment. On March 25, 1945, the First
Army started by surprise the assault crossing of the river, while the Fourth
Army initiated the offensive for piercing the Big Tatra massif through the
Ulmanka-Harmaneč gorge.

Both offensive operations ended successfully. The troops of the First Army assault crossed the Hron—steep banks 50-70 wide and 3 m deep—and after only two days had advanced 10-20 km westwards clearing the Janoveţ (Vel Ianovec) massif of enemy troops. Then, they immediately engaged the enemy fortified in the Nitra Mountains, succeeding in surpassing that obstacle too, after only three days. On April 3, 1945, the First Army crossed the Nitra river and started its advance through that vast area bordering on the Nitra river in the east and on the Váh river on the west. The divisions of the Fourth Army smashed the enemy in the Big Tatra Mountains, recording a daily average advance rate of 3.5 km, and on April 12 they attacked the enemy defenses in the Small Tatra and the White Carpathians. By April 27, the latter two obstacles had been carried also. Over the last ten days of April, the Fourth Army embarked upon an energetic pursuit of the enemy toward the Beskid Mountains.

The area stretching between the Nitra and the Váh would be crossed by the large units of the First Army at an impetuous advance rate. On April 6, 1945, the 3rd Mountain Division was already fighting against the enemy west of the Váh, developing the offensive toward the Morava river alignment. In order to reach sooner the Morava river with the bulk of its forces, the command of the First Army decided to cross the ridge of the White Carpathians. The action started on April 6, 1945, and three days later the bulk of the 2nd Mountain Division would reach the Morava river.

In mid- and late April, the direction of the advance of the First Army turned northwards, to Uhreský Ostroh. In keeping with the plan of the army command, the breaking of the enemy defense, deployed in that direction, was achieved through an offensive mounted on both banks of the Morava. A daring plan that would yield the expected result, and Uherský Ostroh was liberated on April 26, 1945. From that date onward, the advance was aimed at another two targets in the general direction north: the towns of Kroměříž and Kojetin. The Romanian troops advanced on a 30 km-wide front. On May 3, Kojetin was liberated and the Romanians were only 2 km's distance from their other objective, which the 2nd and 19th Infantry Divisions freed, after fierce fighting, the following day. The offensive operation carried out by the First Army along the Morava river recorded a high advance rate—5.5 km a day—with a 44 km-penetration in the depth of the enemy disposition on a 36 km wide front in only eight days. The memory of the soldiers of the IV Army Corps killed in action during the liberation of those Moravian towns toward the end of the war is commemorated through a monument built at Kroměříž by the inhabitants of the town.

The IV Army Corps (the 10th Infantry, 2nd and 3rd Mountain Divisions and, for a while, the 19th Infantry and 9th Cavalry Divisions) continued to pursue the enemy in the general direction of Prague, at a daily advance rate of 6-8 km. The VII Army Corps, which had been regrouped on May 4 and was heading south-westwards for fulfilling some other missions, had again to fight against the enemy on May 9, 1945, when the Wehrmacht troops in Czechoslovakia refused to surrender. For three days on end, until May 12, 1945, the whole First Army pursued the enemy along the Brno-Prague highway. In some directions they advanced at a rate of 12 km per day, and on May 12, when the enemy finally surrendered, the First Army was within some 80 km south-east of Prague, the capital city of Czechoslovakia.

In early May 1945, while energetically pursuing the enemy toward the Beskids, the divisions of the Fourth Army changed their direction of advance. They started powerfully to push the enemy toward Prague. The offensive continued until May 12, 1945, when the pursued enemy forces surrendered.

Mention should be made of the military performance scored by two Romanian armies during the fighting waged on Czechoslovak territory as they are relevant for the dynamism of the fighting, for the heroism displayed by the military, and for the remarkable planning, organization and preparation of the operations.

The Fourth Army pierced the enemy dispositions on a distance of 635 km, at a daily advance rate of 6 km, assault crossed three major rivers (the Hron, Váh and Morava) and corssed the ridges of five mountain massifs (Small Tatra, the Metalic Mountains, Big and Small Fatra, the White Carpathians). Nineteen towns, twelve large localities and 1,211 smaller populated areas in the offensive strip of the army were freed. The casualties inflicted upon the enemy stood at 15,919 men (14,058 prisoners and 1,861 dead found in the field).

The First Army would carry on offensive actions for 124 days, with no respite whatsoever, out of the 138 days it fought in Czechoslovakia. Its main advance direction was Lučenec-Brno-Prague. The enemy dispositions were pierced on a distance of 350 km; they carried five mountain massifs —Javorina, Nitra, Inovec, the White Carpathians and Chirby—and assault crossed or crossed five rivers (Ipel, Hron, Nitra, Váh and Morava). It committed 90,141 men to battle, the casualties sustained rising to 25 percent of that figure.

The campaign waged by the Romanian army in Czechoslovakia actually meant a permanent offensive in the general direction .south-east—northwest. Generally speaking, the offensive strips of the two Romanian armies were flanked by the offensive strips of the Soviet troops. During the Lučenec-Javorina operation the First Army was flanked, on the left, by the Soviet Fifty-Third Army, while on the right, first by the Soviet 27th Army, and later by the Soviet 40th Army. During the fightings carried on in the Nitra Mountains and the While Carpathians, between the Váh and the Morava rivers, and further northwards on the banks of the latter river, it was flanked by the Soviet Seventh Guard Army (on the left) and the Fortieth Army (on the right). During the final stage of the operations, while pushing the offensive in the direction of Brno-Prague, the First Army was flanked, on the left, by the Soviet Seventeenth Guard Army, and, on the right, by the Soviet LI Army Corps, which separated it from the Fourth Army. All throughout the campaign waged on Czechoslovak territory, the Fourth Army was flanked on the right by troops belonging to the 4th Ukrainian Front (the Soviet Eighteenth Army, the Czechoslovak Corps or the Soviet First Armored Guard Army), while on the left by the Soviet Fortieth Army, which permanently "welded" the two Romanian armies. The latter were supposed to act as a "battering ram", namely to apply head-on hits to the enemy dispositions arranged on parallel mountain ridges or along rivers. Difficult terrain, weather conditions unfavorable for an offensive (heavy snowfalls that turned the otherwise scarce roads impassable) were as many obstacles in front of the Romanian troops which, except for the mountain divisions, lacked training in mountain warfare.

The Romanian troops scored outstanding results in Czechoslovakia despite objective difficulties raised by the nature of the operations, of frequent disposition reshuffling or of frequent subordination of the divisions or army corps to other echelons than the respective Romanian ones, the subordination of armies to similar Soviet echelons included. The Romanian forces carried a number of mountain massifs—Muran, the Slovak

Ore Mountains, Small Tatra, Javorina, Big Fatra, Small Fatra, Nitra, Inovec, the White Carpathians and the Beskids, assault crossed major rivers
such as the Hron, the Nitra, the Váh and the Morava, while the wide areas
lying in-between them were crossed at a rapid pace.

On the whole, the Romanian military forces committed to battle on
the Czechoslovak territory were the following: the First Army, consisting
of the IV and VII Army Corps (the 2nd, 10th, 19th Infantry Divisions,
the 2nd and 3rd Mountain Divisions, the 9th Cavalry and 1st Guard
Divisions); the Fourth Army, consisting of the II and VI Army Corps
(the 3rd, 6th, 9th, 11th, 18th and 21st Infantry Divisions, and the 1st and
8th Cavalry Divisions); the "Tudor Vladimirescu-Debreczen" Division
(December 31, 1944-March 25, 1945); the 2nd Tank Regiment (February
25-May 12, 1945); the Pontoneer Regiment (with two battalions for
fluvial bridges and one company for river bridges); five road battalions,
the Operational group of the Railway Brigade, the 1st Anti-Aircraft
Artillery Brigade and the Air Corps (three fighter groups, one heavy
bomber group, one assault group, two observation groups, one air transport group, one reconnaissance squadron and the 6th Anti-Aircraft Artillery Regiment). The total combat strength engaged by Romania in Czechoslovakia raised to 248,430 men, the casualties sustained amounting to
66,495 men (killed, wounded and missing). The enemy lost 22,803 people
(killed and prisoners). In Czechoslovakia the Romanian army freed 1,723
localities, among which 31 towns, from fascist occupation.

Starting April 9, 1945, the 2nd Tank Regiment was committed to
battle in *Austria* to support the actions carried on by two Soviet large
infantry units. On April 11, 1945, it was assigned the mission of breaking
the enemy defenses in the direction of Hohenruppersdorf-Schrick-Mistel-
bach (an important junction 45 km north-east of Vienna). The file of
orders of the Romanian armored regiments shows that on April 11, 12
and 13 it carried on the bitterest fighting throughout its campaign in the
anti-Hitler war (the regiment had been committed to battle in Czechoslovakia on March 25, 1945). During those days, the Romanian tankmen
would be the target of many counter-attacks in the surroundings of
Hohenruppersdorf, where, according to enemy command maps, there
was an armored regiment of the German 101st Jäger Division operating.

The following days until April 25, 1945, the Romanian armor would
be engaged in grim fighting in the areas contiguous to Schrick, Wilfersdorf,

Mistelbach, Aspern, Zisterdorf and Poysdorf, where they had to cope with elements from the German 211th and 48th Grenadier Divisions and from the 25th and 6th Armored Divisions. Throughout the 16 days' fighting carried out on Austrian territory the enemy was inflicted with heavy losses —in war materiel (17 tanks of various types, 13 armored carriers and four assault guns), and casualties (several hundred men).

Romanian subunits belonging to the Operational group of the Railway Brigade were also present on the Austrian territory during the last month of the war and for another six weeks after it had ended. They provided the Soviet forces operating in Austria with valuable logistic support, working on the remaking or repair of bridges on various communication blocks, on increasing the side-track capacity of some railway stations and similar tasks. On the whole, the work done by those Romanian logistic subunits was equivalent to 24,056 man/days.

Generally speaking, the human "capital" invested by Romania in the war she waged against the Reich for 263 days had secured her a top place in the "hierarchy" of the powers in the anti-Hitler coalition (according to assertions made before the British Parliament in January 1945 she ranged fourth, after the USSR, the USA and Great Britain). Romania committed to the battle against fascism 538,536 combatants (308,003 of whom were infantry troops, 73,667 in the air force, 9,468 in the navy, and so forth), with an average strength of 175,000 men in permanent contact with the enemy.

The casualties sustained by Romania raised to 169,822 men, which means that the Romanian army in the filed lost one "turn" of the combat strength permanently kept on the front line, out of whom 21,035 killed, 90,344 wounded and 58,443 missing. The casualties inflicted upon the Romanian field army speak of the dynamism and bitterness of the fighting, of the self-devotion and self-sacrifice evinced by the Romanian fighters, of the steadfastness of the enemy defense and of the exigencies of continuous offensive. The Fourth Army, which had 173,176 men rolled in the front line, lost 52% of the engaged manpower, a percentage that with the First Army stood at 48 (of a combat strength of 130,148 men). The Romanian large units sustained substantial casualties: the 2nd and 3rd Mountain Divisions lost in the Bükk Mountains 25% of their strength, the four divisions engaged in the battle of Szolnok—17%, and so forth. There were divisions whose casualties surpassed the so-called "control" strength ceiling: the 9th Infantry Division—13,838; the 18th Infantry Division—12,118 men; the 11th Infantry Division—11,496 men; the 3rd Mountain Division—13065 men; the 19th Infantry Division—9,382 men, and so forth.

Yet, the Romanian sacrifices were not unavailing. From the Black Sea to the Bohemian quadrilateral, that is 1,600 km "à vol d'oiseau," the Romanian army mopped up over 200,000 sq km (in Romania, Hungary, Czechoslovakia and Austria). It crossed through bitter fighting some 20 mountain massifs, it assault crossed or crossed 12 rivers, and, after successfully carrying out the insurrection, it freed 3,831 localities, among which were 53 towns. The Romanian soldiers inflicted heavy losses in manpower upon the enemy—117,798 prisoners and 18,731 dead found in the field— the equivalent of some 15 standard Wehrmacht divisions. A statistical assessment relevant for the offensive actions uninterruptedly carried on by the Romanian army: 540 enemy military would be daily put out of action (a figure calculated without taking into account the number of wounded and dead taken away or buried by the enemy) with a daily toll of 630 Romanian casualties (killed, wounded and missing).

The Romanian field army was a harmoniously-knit military body, consisting of all categories of arms and special branches of the time. A valuable Air Corps that carried out 4,306 missions throughout the war totalling 8,542 flights with efficient results: 101 enemy aircraft shot down, 15 ships sent to the bottom, 26 batteries and 83 tanks blown up, to give some examples. The Navy carried through important missions on the Danube in support of the Soviet and Romanian troops' actions, inflicting upon the enemy the loss of 498 ships (captured or destroyed). The engineer (pontoneers and sappers), signal, railway and road units made a valuable contribution to the deployment of operations under the best possible conditions. By the end of the war the Romanian field army in Czechoslovakia consisted of: two army commands, four army corps commands, sixteen divisions (eleven infantry, two mountain and three cavalry divisions), one air corps, one antiaircraft artillery division, one tank regiment, one railway brigade, many engineer, signal, etc. units and formations (with 16,617 men meant to bring the above units to their full number on their way to the front by the end of hostilities).

To justly assess the significance of Romania's contribution to the victory over Nazi Germany it is important to consider not only the size of

the armies engaged in combat but also the size of the area in which the
Romanian military activities occurred. In the fall and winter of 1944-1945
Germany lost, as a result of the serious defeats suffered on the eastern
front, the provinces of East Prussia, Silesia, Brandenburg, and Pomerania
which were most valuable to the German military industry because of their
deposits of coal, lead, and iron ore, of their important metallurgical centers, and of their synthetic fuel and rubber plants.[13] Therefore, to the
leaders of the Reich "the German territory itself was less valuable than
foreign lands"[14] namely Austria and the western parts of Hungary and
Czechoslovakia. In these regions were located numerous enterprises that
worked for the Wehrmacht as well as rich deposits of iron ore, magnesium,
lead, zinc and, above all, the only oil resources available to the German
war machine. The importance of the oil fields of Zisterdorf, in Austria,
and of Balaton, in Hungary, was stressed by Hitler at the meeting of the
OKW on January 23, 1945. "The Hungarian oil fields and the sources
of petroleum from Vienna are of primary significance since, without that
oil which provides 80 percent of our supplies, we cannot continue the
war."[15]

To secure the Czech-Hungarian-Austrian perimeter Hitler, as previously
shown, initially tried to stabilize the Carpathian front through his directives of August 29, 1944. Following the failure of that plan he thought—as
indicated on September 12, 1944 by Gen. Vörös Janos, Chief of the Hungarian General Staff—of concentrating the majority of the German troops
that had been withdrawn from the Balkan Peninsula in Hungary and in
northern Transylvania and of setting up a front on the Iron Gates-Deva-
Mureş line which would eventually be advanced to the southern Carpathians.[16] As it is known, the offensive unleashed by the Hitler-Horthy
forces, on September 5, 1944, from Cluj and Tîrgu Mureş toward Alba
Iulia was designed to reach those mountains while that of September 13
1944 sought to penetrate the valley of the Mureş toward the Deva-Huned-
oara zone. Both offensives failed because of the heroic resistance of the
Romanian forces such as the Păuliş detachment which blocked the mouth
of the Mureş chain and, thus, preventing the enemy's advance. Similar defeats were inflicted upon the enemy in its efforts to conquer Timişoara
and reach the Timiş-Cerna corridor.[17]

Also later, through the so-called *Zigeunerbaron* operation, the German
High Command wanted to push the front to the Carpathians. Gen. Hans

Friessner, the commander of the "South" Army Group, explains the plan
in the following manner: "The intent of the army group was, in the event
of an advance by the Russian forces of the Arad zone toward the Hungarian plain, to attack these forces from north to south and to cut them off,
east of Arad, from access to mountain passes. The attack was to be carried
farther, over Timişoara, to the Iron Gates and beyond the Turnu Roşu
pass, to secure the tops of the Southern Carpathians."[18] While this plan
was unrealistic and, thus, bound to fail it is indicative of the intentions of
the OKW to secure the Hungarian-Austrian-Czech perimeter by controlling
the Carpathian rim.

This zone was of constant concern to Hitler who conceived the plan for
a major offensive in Hungary in the hope that it would be a turning point
in the war. A reference to this plan was made during the conversations between Hitler and the head of the fascist regime in Hungary, Szálasi Ferenc,
to whom Hitler told of his intention to stem the advance of Soviet troops
in the Lake Balaton region and, then, launch offensive actions "either to
the west of Budapest, or between the Danube and the Tisza or, lastly, to
the east of the Tisza."[19] The offensive, in which 6-8 tank divisions and
8-12 infantry divisions were to take part had to be coordinated with subversive actions in South-East Europe. We know now, from recently dis-
covered documents, that the first country Hitler had in mind was Romania.[20] Hitler, encouraged by the legionaries located in Germany, was
dreaming of what he thought would be a replaying of the great battle of
the Catalonian Fields of 451 that saved western Europe from Attila, convinced as he was that a victory in South-East Europe would turn the war
in Germany's favor. Despite the objections of the command of the land
forces, which assigned priority to the arresting the advance of the Soviet
armies in eastern Germany, Hitler ordered the concentration of massive
forces in western Hungary. As told, after the war, by Gen. Sepp Dietrich
—the commander of the 6th SS Tank Army—to Albert Speer "when the
battle of Bastogne was lost Hitler's last war effort was aimed at the south-
east, against the Balkans. . . . The 6th SS Tank Army, which had suffered
great losses at Bastagone, was ordered to recapture the Sava-Danube triangle. Afterwards, as an optimistic Hitler explained while standing before
the map, that army was to advance through Hungary toward the south-
east. . . . This, Gentlemen, because I was always determined to stage an
offensive in the east."[21] In Joseph Goebbels' diary there are numerous

references to this action, tied to so many hopes, which was to bring the Wehrmacht back all along the Danube.[22] The German soldiers who were to take part in the offensive unleashed on March 6, 1945 in the Lake Balaton region were told that, through their action, they wereto make the Ploieşti oil a present to the Führer on the occasion of his birthday, on April 20th.[23] All these plans, of course, were unrealistic; nevertheless, they cast much light on Hitler's strategic-political views during the final phase of the war. They reveal that the Hungarian-Czech-Austrian zone, the very area in which the Romanian war effort occurred, was assigned the greatest importance for changing the course of the war and, albeit illusory, to win the war for Hitler. Thus, the Romanian army did not participate in a theater of war of secondary importance but, as shown by the sources, in one of the greatest significance.

Constantly making an intense military effort, as well as the maintenance of an army of almost 200,000 men beyond the national borders required a huge economic contribution, the mustering up of national energies, a process whose active ferment was the Communist Party. Huge quantities of armament and munitions, of military equipment, foodstuffs, and the like would be sent over to the front. Here are a few figures testifying to the notable performance made by the Romanian war economy: the ammunition demands were met 200% with the antitank guns shots; on February 10, 1945, there were availabilities of howitzer shots for another 29 months of war, of mines for mine-throwers for another six months, and so forth; over 360,000 tons of flour, wheat, meat, lard and edible oil, fodder and other goods were sent to the front, which not only met the needs of the Romanian troops, but were also distributed to the population in the zones of operations in Hungary and Czechoslovakia. Moreover, Romania used for front requirements her entire system of railway communications (the rolling stock included: 52,000 railway carriages and wagons, and 2300 engines), of road, air, fluvial and maritime (92% of the national fleet) communications, the telephone and telegraph networks.

During the anti-Hitler war, Romania also had to ensure the expenditures and goods deliveries from the Armistice Convention. In hard currency, those expenditures and the economic war effort reached the fabulous sum of $1,120,000,000 (the 1938 rate of exchange), which means four times Romania's budget for the 1937-1938 fiscal year.

Romania's contribution to the anti-Hitler war amounted to 630 casualties and almost five million dollars a day.

Naturally, such a huge war effort required that Romania be granted the status of a co-belligerent in the fight against Hitler's Reich. That the more so as Romania, which had constantly had an effective strength of some 175,000 men on the front, ranked, from this point of view, before other nations in the anti-Hitler coalition (Italy—over 100,000 men during the last months of war, partisans for their greatest majority; Bulgaria—some 100,000 men from October 1944 until May 1945; Yugoslavia—some 150,000 men; France—an army totally 11 divisions, between June 1944-May 1945; Belgium and Holland—one brigade each; Poland—seven divisions in the West and one army on the Soviet-German front; Czechoslovakia—one army corps on the eastern front and one brigade on the western one).

According to international law regulations, the co-belligerency status defines the situation of a State which upon the end of the war is in the camp opposite to the one it had belonged to at the beginning of the war. Such a status is consequential in terms of international responsibilities, the "respective State benefiting by certain circumstances upon the conclusion of peace."[24] The favoring effects of such a status, deriving from the very contribution to the obtaining of victory, refer to the right of the respective State to being paid war compensations or to the annulment or lessening of those imposed on it, to unrestricted conditions in the field of military or economic policy, etc.

Romania made sustained diplomatic efforts for being granted the co-belligerency status. Thus, during the last meeting held in Moscow on the occasion of the conclusion of the armistice of September 12, 1944, the Romanian delegation asked for the co-belligerency status, motivating that Romania "has been fighting against the Geman-Hungarian armies ever since August 24, 1944, 4:00 a.m. [and], by signing the armistice, she has pledged fully to collaborate with te Allies in all fields."[25] The Foreign Minister of the Soviet Union declared, on behalf of the USSR, Great Britain and the USA: "I agree in principle to Romania's being granted the status of a co-belligerent and to its carrying into effect as the action of the Romanian army is felt."[26] In the latter half of October 1944, the Romanian General Staff worked out a study in which Romania's claiming the co-belligerency status was provided with solid arguments. The conclusions of the study were the following: "Taking into account these results [military results, detailed in the study], the Romanian Commission for the implementation of the armistice considers that the Romanian Government and High Command have carried into effect—within the limits of the exceptional situations aroused as a result of operational needs and transport difficulties—all stipulations in the Armistice Convention and even more than stipulated there."

"Therefore, taking into account our contribution and comparing it with the precedent of Italy and with the recent events in Hungary [the announcement by Horthy of the armistice with the United Nations], we think that Romania can be granted the co-belligerency status.

"Indeed, Italy's co-belligerency has been acknowledged two months or so after the armistice, although she has not brought anything in support of the Allies except for her fleet, while half of Italy is even now occupied by the Germans."

"Things are the same in Hungary, where Horthy, the regent, who had sued for armistice, has been arrested, and the Hungarian territory and army are probably going to share the fate of the Italian territory and army."[29]

While war was still under way, authorized opinions would be expressed abroad as to the value of the Romanian contribution to the fighting against Hitler's Reich which pointed to the need of recognizing Romania as a co-belligerent. Thus, during the debates in the House of Commons in January 1945, it was suggested, in the course of an interpellation, that, taking into account Romania's military share in the anti-Hitler war, she should be acknowledged the status of a co-belligerent: "Since Romania ranks the fourth country actually fighting on the front against Germany," Labour Deputy Ivor Thomas showed in the House of Commons, "it would be proper to suggest that she should be granted the co-belligerency status."[28] Answering the interpellation, Anthony Eden, the British Foreign Secretary, pointed out Romania's substantial contribution to the war effort of the United Nations; the same opinion would be expressed by the American official broadcasting station on February 9, 1945.

The Romanian government had specified its stand regarding the draft of the peace treaty of the United Nations with Romania on August 12, 1946, when it had stated that "Romania has the right to ask for and get acknowledgement of her co-belligerency from the United Nations." By virtue of such a just claim, the Romanian government considered itself entitled to "ask for and obtain an essential improvement of the conditions regarding the limitations of armament and of the armed forces," not to pay greater compensation than stipulated in the Armistice Convention, to claim "complete liberty in its economic policy," a special convention on the Danube regime "in the conclusion of which only the riparian states should take part."[29]

During the debates of the Peace Conference in Paris, General Heliodor Pika, the Czechoslovak delegate, upheld Romania's claim to co-belligerency, showing that: "The contribution of the Romanian army to the victory has been by far greater than, for instance, that of Italy, which has been acknowledged as a co-belligerent State. The proportion is more obvious if one takes into account the number of inhabitants. Romania, with a population of 14,000,000 inhabitants has successively committed to battle 15 to 29 divisions, while Italy, whose population stands at 47,000,000 inhabitants could hardly send six divisions to the front line. This is a brilliant, undisputed proof. Moreover, the Romanian army has captured over 100,000 German and Hungarian military [. . .] I believe that we, the military, shall give new and democratic Romania what she deserves, for since the very first day of her breaking off with Germany, she has committed all human, material and economic availabilities to the fight against the Axis." Quite a remarkable plea for Romania's right to be granted the co-belligerency status was the demonstration made by two French officers in a study entitled *Romania on the Side of the United Nations*, published in 1946.[30] Synthesizing the Romanian military contribution to the defeat of Hitler's Reich, the two pointed out: "The Romanians have participated in 16 great battles and 360 fights, have penetrated more than 1,000 km into the enemy defenses (from the Mureș River up to Bohemia, crossing 12 mountain massifs in winter and in regions completely lacking shelter and communications, liberating 3,830 towns and villages and making 100,000 prisoners."

The co-belligerency status would not be obtained despite the frequent demarches of the Romanian diplomacy to the Allies, and that deprived Romania of the right to "capitalize her claims on Germany, and of the right to be paid compensations by the latter for the damages sustained during the war waged side by side the Allies for the triumph of the right and of liberty."[31]

The peace treaty signed with Romania on February 10, 1947, recognized her legitimate sovereignty over northern Transylvania: "The decisions of the Vienna sentence of August 30, 1940, were proclaimed null and void" the border between Romania and Hungary going back to "where it had been on January 1, 1938." Moreover, it stipulated, among other things, that the compensations due to the Soviet Union stood at 300 million dollars, "payable within eight years from September 12, 1944"; the frontier with the USSR was set "in keeping with the Soviet-Romanian Agreement of June 28, 1940, and the Soviet-Czechoslovak Agreement of June 24, 1945", and the withdrawal of all Allied troops from Romania's territory within 90 days from the signing of the treaty was stipulated ("The Soviet Union reserved the right to maintain on the Romanian territory those armed forces that she might need for ensuring the communications of the Soviet Army with the Soviet zone in Austria.")

The Romanian government signed the peace treaty, stating that "Romania wants to make her contribution to building up a peace and to international collaboration." At the same time, in a statement of February 8, 1947, the Romanian government expressed the regreat that, by not taking into account Romania's important military and economic contribution to the war waged on Hitler's Germany and her satellites, the "Peace Treaty has created extremely bad circumstances for Romania's future development."[32]

NOTES

Notes to Foreword

1. Hugh Seton-Watson, *The East European Revolution*, Ed. F. A. Praeger, New York, 1961, p. 89.
2. L. F. Ellis, *The War in Flanders and France*, London, H.M.S.O., 1953, p. 241; E. Wanty, *L'art de la guerre*, vol. 3, Verviers, 1968, p. 54.
3. Ibid., p. 46; see the analysis made by H. A. Jacobsen in *Dünkerchen 1940*, in *Entscheidungsschlachten des zweiten Weltkrieges*, ed. H. A. Jacobsen-J. Rohwer, Frankfurt am Main, Bernard and Graefe, 1960, pp. 36-46.

Notes to Chapter I

1. Arhiva Ministerului Apărării Naţionale (Archives of the Ministry of National Defense—further quoted as Arh. M. Ap. N.), stock 948, file 224, p. 619.
2. For a broader approach, see C. Botoran, I. Calafeteanu, E. Campus, V. Moisuc, *România şi Conferinţa de pace de la Paris (1918-1920), Triumful principiului naţionalităţilor* (Romania and the Paris Peace Conference 1918-1920. A Triumph of the Principle of Nationalities). Cluj-Napoca, Editura Dacia, 1983.
3. For the genesis and activity of the Little Entente, see Eliza Campus, *Mica Inţelegere* (The Little Entente), Bucharest, 1968.

202   A TURNING POINT IN WORLD WAR II

4. Nicolae Titulescu, *Documente diplomatice* (Diplomatic Documents), Bucureşti, pp. 337-355. The speech, entitled "The Progress of the Idea of Peace," is a deep analysis of the international affairs and of the ways of restoring confidence among peoples. The volume also benefits by a comprehensive introductory essay owed to George Macovescu, which tackles all great issues of foreign policy related to Nicolae Titulescu's activity.

5. Nicolae Titulescu, op. cit., p. 401.

6. Ibid., p. 347.

7. Ibid., p. 487. For disarmament and Romania's stand in this respect, see Gh. Matei, *Dezarmarea în contextul problemelor internaţionale şi atitudinea României (1919-1934)* (Disarmament in the Context of International Affairs and Romania's Stand. 1919-1934), Bucureşti, 1971.

8. Nicolae Titulescu, op. cit., p. 511.

9. Ibid., p. 554.

10. I. Chiper, *L'expansion économique de l'Allemagne nazie dans les Balkans: objectifs, méthodes, résultats (1933-1939),* "Studia balcanica," 7, 1973, pp. 122-123.

11. Nicolae Titulescu, op. cit., p. 474.

12. Ibid., p. 581. For details on the activity of the Balkan Entente, see Eliza Campus, *Înţelegerea balcanică* (The Balkan Entente), Bucureşti, 1974; for the military conventions, Mihail E. Ionescu, *Preliminariile încheierii convenţiilor militare balcanice (1934-1936)* (Preliminaries to the Conclusion of the Balkan Military Conventions 1934-1936), in *File din istoria militară a poporului român* (Pages on the Military History of the Romanian People), vol. 1, Bucureşti, 1973, pp. 143-146.

13. B. H. Liddel-Hart, *The History of the Second World War,* New York, 1971, p. 701.

14. *Documents diplomatiques, Français,* 2e série, T. I, do. 518. See also Mihail E. Ionescu, *Prognozele diplomaţilor români privind evoluţia situaţiei internaţionale în ajunul declanşării celui de-al doilea război mondial* (Prognostications of Romanian Diplomats on the Course of World Affairs on the Eve of World War II), in "Studii de istorie şi teorie militară," Bucureşti, 1980, pp. 122-125.

15. Nicolae Titulescu, op. cit., p. 726; cf. also, *Documents,* the quoted edition, t. II, doc. 158. For the reaction of the Balkan states, see G. Castellan, *Les Balkans dans la politique française face a la réoccupation de la Rhénanie (7 mars 1936),* in "Studia balcanica," 6, 1973, pp. 33-34.

16.   I. Chiper, Florin Constantinu, *Din nou despre cauzele înlăturării din guvern a lui Nicolae Titulescu* (Again on the Causes Underlying Nicolae Titulescu's Removal from the Government), in "Revista română de studii internaționale," 1969, 2 (6), p. 53.

17.   Gh. Zaharia, I. Cupșa, Al. Vianu, *Al doilea război mondial* (World War II), București, 1975, p. 36; also Gh. Zaharia, *Le caractère de la politique militaire de la Roumanie durant la période de l'entre-deux-guerres mondiales*, "Nouvelles études d'histoire," 5, București, 1975, pp. 203-205 and Mihail E. Ionescu, op. cit.

18.   Ph. Marguerat, *L'Allemagne et la Roumanie à l'automne 1938: économie et diplomatie*, "Relations internationales," I (1974), 1, pp. 173-179. Cf. also Mihail E. Ionescu, op. cit., pp. 127-133.

19.   For details, see Viorica Moisuc, *Diplomația României și problema apărării suveranității și independenței naționale in martie 1938—mai 1940* (Romania's Diplomacy and the Defense of National Sovereignty and Independence during March 1938—May 1940), București, 1971.

20.   Ph. Marguerat, op. cit., pp. 176-179.

21.   *Documents on German Foreign Policy*, vol. V., doc. No. 306.

22.   David B. Funderburk, *Politica Marii Britanii față de România. 1938-1940* (Great Britain's Policy Toward Romania, 1938-1940). București, 1983, p. 106.

23.   Apud Viorica Moisuc, op. cit., p. 149.

24.   Eliza Campus, *Din politica externă a României* (From Romania's Foreign Policy), București, 1980, p. 447.

25.   Ph. Marguerat, op. cit., pp. 176-179.

26.   Eliza Campus, op. cit., p. 473.

27.   Ibid., p. 506 ff.; cf. also B. Vago, *Le second diktat de Vienne: les préliminaires*, in "East European Quarterly," III (1969), 4, pp. 415-437 and idem, *Le second dikтат Vienne: le partage de la Transylvanie*, ibid., V (1971), pp. 47-73.

28.   For the history of fascism in Romania, see Lucrețiu Pătrășcanu, *Sub trei dictaturi* (Under Three Dictatorships), 5th edition, București, 1970; Mihai Fătu, Ion Spălățelu, *Garda de Fier, organizație teroristă de tip fascist* (The Iron Guard. A Terrorist Organization of Fascist Type), 2nd edition, București, 1980. Nicholas M. Nagy-Talavera, *The Green Shirts and Others*, Stanford, 1970.

29.   Nicolae Iorga, *Ultimele* (The Last Writings), Scrisul românesc Craiova, 1979, p. 97.

30. Ibid., p. 93.

31. Ibid., p. 95.

32. Arhiva Institutului de Studii Istorice și Social-Politice de pe lingă C.C. al P.C.R. (Archives of the Institute for Historical and Social-Political Studies of the C.C. of the R.C.P.—hereafter cited as Arhiva I.S.I.S.P.), Catalogue No. Ab—XX—3, inventory No. 956.

33. See, for a comprehensive approach, Titu Georgescu, *Organizații de masă legale conduse de P.C.R. (1932-1934)* (Legal Mass Organizations Led by The R.C.P. 1932-1943), București, 1967; Gheorghe Ioniță, *P.C.R. și masele populare* (R.C.P. and the People's Masses), 2nd edition, București, 1978, pp. 145 ff.

34. General-Colonel Dr. Constantin Olteanu, General-Locotenent Dr. Ilie Ceaușescu, Colonel Dr. Vasile Mocanu, Colonel Dr. Florian Tucă, *Mișearea muncitorească, socialistă, democratică, activitatea Partidului Comunist Român și apărarea patrici la români. Repere cronologice* (The Working-Class, Socialist and Democratic Movement, the Activity Carried on by the Romanian Communist Party and Defense of the Homeland with the Romanians. Chronological Reference Points), Editura militară, București, 1983, pp. 431, 436.

35. An impressively bigh oak tree, around which Horea (1731-1785), the leader of the 1784 Revolution of the Romanian peasants in Transylvania, allegedly gathered a large number of peasant-fighters and spoke to them before the battle.

36. Born in 1824, he was one of the leaders of the 1848-1849 Revolution in Transylvania, and was buried at Țebea in 1872.

37. Ibid., p. 441.

38. Arhiva I.S.I.S,P., catalogue No. A—XXII—9, inventory,No. 1039.

39. A. Hillgruber, *Hitler, König Carol und Marschall Antonescu. Die deutsch-rumänischen Beziehungen 1938-1944,* 2nd edition. Wiesbaden, 1965, pp. 119-122.

40. M. Fenyo, *Hitler, Horthy and Hungary. German-Hungarian Relations 1941-1944,* New Haven, Lond, 1972.

41. Ph. Marguerat, *Le IIIe Reich et le pétrole roumain 1938-1940,* Leiden, 1977, p. 205.

42. M. Covaci, Fl. Dragnea, *Unele aspecte ale luptei clasei muncitoare din România impotriva dictaturii militare-fasciste și a războiului anti-sovietic* (Some Aspects of the Struggle Carried on by the Working Class

in Romania against the Military-Fascist Dictatorship and the Anti-Soviet War), "Revista arhivelor," V (1962), no. 2, p. 86, footnote 13.

43.   General-Colonel Dr. Constantin Olteanu, General-Locotenent Dr. Ilie Ceauşescu, Colonel Dr. Vasile Mocanu, Colonel Dr. Florian Tucă, *Mişcarea muncitorească, socialistă, democratică, activitatea Partidului Comunist Român şi apărarea partriei la români. Repere Cronologice* (The Working-Class, Socialist and Democratic Movement, the Activity Carried on by the Romanian Communist Party and Defense of the Homeland with the Romanians. Chronological Reference Points), Editura militară, Bucureşti, 1983, pp. 502, 507-508.

44.   Arhiva I.S.I.S.P., catalogue No. A–XXX–10.

45.   Ibid., catalogue No. Ab. XXV–2.

46.   Ibid., catalogue No. AB XXVI.

47.   For details see N. Jurcă, *Mişcarea socialistă şi social democratică din România. 1940-1944* (The Socialist and Social-Democratic Movement in Romania. 1940-1944), Bucureşti, 1978, pp. 141 ff.

48.   The matter has been widely approached by Major-General Dr. Ilie Ceauşescu, *Aspecte contradictorii în atitudinea unor forţe politice burgheze din România faţă de problemele militare şi politice ale ţării în perioada septembrie 1940-august 1944* (Contradictory Aspects in the Stand of Some Bourgeois Political Forces in Romania on Military and Political Matters over September 1940-August 1944), in *File din istoria militară a poporului român* (Pages on the Military History of the Romanian People), vol. 1, Bucureşti, 1973, pp. 181 ff.; also Dr. Ilie Ceauşescu, *Aspecte privind poziţia partidelor burgheze faţă de dictatura antonesciană şi războiul împotriva U.R.S.S.* (On the Stand of the Bourgeois Parties Regarding Antonescu's Dictatorship and the War Waged against the U.S.S.R.), in *Insurecţia din august 1944 şi semnificaţia ei istorică* (The August 1944 Insurrection and Its Historic Significance), Bucureşti, 1974, pp. 64-78.

49.   Ibid., p. 205.

50.   Ibid., pp. 204-205.

51.   Ibid., pp. 205-206.

52.   Ibid., p. 205.

53.   On the demarches, see Aurică Simion, *Preliminariile politico-diplomatice ale insurecţiei române din august 1944* (Political-Military Preliminaries to the Romanian Insurrection of August 1944), Cluj-Napoca, 1979. Cf. also, J. Forester, *Stalingrad: Risse im Bündnis. 1942-1944,*

Freiburg, 1975, pp. 69-79, 108-113; Florin Constantin, *L'agonie d'une dictature: la diplomatie du régime d'Antonescu à la veille de l'insurrection* in *"Revue roumaine d'histoire,"* XXII (1983), 3, pp. 201-212. Gh. Buzatu, A. Simion, *Preliminariile diplomatice ale actului de la 23 August 1944* (Diplomatic Preliminaries of August 23, 1944), in vol. *Actul de la 23 August 1944 în context internațional. Studii și documente* (August 23, 1944 in the International Context), Gh. Buzatu, ed., p. 200 ff. Diplomatic data and reports on the demarches of the Romanian government and opposition in *23 August 1944. Documente* (August 23, 1944. Documents), Ion Ardeleanu, Vasile Arimia and Mircea Mușat, eds., vol. 2, Editura științifică și enciclopedică, București, 1984.

54. See, at large, F. C. Nano, *The First Soviet Double Cross. A Chapter in the Secret History of World War II,* in "Journal of Central European Affairs," vol. 12 (1952), 3, pp. 236-258.

55. Arhivele Statului București (Bucharest State Archives—further referenced as Arh. St. Buc.), Microfilms England, reel 405, frame 571.

56. Ibid., Microfilms U.S.A. T. 120-776, reel 280, frame c. 370 536.

57. *23 August 1944. Documente,* vol. 2, p. 156.

58. Ion Gheorghe, *Rumäniens Weg zum Satellitenstaat,* Heidelberg, 1952.

59. *23 August 1944. Documente,* vol. 2, pp. 171-172.

60. Ibid., frame 641.

61. Ibid., frames 841-842.

62. Ibid., reel 406, frame 789.

63. Arhiva Ministerului Afacerilor Externe (Archives of the Ministry of Foreign Affairs—hereafter Arh. M.A.E.), file S. 5, Madrid, 1944, vol. 3, p. 63.

64. Arh. St. Buc., Microfilms England, reel 406, frame 899.

65. Ibid., frames 877, 891, 892.

66. Florin Constantinin, *23 August 1944 în memoriile unui general german* (August 23, 1944 in the Memoires of a German General), in "Revista de istorie," t. 35 (1982), no. 10, p. 1141.

67. Arh. St. Buc., Microfilms England, reel 406, frame 904. See also *23 August 1944. Documente,* vol. 2, p. 413.

68. On the evening of August 22, General C. (Piky) Vasiliu asked British agent G. de Chastelain, detained in the building by the Gendarmerie Inspectorate in Bucharest (on the mission of the "Autonomous" Group,

of which he was a member, see Elisabeth Barker, op. cit., pp. 228 ff.), if he agreed to leave immediately for Cairo, with Mihai Antonescu, for the peace negotiations. See Florin Constantiniu, *Însemnările unui agent britanic în ajunul insurecției române din august 1944 (II)* (The Notes of a British Agent on the Eve of the Romanian Insurrection of August 1944–II), in "Revista de istorie," t. 3 (1982), Nos. 5-6, p. 737. See also *23 August 1944. Documente*, vol. 2, pp. 796 ff.

69. *Documente privind istoria militară a poporului român. 23-31 august 1944.* (Documents on the Military History of the Romanian People, August 23-31, 1944–hereafter DIMPR), vol. 1, București, Editura militară, 1977, pp. 117-118.

70. Arh. I.S.I.S.P., catalogue No. AB XXVII–1.

71. Nicolae Jurcă, op. cit., p. 162.

72. Arhiva Comitetului Central al Partidului Comunist Român (Archives of the Central Committee of the Romanian Communist Party—hereafter Arh. C.C. al P.C.R.), file 7951, paper case 166, pp. 36-40, apud Gheorghe Zaharia, *Insurecția națională antifascistă și antiimperialistă din august 1944* (The Antifascist and Anti-Imperialist National Insurrection of August 1944), București, 1977, p. 42.

73. Arh. I.S.I.S.P., stock 8, file No. 481.

74. *23 August 1944. Documente.* Vol. 2, p. 802.

75. Gheorghe Zaharia, op. cit., p. 43.

76. For these negotiations, see A. Simion, op. cit., passim; Elisabeth Barker, op. cit., ; P. Quinlan, *Clash over Romania*, Los Angeles, 1977, pp. 90-100; Gh. Buzatu, A. Simion, op. cit., pp. 233 ff.

77. Hoover Institution on War, Revolution and Peace (Stanford University, U.S.A.), George Duca stock, *Memoirs* (MS) and *Secret Diary*.

78. Gheorghe Zaharia, op. cit., pp. 47-48.

79. Arh. St. Buc., Microfilms USA, 77-882 17/58, reel 58, frame 6 311 433.

Notes to Chapter II

1. Nicolae Ceaușescu, *Romania on the Way of Building up the Multilaterally Developed Socialist Society*, vol. 24, Meridiane Publishing House, Bucharest, 1983, p. 17.

2. DIMPR, I, documents Nos. 1, 2, 3.

3. Arh. M. Ap. N., stock 948, file 327, p. 290; see also stock 948, 3rd section, file 2 906, p. 53.

4. The table has been drawn up by collating the data in Arh. M. Ap. N., stock 948, file 847, pp. 104-133.

5. Cf. also Gordon A. Harrison, Cross-Channel Attack, United States Army in World War II, Washington, D.C., 1951, Appendix G., Divisions Available to Germany on 6 June 1944 (Based on German Situation Maps), p. 471.

6. Major-General Dr. Ilie Ceaușescu, The Entire People's War for the Homeland's Defense with the Romanians, Editura Militară, București, 1980, pp. 274-276.

7. România în războiul antihitlerist, 23 August 1944–9 Mai 1945 (Romania in the Anti-Hitler War, August 23, 1944–May 9, 1945), Editura militară, București, 1966, pp. 600-620.

8. Hans Kissel, Die Katastrophe in Rumänien 1944, Darmstadt, 1966, pp. 26-27.

9. Istorya Velikoy Otechestvennoy Vojny Sovietskogo Sojuza 1941-1945, vol. IV, Moskva, 1961, p. 260.

10. DIMPR, I, document No. 11.

11. Paul Klatt, 3. Gebirgs Division. 1939-1945, Bad Nauheim, 1958, p. 285.

12. Pentru eliberarea patriei. Documente, extrase din presă, memorii cu privire la lupta poporului român pentru eliberarea patriei de sub jugul fascist (For the Liberation of the Homeland. Documents, Press, Excerpts, Memoirs on the Romanian People's Fight for the Liberation of the Homeland from under the Fascist Yoke—herafter P.E.P.), Editura militară, București, 1972, pp. 289-292.

13. Arh. M. Ap. N., stock 948, file 1257, p. 246.

14. Arh. St. Buc., Microfilms U.S.A., reel 130, frame 48.

15. Ibid., reel 116, frame 986.

16. Ibid., reel 130, frame 85.

17. Ibid., reel 280, frames 370, 512.

18. Arh. I.S.I.S.P. catalogue No. Ab XXVII–1.

19. Major-General Dr. Constantin Olteanu, Colonel Dr. Ilie Ceaușescu, Colonel Dr. Vasile Mocanu, Activitatea Partidului Comunist Român în armată 1921-1944 (The Activity Carried on by the Romanian Communist Party Within the Army), Editura militară, București, 1974, pp. 255-256.

20. Arh. M. Ap. N., file 225, p. 177.
21. Major-General Dr. Ilie Ceauşescu, op. cit., pp. 275 ff.
22. Over August 24-28 around 1,000 soldiers and officers retreating from the Moldavian front joined the Păuleşti fight group—Arh. St. Buc., Microfilms U.S.A., reel 247, frames 6 067 762–765, 6 068 14; 6 068 243–259; 6 067 826, etc.
23. Ibid., frame 6 067 762.
24. Arh. M. Ap. N., stock, 998, 3rd section, file 2 905, p. 336.
25. Arh. St. Buc., Microfilms U.S.A., reel 247, frames 6 067 775-78.
26. Arh. M. Ap. N., stock 948, file 1 181, p. 567.
27. Ibid., stock 321, file 1, p. 121.
28. Ibid., stock 355, file 44, p. 39.
29. Ibid., stock 948, file 861, p. 83.
30. Ibid., stock 948, file 1 404, vol. 1, p. 35.
31. P.E.P., p. 345.
32. "Timpul" (The Time) of August 27, 1944.
33. Arh. M. Ap. N., stock 3, file 181, p. 202.
34. Ibid., p. 242.
35. Ibid., p. 251.
36. P.E.P., p. 435.
37. Arh. M. Ap. N., stock 647, file 3, p. 14.
38. Arh. M. Ap. N., stock 948, file 224, pp. 629, 619.
39. Ibid., p. 629, BBC broadcast of August 24, 1944, 7:00 a.m. (in German).
40. Ibid., p. 630, BBC broadcast of August 24, 9:00 a.m. (in Greek).
41. Ibid., pp. 637-638.
42. Ibid., p. 638.
43. Ibid., p. 646.
44. Ibid., p. 652.
45. Ibid., p. 674.
46. Ibid., p. 708.
47. Ibid., p. 635.
48. Ibid., p. 694.
49. Ibid., p. 733.
50. Ibid., stock 948, file 2, 905, p. 341.
51. Ibid., p. 650.
52. Ibid., p. 712.

53. Ibid.
54. Ibid., file 223, p. 324.
55. Ibid., file 224, p. 657.
56. Ibid., p. 723.
57. Ibid., p. 635.
58. Ibid., pp. 716-717.
59. Ibid., 676.
60. Ibid., p. 638.
61. Ibid., p. 649.
62. Ibid., passim.
63. Ibid., p. 674.
64. Ibid., p. 692.
65. Ibid., p. 728.
66. Arh. St. Buc., Microfilms U.S.A., reel 781, frame 5 507 758.
67. Ibid., reel 130, frame 68.
68. Arh. M. Ap. N., stock 948, file 224, f. 99.
69. Andreas Hillgruber, *Staatsmänner und Diplomaten bei Hitler*, vol. II, Frankfurt, Bernard und Graefe Verlag, 1971, p. 511.
70. Arh. St. Buc., Royal House Stock, file 20/1945.
71. Ibid.

Notes to Chapter III

1. David Irving, *Hitler's War*, New York, 1977, p. 692.
2. *Hitlers Tischgespräche im Führerhauptquartier*, ed. I and R. Picker, Stuttgart, 1976, p. 83.
3. It is true that the High Command of the Wehrmacht, taking into consideration the possibility of Romania's defection, had worked out a plan, the so-called *Margarethe II*, which called for common German-Hungarian military action to reestablish German control over Romania. Following Hitler's meetings with Antonescu of February 26-27, 1944, *Margarethe II* was laid aside on the Führer's orders. See *Staatsmänner und Diplomaten bie Hitler*, ed. A. Hillgruber, vol. II, Frankfurt am Main, 1970, p. 362.
4. Andreas Hillgruber, op. cit., pp. 216-217, mentions the warnings of the chiefs of the *Abwehr* in Romania, colonels Rodler and Bauer, which wre disregarded by the German minister to Bucharest, von Killinger. See also *Neues um Rumäniens Frontwechsel am 23. August 1944*, Starnberg,

1970, p. 5, where it is claimed that the original date for which the Romanian insurrection was scheduled, August 26, and even the list of the government that was to be installed, were known to certain Germans. Additional data in Fl. Constantiniu, *Aspecte ale crizei regimului antonescian* (Aspects of the Crisis of the Antonescu Regime), "Revista de istorie," vol. 32 (1979), no. 7, pp. 1310-1311.

5. Hans Friessner, *Verratene Schlachten*, Hamburg, 1956, p. 58; A. Hillgruber, op. cit., p. 344; Hans Kissel, op. cit., p. 20; Peter Gostzony, *Endkampf an der Donau 1944-1945*, Wien, 1969, p. 19.

6. According to this general's opinion a single anti-aircraft battery would have been sufficient to prevent any Romanian attempt at cutting off ties with the Reich.

7. D. Irving, op. cit., p. 681; then repeated because Antonescu did not understand "Do not go to the royal palace!"

8. Ibid., p. 692. It is true that after the assassination attempt of 20 July 1944 the SS insured its preponderance over the army but it is surprising that given the alarming reports sent to Himmler by the chief of the ethnic German group in Romania, Andreas Schmidt, the SS could have been as optimistic as it was.

9. Walter Warlimont, *Inside Hitler's Headquarters (1939-1945)*, New York, 1964, p. 469.

10. H. Kissel, op. cit., p. 109; D. Irving, op. cit., p. 692.

11. Arh.St. Buc., Microfilms USA, reel T-311-298, frame 130.

12. H. Friessner, op. cit., p. 84.

13. Arh. M. Ap. N., stock 3, file 103, p. 254.

14. "Revista arhivelor," LI (1974), vol. XXXVI, nr. 3, pp. 411, 414.

15. Arh. St. Buc., Microfilms R.F.G., reel 61, frame 124.

16. It was only on August 24 that a summary statement issued by the Reich's Ministry of Foreign Affairs, for the use of the highest echelons, mentioned that after confirmation of the arrest of Ion and Mihai Antonescu, on "22.8. in the evening. The Marshal, in the presence of Mihai (Antonescu) and the minister of war (of Romania), told minister Clodius that despite the untenable situation created by the withdrawal of the German divisions he threw into battle the last reserves to stop the Soviets south of Iași and on the Bug (probably the Prut). This situation does, however, raise a political problem: after, out of loyalty, he rejected Wilson's conditions set in Cairo, the southern front has been weakened continuously in a

manner contrary to his assumptions. He, therefore, must request the regaining of freedom of action. Clodius's impression is that only in the event
of the collapse of the front will he (Antonescu) act independently in a
desperate move to leave the war."

17.   F. Nano, op. cit., pp. 236-258.
18.   DIMPR, p. 118. Textually: *"nicht ganz durchsichtichtig."*
19.   Arh. St. Buc., Microfilms USA, reel T311-190, frame 000993.
20.   Arh. St. Buc., Microfilms USA, reel T-120-775, Rr. 280, frame
370 503.
21.   "Revista arhivelor," loc. cit., pp. 413, 416.
22.   H. Kissel, op. cit., p. 119. Gen. Schultz was the chief of the general staff of the 4th fleet of the Luftwaffe which was operating in Romania. He prepared an extensive report on the events of August, drafted
on January 29, 1945, which is to be found in the appendix of Kissel, ibid.,
pp. 196-231.
23.   "Revista arhivelor," loc. cit., pp. 411 and 414.
24.   The presidency of this government was offered, in Berlin, to Gen.
Ion Gheorghe, Romania's minister to Germany, but he declined that offer.
See A. Hillgruber, op. cit., p. 227. In his memoirs (*Rumänien Weg zum
Satellitenstaat,* Heidelberg, 1952), Gheorghe does not refer to this episode.
Hillgruber's statement is based on a personal conversation with the general.
25.   A. Hillgruber, op. cit., p. 227. Preoccupied over the situation in
Romania, whose leader—in Hitler's opinion—lacked any kind of public support (Hitler himself stated on 18 January 1942: "If Antonescu does not
reach the people he is lost"), Hitler once again considered the alternative
of bringing the Iron Guard to power. See *Hitlers Tischgespräche,* ed. cit.,
p. 83.
26.   Mihail Sturdza, *The Suicide of Europe,* Boston-Los Angeles, 1968,
pp. 256-257.
27.   Ibid., p. 260. (Atlenburg belonged to the mixed German-Italian
commission which investigated the complaints of the Romanian government with respect to the treatment of the Romanians of northern Transylvania by the Hungarian government following the Vienna Diktat. See A.
Hillgruber, op. cit., p. 351).
28.   Arh. St. Buc., Microfilms USA, reel T 120-2822, Rr. 407, frame
E 449 068.
29.   Ibid., reel T-120-776, Rr. 280, frame 370 503.

30. Ibid., frame 370 513.
31. Ibid., reel T-120-2961, Rr. 415, frame E 474 102. Pending the
establishment of the government he thought that it was necessary to announce "the establishment of a command of the Romanian-legionary armed forces."
32. Ibid., reel T 120-776, Rr. 280, frame 370 513.
33. The last foreign policy act of the Sima government was a meeting
between Sima and Baron L. Kemény, foreign minister in the Szálasi government, during which the two men discussed—belatedly and uselessly—
means for solving conflicting views on Transylvania. See M. Sturdza, op.
cit., pp. 266-267.
34. Arh. St. Buc., Microfilms USA, reel T-120-776, Rr. 280, frame
370 507-370 508.
35. M. Sturdza, op. cit., p. 260.
36. H. Kissel, op. cit., p. 106.
37. Supra.
38. Ibid.
39. Ibid., p. 57.
40. Cf. General-major (ret.) Valeriu Selescu, Onoarea generalului
(The General's Honor), in "Magazin istoric," no. 7-8, 1969.
41. KTBSU, p. 57.
42. Ibid.
43. Arh. St. Buc., Microfilms USA, reel T 120-776, Rr. 280, frame
360. See also R. Bova Scoppa, Colloqui con due dittatori, Roma, 1949, p.
183 and Mihail E. Ionescu, Strategia insurecţiei naţionale armate anti-
fasciste şi antiimperialiste din august 1944 (The Strategy of the Armed National Anti-fascist and Anti-Imperialist Insurrection of August 1944) in
File din istoria militară a poporului român, vol. 5-6, Bucureşti, Editura
militară, 1979, pp. 271-272.
44. KTBSU, p. 50.
45. Ibid., p. 58.
46. Ibid., p. 60.
47. Ibid., p. 71.
48. Kriegstagebuch des Oberkommandos der Wehrmachtsführungs-
stab, Vol. IV/1, Frankfurt am Main, 1961, p. 806.
49. Mihail E. Ionescu, Stuka-uri atacă Bucureştii (The Stukas Attack
Bucharest), in "Magazin istoric," 1974, nr. 7.

50. KTBSU, p. 58. From the "South Ukraine" Army Group there were sent two companies to protect the airport.

51. According to an account of the "F" Army Group related to the air shipment of troops from Yugoslavia to Romania, on August 25, 26, and 27 approximately four companies of the parachute battalion Brandenburg and of the training batallion of the military school of Nish, landed at Otopeni, while four companies were launched in the Mizil area where they were subordinated to the 6th German army. Approximately two companies were downed by Romanian anti-aircraft forces at Drăgănești-Prahova, Glîmbocata-Dîmbovița, Cotești-Argeș, and elsewhere.

52. D. Irving, op. cit., pp. 693-694.

53. KTBSU, p. 72.

54. Mihail E. Ionescu, *Apogeul crizei politico-militare a regimului antonescian in prejma declanșării insurecției din august 1944* (The Height of the Political-Military Crisis of the Antonescu Regime on the Eve of the Unleashing of the Insurrection of August 1944), in "Revista de istorie," no. 9, 1980, pp. 1662-1663.

55. On Phleps see Franz Herberth, *Neues um Rumäniens Frontwechsel am 23. August 1944*, pp. 9-14.

56. Ibid.

57. DIMPR, I, doc. no. 257.

58. KTBSU, p. 63.

59. Ibid., p. 99.

60. Report of April 6, 1944. *Meldungen aus dem Reich. Auswahl aus den geheimen Lageberichten der Sicherheitsdienstes der SS 1939-1943*, ed. Heinz Boberbach, Neuwied-Berlin, 1965, p. 499.

61. Report of April 30, 1944. Ibid.

62. Ibid., p. 516, however, in the context of rumors regarding the launching of German paratroopers in England.

63. Ibid., p. 528.

64. Erich Murawski, *Der deutsche Wehrmachtbericht 1939-1945. Ein Beitrag zur Untersuchung der geistigen Kriegführung*, 2nd ed., Boppard am Rhein, p. 246.

65. Ibid., p. 248.

66. Ibid., p. 249.

67. Arh. M. Ap. N., stock 948, file 224, p. 632.

68. Erich Murawski, op. cit., p. 251.

69. Ibid., p. 254.
70. Arh. M. Ap. N., stock 948, file 224, p. 632.
71. Helmut Sündermann, *Tagesparolen. Deutsche Presseweisungen 1939-1945. Hilters Propaganda und Kriegsführung,* Leoni am Starnberger See, 1973, p. 281.
72. F. Gruber, *Der Stoss in die Luft,* in "Südostdeutsche Vierteljahrsblätter," 1960, no. 4, pp. 208-218.
73. H. Kissel, op. cit., p. 200.
74. DIMPR, vol. IV, 1979, p. 130. According to A. Phleps's diary it would appear as if his attentions were to issue a proclamation to the mountain infantry and another to the army. See F. Herbeth, op. cit., p. 10.
75. Arh. St. Buc., Microfilms USA, reel T-120-776, Rr. 280, frame 370 505.
76. Ibid., frame 270 506.
77. D. Irving, op. cit., p. 681.
78. General-maior dr. Ilie Ceaușescu, *Războiul întregului popor pentru apărarea patriei la romăni* (The Entire People's War for the Defense of the Fatherland for Romanians), pp. 308-309.

Notes to Chapter IV

1. *Istorya vtoroy mirovoy vojny* (hereafter IVMV), volume IX, Moskva, 1978, p. 19.
2. Ibid., 1962, tom IV, pp. 260-261.
3. Robert W. Coakley and Richard M. Leighton, *Global Logistic and Strategy 1943-1945,* Washington, D.C., 1968, pp. 374-375.
4. Martin Blumenson, *Breakout and Pursuit,* Washington, D.C., 1961, Map XVI—Pursuit to the German border.
5. Cf. Henri Michel, *La guerre de l'ombre. La Résistance en Europe.* Paris, 1970, pp. 342-355.
6. W. F. Craven, J. L. Cate, *The Army Air Force in World War Two,* vol. III, Chicago, 1951, pp. 173, 280-281.
7. Constantin C. Giurescu, Dinu C. Giurescu, *Istoria romănilor* (History of the Romanians), vol. I, Editura științifică, București, 1974, p. 16.
8. Simion Mehedinți, *Opere alese* (Selected Works), Editura științifică, București, 1967, p. 100. See also Colonel (Rtd.) Mihai Cucu,

Factorul geografic în acţiunile militare (The Geographical Factor and Military Actions), Editura militară, Bucureşti, 1981, pp. 42-50.

9. *The Second Great War*, vol. VIII, Sir John Hammerton, ed., The Waverly Book Company, London, p. 475.

10. "Scînteia" of August 16, 1946.

11. IVMV, t. 9, p. 17.

12. Ibid., p. 18.

13. *Command Decisions*, Washington, D.C., 1960, pp. 429 ff.

14. B. H. Liddell-Hart, *The Other Part of the Hill*, London, 1949, p. 446.

15. Idem, *History of the Second World War*, p. 659.

16. Apud, E. Koulikov, *Le front sovieto-allemand et les Ardennes*, in "Revue militaire soviétique," No. 12, 1974, p. 45.

17. B. H. Liddell-Hart, *The Other Part of the Hill*, p. 446. See also Hasso von Manteuffel, *Die Schlacht in den Ardennen 1944-1945*, in *Entscheidungsshlachten des Zweiten Welt Krieges*, H. A. Jacobsen and J. Rohwer eds., Frankfurt am Main, 1960, pp. 527 ff.

18. P.Gosztony, *Endkampf an der Donau*, Wien, 1964, p. 217.

19. IVMV, t. 9, p. 469.

20. Charles B. MacDonald, *The Last Offensive*, Washington, D.C., 1973, p. 7.

21. Forrest, C. Pogue, *The Supreme Command*, Washington, D.C., 1954, p. 252.

22. Ph. Masson, *Les armes secretes allemandes*, in "La deuxième guerre mondiale. Historia Magazine," 1969, Nd. 96, p. 2673. As far as the use of ground-to-air missiles is concerned, they could not have a decisive effect before the discovery of the transitor, microelectronics, etc. Karl Heinz Ludwig, *Fabrication de fusées et stratégie*, in "RHDGM," XXI (1971), 84, p. 90.

23. Martin Blumenson, *Breakout and Pursuit*, Washington, D.C., 1961, pp. 34-35.

24. Charles B. Macdonald, op. cit., p. 8.

25. IVOV, tom. IV, pp. 260-261.

26. Hans Friessner, *Verratene Schlachten. Die Tragödie der deutschen Wehrmacht in Rumänien und Ungarn*, Hamburg, Holstein Verlag, 1956, p. 46.

27. Ibid., p. 83; V. A. Matsulenko, *Razgrom nemetsko-fashistkyh*

voisk na Balkanskom napravlenyi avgust-senteabr 1944 goda, Moskva, 1957, p. 71; Hans Kissel, op. cit., pp. 123 ff.

28.   Arh. M. Ap. N., stock 4, file 255, pp. 185-186.

29.   Arh. St. Buc., Microfilms USA, reel 130, *Kriegstagebuch des Oberkommandos der Heeresgruppe Südukraine* (hereafter KTBSU), p. 47.

30.   KTBSU, p. 63.

31.   Ibid., p. 68.

32.   Ibid., pp. 70-71.

33.   *Documente privind istoria militară a poporului român 23-31 August 1944* (Documents on the Military History of the Romanian People. August 23-31, 1944—hereafter cited as DIMPR), Editura militară, București, 1977 I, document No. 257.

34.   Arh. St. Buc., Microfilms England, reel 408, frame 3, Telegram No. 1 962 from Minister Resident's Office Cairo to Foreign Office, August 25, 1944, 11:50 a.m.

35.   Ibid., Telegram No. 2 242 from Moscow to Foreign Office, August 26, 5:40 a.m.

36.   Documents worked out by Romanian commanding officers at the time stand proof to that. On August 25, 1944, Brigadier General Dumitru Tudose, Deputy Commander of the III Army Corps, confirmed to a Soviet military delegation during a meeting in the Danube Delta the "orders received by the Romanian troops to the effect of ceasing hostilities and also that the Russian troops that had passed in Dobrudja be withdrawn north of the Chilia branch, *which is the demarcation line* [our italics]." DIMPR, I, document No. 240; Cf. *File din istoria militară a poporului român* (Pages on the Military History of the Romanian People), Major-General Dr. Ilie Ceaușescu, ed., vol. 5-6, Editura militară, București, pp. 274-276.

37.   Ibid., p. 275. "The Russian officers"—General Dumitru Tudose wrote down in his report of August 25, 1944—"also said that they had to pursue the Germans, hinting that for that purpose their troops would cross the demarcation line."

38.   G. K. Zhukov, *Amintiri și reflecții* (Reminiscences and Reflections), Editura militară, București, 1970, pp. 596-620, 641.

39.   Colonel A. Orlow, *L'offensive au nord*, in "Revue militaire soviétique," 10, 1979, pp. 43-46.

40.   V. Gurkin, *Osvobozhdenje Vengryi*, in "Voenno-istoricheskyi zhurnal," 4, 1981, p. 68.

41. V. A. Matsulenko, *Razgrom nemetsko-fashistaskih voisk na Balkansokom napravlenie*, Moskva, 1957, pp. 92-93.

42. Arh. M. Ap. N., stock 948, file 1404–1, p. 170.

43. *România și războiul antihitlerist*, (Romania and the Anti-Hitler War), București, 1966, p. 53.

44. *Kriegstagebuch des Oberkommandos der Wehrmacht, 1940-1945* (hereafter cited as KTB des OKW), vol. IV: 1944-1945, 2, Frankfurt am Main, 1961, p. 1550.

45. B. H. Liddell-Hart, *History of the Second World War*, p. 23.

46. Albert Speer, *Au coeur du troisième Reich*, Fayard, Paris, 1971, pp. 450-451.

47. Cf. Ralph S. Mavrogordato, *Hitler's Decision on the Defense of Italy*, in *Command Decisions*, Washington, D.C., 1960, pp. 309-310.

48. Gordon A. Harrison, *Cross-Channel Attack*, Washington, D.C., 1951, p. 471.

49. Earl Ziemke, *Stalingrad to Berlin: The German Defeat in the East*, Washington, D.C., 1968, p. 369.

50. V. I. Dashichev, *Bankrostvo strategii ghermanskogo fashizma*, t. 2, Moskva, 1973, p. 521.

51. Gordon A. Harrison, op. cit., p. 122.

52. Maurice Matloff, *Strategic Planning for Coalition Warfare, 1943-1944*, Washington, D.C., 1959, pp. 360-363; Ray S. Cline, *Washington Command Post: The Operations Division*, Washington, D.C., 1951, pp. 226-232; Trumbull Higgins, *Soft Underbelly*, London, 1972.

53. M. V. Zaharov, *Molnienosnaia operatsyia*, in "Voennoistorichesky zhurnal," 8, 1964, p. 27.

54. Iltcho Dimitrov, *La politique extérieure du gouvernment d'Ivan Bagrianov*, in "Revue d'histoire de la deuxième guerre mondiale," No. 93, January 1974, pp. 32, 43.

55. Arh. St. Buc., Microfilms USA, reel 116, frame 42.

56. B. H. Liddell-Hart, op. cit., p. 585.

57. Albert Seaton, *The Russo-German War. 1941-1945*, Arthur Barker, Ltd., 1971, p. 484.

58. Andre Latreille, *La seconde guerre mondiale*, Libairie Hachette, 1966, p. 256.

59. Earl F. Ziemke, op. cit., p. 371.

60. KTBSU, p. 99.

61. Hans Friessner, op. cit., pp. 113, 107.

62. Arh. M. Ap. N., stock 948, 3rd Section, file 2 925, p. 8.

63. KTB des OKW, p. 15.

64. Arh. M. Ap. N., stock 948, file 1 404, vol. II, p. 380.

65. Ibid., p. 646.

66. Ibid., p. 647.

67. Ibid., p. 657.

68. *România în războiul antihitlerist—23 august 1944-9 mai 1945* (Romania in the Anti-Hitler War. August 23, 1944-May 9, 1945), București, 1966, pp. 143-144.

69. Arh. M. Ap. N., stock 948, file 224, p. 675.

70. *România în războiul antihitlerist*, (Romania in the Anti-Hitler War), București, 1966, p. 144.

71. Henri Bernard, *Histoire de la résistance européenne: la "quatrième force" de la guerre 39-45*, Marabout Université, 1968, p. 91.

72. B. H. Liddell-Hart, op. cit., p. 585.

73. IVOV, t. IV, pp. 20-21. The superiority of the Soviet forces in combat strength was 1.3:1.

74. Ibid.

75. Forrest C. Pogne, *The Supreme Command*, Washington, D.C., 1954, pp. 542-543; Appendix E., *Strength and Casualty Figures* (U.S. Army, British and Canadian Armies).

76. *La contribution de la Pologne à la victoire sur l'Allemagne hitlerienne 1939-1945*, Varsovie, 1980, pp. 51, 72.

77. Marcel Vigneras, *Rearming the French*, Washington, D.C., 1957. Map: Operations and Participating Forces.

78. Gordon A. Harrison, op. cit., p. 471.

79. Charles B. MacDonald, *The Siegfried Line Campaign*, Washington, D.C., 1963, p. 15; Hugh M. Cole, *The Lorraine Campaign*, Washington, D.C., 1950, p. 30.

80. Arh. M. Ap. N., stock 948, file 224, p. 733. The specialized bodies of the Romanian General Staff assessed that the combat strength of the Romanian forces available on August 23, 1944, raised to *40 divisions* able to be immediately sent over on the front line against the Wehrmacht (cf. Arh. M. Ap. N., stock 948—3rd Section—file 2, 931, p. 7).

81. Ibid., file 1 404—I, pp. 17-18.

82. Ibid., file 1 404—II, p. 368.

83. Ibid.
84. Ibid., p. 369.
85. Ibid.
86. Charles B. MacDonald, op. cit., p. 15.
87. *La contribution de la Pologne à victoire sur l'Allemagne hitlerienne 1939-1945*, p. 223.
88. Hugh M. Cole, op. cit., p. 31.
89. Ibid., p. 32.
90. IVOV, t. 4, p. 7.
91. Ibid., pp. 143-147.
92. *La contribution de la Pologne à la victoire*, pp. 64, 101.
93. Ibid., pp. 64, 101—The operations of the Polish forces were carried out within the framework of some Allied strategic operations.
94. For comparison we have chosen this tactical operation too—cf. Hugh M. Cole, op. cit.
95. Major-General V. Gurkin, op. cit., p. 68. The freed area has been obtained by taking into account the width of the front and the depth of the advance.
96. Hugh Seton-Watson, *The East European Revolution*, F. A. Praeger, New York, p. 89.
97. John Erickson, *The Road to Berlin*, London, 1983, p. 360.
98. Arh. M. Ap. N., stock 948, 3rd Section, file 2 905, p. 342.

Notes to Chapter V

1. During World War I, after having checked the advance of the German, Austro-Hungarian, Bulgarian and Turkish forces in southern Moldavia and after having won the victories of Mărăşti, Mărăşeşti and Oituz, the Romanian army found itself in a predicament as a result of the fact that the Entente did not keep the military pledges assumed (offensive actions of General Sarrail's army, deliveries of armament and ammunition), and the Russian army ceased hostilities, followed by the conclusion of the Peace of Brest-Litovsk. Unable to continue the fight because of the disproportion in forces and of an unfavorable geo-strategic position, Romania saw herself forced to conclude with the Quadruple Alliance the Peace of Bucharest (April 24/May 7, 1918), whose terms were extremely hard (territorial cessions, great economic advantages granted to the Central Powers,

etc.). For details, see *România în timpul primului război mondial* (Romania during World War I), București, Editura militară, 1979.

2. With respect to the exploitation of the Romanian territory temporarily occupied by the Central Powers and their allies, see E. Răcilă, *Contribuții privind lupta românilor pentru apărarea patriei în primul război mondial* (Contributions to the Research on the Romanians' Struggle for the Homeland's Defense in World War I), București, Editura stiinтifică și enciclopedică, 1981, pp. 117-198.

3. J. F. Fuller, *La conduite de la guerre*, Paris, Payot, 1963, p. 165.

4. B. H. Liddell-Hart, *History of the Second World War*, p. 23.

5. Ibid., p. 24.

6. A fundamental work in this respect is W. Birkenfeld's *Der synthetische Treibstoff 1933-1945. Eim Beitrag zur nazional-sozialistische Wirtschafts- und Rüstungs-politik*, Göttingen, 1964.

7. Ph. Marguerat, *Le IIIe Reich et le pétrole roumain (1938-1940)*, Leiden, 1977, p. 18.

8. Ibid., p. 19. For the Krauch plan, see D. Petzina, *Autarkienpolitik im Dritten Reich. Der nazional-sozialistischen Vierjahresplan*, Stuttgart, 1968, pp. 118-125.

9. In 1936 it amounted to 8,703,000 tons, and in 1937 to 7,147,000 tons.

10. Ph. Marguerat, op. cit., p. 20.

11. Idem, *L'Allemagne et la Roumaine à l'automne 1938: économie et diplomatie*, in "Relations internationales," I (1974), pp. 173-179.

12. Arh. St. Buc., Microfilms USA, reel 35, frame 1 666 893; Ph. Marguerat, op. cit., p. 138.

13. This is yet another proof of the fact that the Romanian-German trade treaty of March 23, 1939, did not entail the expected subordination of the Romanian economy to the Reich's demands.

14. Arh. St. Buc., Microfilms USA, reel 35, frame 1 667 073.

15. Romania's oil supplies in winter 1939-1940 amounted to: 98,000 tons (October); 66,000 tons (November); 60,000 tons (December); 28,000 tons (January); 21,000 tons (February); See A. Hillgruber, *Hitler, König Carol und Marschall Antonescu. Die deutsch-rumänischen Beziehungen, 1938-1944*, 2nd edition, Wiesbaden, 1965, p. 251.

16. Ibid., p. 85. A proof of the alarm this reduction aroused in Berlin was Dr. Neubacher's appointment as "special representative in charge of

economic affairs by the German Legation in Bucharest." See also the latter's memoirs, *Sonderauftrag Südost,* Göttingen, 1956. In December 1939,
a German memorandum pointed out that Germany had to be ready to
take hold of Romania's oil-fields by a surprise action. The same document
stressed the idea that Romania had to be led into giving up her sovereign
rights over the Prahova and Buzău Counties (the oil-field area) in favor
of Germany during the war (Arh. St. Buc., Microfilms USA, reel 37, frame
1783 279).

17.   An expert in economic affairs of the German Legation in Bucharest.

18.   A Hillgruber, op. cit., p. 249; the author details the amount of
petrol, plane fuel, black oil and petroleum as well as the supplies for the
Protectorate of Bohemia and Moravia, p. 250, and the monthly supply
rates, p. 251.

19.   A. Hillgruber, op. cit., p. 250.

20.   Ibid.

21.   *Rezultatele "colaborării" economice cu Germania și ale parti-
cipării noastre la războiul hitlerist* (The Results of the Economic "Collaboration" with Germany and of Our Participation in Hitler's War), București, 1945, pp. 5, 9.

22.   *Hitlers Weisungen für die Kriegsführung,* W. Hubatsch ed., Frankfurt am Main, 1965, p. 244.

23.   A. Hillgruber, op. cit., p. 200.

24.   N. N. Constantinescu, *L'exploitation et le pillage de l'économie
roumaine par l'Allemagne hitlérienne dans la période 1939-1944,* in *La
Roumaine pendant la deuxième guerre mondiale,* Bucharest, 1964, p. 111.

25.   Ibid., p. 110.

26.   Arh. St. Buc., Microfilms USA, reel T 77-607, no. 44, frame 1792
189; A. Hillgruber, op. cit., p. 201; Eugen Preda, *Miza petrolului în vil-
toarea raăboiului* (The Oil Stake in the War Vortex), București, Editura
militară, 1983, p. 185.

27.   A. Hillgruber, op. cit., p. 252. Those supplies were a burdensome
strain on the Romanian economy, bringing about food penury in the
country. In December 1941, the German Legation in Bucharest expressed the satisfaction of the German government at the "reduction in the
home [Romanian—a.n.] consumption of wheat and bread ration, with
two breadless days in Bucharest and three in the provinces, with a view

to thereby increasing export availabilities." (N. N. Constantinescu, op. cit., p. 112).

28. N. N. Constantinescu, op. cit., p. 113.

29. Ibid., pp. 113-114.

30. As a result of such attempts there were harsh recriminations with both sides which brought about periods of strained economic relations between Romania and Germany—see A. Hillgruber, op. cit., passim.

31. V. I. Dashichev, *Bankrostvo strategii germanskogo fashizma*, vol. II, Moskva, 1973, p. 490.

32. Col. J. de Tarlé, *Bombes sur Ploieşti*, in "Forces aériennes françaises," April 1950, No. 43, pp. 20-43. The first American air attack on Ploieşti occurred on June 12, 1942, being the first operation carried on by the American Air Force in Europe after the United States' joining the war. As it ended in a failure, air attacks no longer took place before August 1943, when 44 of the 177 participating bombers were lost. Starting April 5, 1944, the oil-field area was the target of heavy bombings by the Anglo-American air forces, a fact which entailed a rapid fall in oil output. Thus, while in March 1944 385,000 tons of crude oil had been processed, in April they fell to 176,000 tons, in May to 152,000 tons, in June to 77,000 tons and in July to 63,000 tons (Arh. St. Buc., Microfilms USA, reel 44, frame 792 189). See also E. Preda, op. cit., pp. 172-177.

33. Arh. St. Buc., Microfilms USA, reel 44, frame 1 792 854.

34. Ibid., frame 1 792 858.

35. D. Irving, *Hitler's War*, New York, 1977, p. 681. According to General W. Warlimont, Hitler allegedly said that the war was lost; W. Warlimont, *Inside Hitler's Headquarters 1939-1945*, New York, 1964, p. 462.

36. H. Kissel, op. cit., p. 202.

37. For details, see A. Speer, op. cit., p. 348, who underlines the coincidence of those attacks with the Anglo-American bombings of the Romanian oil-field area, started already in April. Cf. *Encyclopedie de la guerre 1939-1945*, Tournas, 1977, pp. 58-59, and Chester Wilmot, *The Struggle for Europe*, who draws the attention to the contradictory data in German sources: he speaks of a fall in the 1944 oil output in Hungary and Romania from 200,000 tons in February to 40,000 tons in June and 11,000 tons in August.

38. J. F. C. Fuller, op. cit., p. 265.

39. See the chapter below: *The Political Consequences.*

40. P. Gosztony, op. cit., p. 217. See also F. Herberth, *Neues um Rumäniens Frontwechsel am 23 August 1944,* Starmberg, 1970, pp. 16-17. General H. Guderian shows that Hitler's decision to embark upon an offensive was partially justified by the need of preserving the last oil deposits (Zisterdorf in Austria, and Nagy Kanisza in Hungary) as well as the Hungarian oil processing facilities. He mentions that most of the German fuel plants had been destroyed (her refers to the bombing of the hydrogenation plant at Poelitz, of the Magdeburg, Derten, Ehmen, Braunschwag facilities, of the Leuna works). His testimony stands proof of the weight the oil factor had in the mounting of the Balaton offensive (H. Guderian, *Erinnerungen eines Soldaten*). For the strategic and political goal of the offensive—regaining the Balkans—see General Sepp Dietrich's account given to A. Speer while in prison in Nüremberg, A. Speer, *Journal de Spandau,* Paris, 1975, p. 30.

41. K. Hnilicka, *Das Ende auf dem Balkan 1944/45. Die militarische Räumung Jugoslaviens durch die deutsche Wehrmacht,* Gottingen, 1970, p. 51.

42. V. I. Dashichev, op. cit., p. 487.

43. A. Speer, *Journal de Spandau,* p. 30, cf. *Staatsmänner und Diplomaten bei Hitler,* vol. II, A. Hillgruber, ed., Frankfurt am Main, 1970, p. 523 (the talk between Hitler and Szálasi of December 4, 1944).

44. A. J. P. Taylor, *The Second World War,* London, 1970, p. 209.

45. An interview granted to Jacques de Launay in "Magazin istoric" (Historical Magazine), XVI (1982), No. 11, p. 60.

Notes to Chapter VI

1. *Staatsmänner und Diplomaten bei Hitler,* vol. II, A. Hillgruber, ed., Frankfurt am Main, 1970, p. 511. For a better understanding of the comparison terms used by Hitler, let us remember that in Byelorussia the Wehrmacht lost 28 divisions (350,000 men), a "double Stalingrad" according to a German historian. See Hermann Gackenholtz, *Der Zusammenbruch der Heeresgruppe Mitte 1944,* in *Entscheidungsschlachten des Zweiten Weltkriegs,* ed., cit., p. 474.

2. David Irving, op. cit., p. 698.

3. See in detail Jürgen Förster, *Stalingrad, Risse im Bündnis 1942-*

1943, Freiburg, 1975, pp. 79-85, 113-117, and Elisabeth Barker, op. cit., pp. 266-269.

4. For the political situation in Hungary see A. I. Puşkaş, *Vengriya v gody vtoroy mirovoy voyny*, Moskva, 1966, pp. 422-425, and C. A. Macartney, *October Fifteenth. A History of Hungary 1939-1945*, vol. II, New York, pp. 318 ff.

5. Nicholas M. Nagy-Talavera, *The Green Shirts and the Others*, Stanford, 1970, p. 218.

6. Ibid., p. 219; A. I. Puşkaş, op. cit., pp. 426-427.

7. A report of Werkmeister, the representative of the German Ministry of Foreign Affairs by the "South Ukraine" Army Group, shows that with the Hungarian military the opinion according to which the involvement of the Hungarian army in military actions in southern Transylvania would have meant an acknowledgement of Hungarian possession of Transylvania as a whole and of the Banat was quite frequent (Arh. St. Buc., Microfilms USA, reel T-120-776, Reel 280, frame 370, 513).

8. Csima Janos. *A horthysta diplomácia elozetes fogyverizuneti targyalásai Bernten . . .* in "Hadtörténelmi Közlemenyek," 1965, No. 4, p. 732.

9. I. Cupşa, *Armata română pe frontul antihitlerist* (The Romanian Army on the Anti-Hitler Front), Bucureşti, Editura militară, 1973, pp. 50-52.

10. A. I. Puşkaş, op. cit., pp. 429-430.

11. Janos Vörös, *Diary*, edited by P. Gosztony in "Wehrwissenschaftliche Rundschau," XX (1970), No. 12, p. 703.

12. Csátari Daniel, *Fonnógeszélben. Magyar-roman viszony, 1940-1945*, Budapest, 1969, p. 404.

13. "Szabad Nép" of September 1, 1944, quoted by Ladislau Gergely, chapter *Ungaria* (Hungary), in *Rezistenţa europeană în anii celui de-al doilea război mondial 1938-1945* (European Resistance during World War II, 1938-1945), vol. I, *Tările din Europa centrală şi de sud-est* (The Countries in Central and South-East Europe), Bucureşti, Editura militară, 1973, p. 373.

14. As for the circumstances of Tsar Boris III's death, see Helmut Heiber, *Der Tod des Zaren Boris*, in "Vierteljahrshefte für Zeitgeschichte," 1964, No. 4, pp. 384-416, and Ilcho Dimitrov, *La mort du roi Boris IIIe*, in "Revue d'histoire de la deuxième guerre mondiale," XXI (1971), No. 83, pp. 16-30.

15. A. Hillgruber, op. cit., pp. 498-499.

16. Hans-Joachim Hoppe, *Deutschland und Bulgarien 1918-1945*, in vol. *Hilter, Deutschland und die Mächte*, Manfred Funke ed., Düsseldorf, 1977, p. 609.

17. See at large chapter *Bulgaria* (author: Crişan Iliescu), in vol. *Rezistenţa europeană în anii celui de-al doilea război mondial. 1938-1945* (European Resistance during World War II, 1938-1945), vol. I, pp. 340 ff.

18. For the activity of this commission concerning the Bulgarian question, see Mihail-Dimitrie Sturdza, *La Commission Consultative Européene et l'armistice bulgare de 1944*, in "Südost-Forschungen," Band XXXII (1973), pp. 211 ff.

19. *Foreign Relations of the United States—Diplomatic Papers*, vol. 1944–III, Washington, 1965, p. 355. M. D. Sturdza, op. cit., p. 216.

20. L. Woodward, *British Foreign Policy during the Second World War*; Stephen G. Xydis, *Greece and the Great Powers 1944-1947. Prelude to the "Truman Doctrine,"* Thessaloniki, 1963, pp. 43-48; Daniel Yesgin, *Shattered Peace. The Origins of the Cold War and the National Security State*, Boston, 1977, pp. 59-61.

21. Marshall Lee Miller, *Bulgaria during the Second World War*, Stanford, California, 1975, pp. 187-188.

22. Elisabeth Baker, op. cit., p. 220.

23. Crişan Iliescu, op. cit., p. 350.

24. Ibid., pp. 350-351, *Istorija Bolgarii*, P. A. Tretyakov, S. A. Nikitin and L. B. Valey, vol. II, Moskva, 1955, pp. 344-345.

25. H. J. Hoppe, op. cit., p. 611.

26. *Istorija Bolgarii*, vol. II, p. 347.

27. Ibid.

28. Johann Wuescht, *Jugoslawien und das Dritte Reich*, Stuttgart, 1969, pp. 320-321.

29. Ibid., p. 323.

30. J. Wuescht, op. cit., p. 55.

31. *Staatsmänner und Diplomaten bei Hitler*, ed. cit., vol. II, p. 508.

32. Ibid.

33. P. Gosztony, op. cit., p. 276.

34. For the developments in Finland, see H. G. Dahms, *La deuxième guerre mondiale*, Paris, 1961, pp. 328-329, 334-335.

35. *Documente privind istoria militară a poporului român, 23-31*

August 1944, (Documents on the Military History of the Romanian People, August 23-31, 1944), pp. 118-119.

36. Ibid., pp. 234-235.

37. Ibid.

38. Eddy Bauer, *The History of World War II*, New York, 1979, p. 539.

39. *The Grand Strategy*, vol. V, p. 402.

40. Ștefan Lache and Gh. Țuțui, *România la Conferința de pace de la Paris din 1948* (Romania at the Paris Peace Conference in 1948), Editura Dacia, 1978, Cluj-Napoca; Daniel Yergin, op. cit., pp. 58-61; Albert Resis, *The Churchill-Stalin "Percentages" Agreement on the Balkans, Moskow, October 1944*, in "The American Historical Review," vol. 83 (1978), No. 2, pp. 368-387.

Notes to Chapter VII

1. Nicolae Ceaușescu, *Romania on the Way of Building up the Multilaterally Developed Socialist Society*, vol. 10, Bucharest, Meridiane Publishing House, 1976, p. 582.

2. M. Fătu, *Un vot decisiv (noiembrie '46)* (A Decisive Vote—November '46), București, Editura Politică, 1972.

3. C. Olteanu, *Un an de transformări revoluționare în România* (A Year of Revolutionary Transformation in Romania), Editura politică, București, 1972.

4. M. Fătu, *Sfîrșit fără glorie* (End without Glory), Editura politică, București, 1972.

5. "Scînteia" of January 29, 1945.

6. *Partidul-Național Țărănesc. Manifest-program* (The National-Peasant Party. The Program-Manifesto), 1944, p. 4.

7. "Scînteia" of December 14, 1944.

8. *Documente privind istoria militară a poporului român, 23-31 August 1944* (Documents on the Military History of the Romanian People), IV, Editura militară, București, 1979, p. 72.

9. Arh. M. Ap. N., stock 948, file No. 1 404/II, p. 137.

10. Mesajul patriotic al unor ordine de zi. Documente care elogiază vitejia și eroismul armatei române în războiul antihitlerist (The Patriotic Message of Some Orders of the Day. Documents Eulogizing the Bravery

and Heroism of the Romanian Army in the Anti-Hitler War), a volume edited by Colonel Dr. Leonida Loghin, Colonel Petre Ilie and Captain Alesandru Duțu, Editura militară, București, 1980, pp. 30-31.

11. În numele libertății și prieteniei (In the Name of Freedom and Friendship), Editura militară, București, 1972, I, p. 67.

12. Colonel Antone Marinescu, Colonel Gheorghe Romanescu, Armata română în războiul antihitlerist—Album de scheme (The Romanian Army in the Anti-Hitler War.—An Album of Maps and Sketches), Editura militară, București, 1980, p. 133.

13. Budapest-Vienna-Prague [in Russian], edited by Marshal R. I. Malinovski, Moscow, 1965, p. 185.

14. Ibid.

15. Ibid., p. 186.

16. See the works of Janos Vörös in "Wehrwissenschaftliche Rundschau," XX (1970), no. 12, pp. 703 ff.

17. Col. Antone Marinescu, Maj. Dr. Ioan Talpeș, Capt. Alexandru Duțu, Pe drumurile biruinței 23 August 1944-12 mai 1945 (On the Road to Victory 23 August 1944-12 May 1945), București, 1984, pp. 129-131.

18. Hans Friessner, Verratene Schlachten, Hamburg, 1956, p. 130.

19. Staatsmänner und Diplomaten bei Hitler, vol. II, ed. A. Hillgruber, Frankfurt am Main, 1970, pp. 531-532.

20. Franz Herberth, Neues um Rumäniens Frontwechsel am 23 August 1944, Starenburg, 1970, pp. 16-17. On the legionaries' manipulation see Horia Sima's confessions, Pentru ce am pierdut războiul. . . (Why did We Lose the War. . .), Madrid, 1973, pp. 42-47.

21. Albert Speer, Journal de Spandau, Paris, 1975, p. 30.

22. The Diaries of Joseph Goebbels. Final Entries, 1945, ed. Hugh Trevor-Roper, New York, 1979, p. 249.

23. Peter Gosztony, Endkampf an der Donau, Wien, 1969, p. 217.

24. Lexicon militar (Military Lexicon), Editura militară, București, 1980, p. 184.

25. Arh. M. Ap. N., stock 948, file 878, p. 10.

26. Ibid. The declaration of the Soviet Foreign Minister had been agreed upon during a meeting of the representatives of the three countries held in Moscow on September 12, 1944. Here is the shorthad record of that conference: "Mr. Harriman [the representative USA] asks about the stand of the Soviet government regarding the proposal that Romania should be granted the co-belligerency status.

Mr. *Vyshinsky* [the representative of the U.S.S.R.]: he thinks it is prematurely for such a concession to be made to Romania immediately, but agrees to it.

Mr. *A. Clark Kerr* [the representative of Great Britain]: they [the Romanians] may be allowed to hope they will get that [concession].

Mr. *Harriman*, too, agress to that point of view. The discussion turned to other additional items in the note submitted by the Romanian delegation.

Mr. *Vyshinsky* declared that the Soviet government would not accept the first Romanian proposal (the adding of a paragraph specifying the obligation of the Allied forces to leave the Romanian territory upon the end of hostilities wit the Germans and the Hungarians).

Mr. *A. Clark Kerr* and Mr. *Harriman* agreed on that proposal having to be rejected." (Arh. St. Buc., Microfilms England, reel 408, frame 285).

27. Arh. M. Ap. N., stock 948, file 882, p. 13.

28. Apud Ion Enescu, *Politica externă a României în perioada 1944-1947* (Romania's Foreign Policy in 1944-1947), Editura științifică și enciclopedică, București, 1979, p. 72.

29. Constantin Bușe, Zorin Zamfir, Alexandru Vianu, Gheorghe Bădescu, *Relațiile internaționale în acte și documente* (International Relations in Acts and Documents), vol. III (1945-1982), Editura didactică și pedagogică, București, 1983, pp. 17-18.

30. General Cochet, Lieutenant-Colonel Paquier, *La Roumanie aux cotés des Nations Unies*, in *Cahiers France-Roumanie*, No. 5, septembre-octobre 1946.

31. Constantin Bușe, Zorin Zamfir, Alexandru Vianu, Gheorghe Bădescu, op. cit., p. 19.

32. Ibid.

INDEX

Aegean Sea, 123, 127-8, 161
Africa, 7, 114
Alba Iulia, 59, 194
Albania, 6, 105, 127
Ankara, 23-5, 160
Ansberg, Erik von, 83, 92
Anti-Hitler Patriotic Front, 30-1
Antonescu, Ion, 1, 19, 20-9, 20-6,
  42, 66, 68, 84, 86-89, 92, 115-
  6, 118, 120, 130, 134, 147, 150,
  155, 158, 169, 210n-2n
Antonescu, Mihai, 23-4, 26-7, 149,
  207n, 211n
"Anvil," Operation, 104, 123
Apuseni Mountains, 61, 130, 176
Arad, 37, 57, 108, 177, 195
Argeş, 73, 126, 214n
Asia, 79, 105-6
Atlantic Charter, 25, 27
Austria, 25, 51, 100, 105, 112, 134,
  141, 148, 151, 166, 191-4, 200,
  224n
Axis, 21-3, 33, 76-8, 84, 99, 100,
  122, 127, 133, 144, 165, 199

Bagrianov, I., 159, 160, 162
Balaton Lake, 151, 194-6, 224n
Balkans, 1, 10, 24, 32, 38, 56, 75-
  7, 79, 81, 122-4, 127, 129, 134-
  5, 137, 152, 162, 195, 224n
Balkan Peninsula, 71, 75, 78-9,
  100, 107-8, 114, 126, 128, 155,
  159, 163, 168, 194

Banat, 40, 57, 62-3, 74, 91, 95-7,
  127-8, 132, 173-4, 176, 225n
Banska-Bystrica, 185, 187
Băneasa, 44, 47, 93
Belgium, 69, 114, 139, 197
Belgrade, 107, 127, 134, 168
Berlin, 5, 9, 10, 12, 42, 75, 77, 79,
  89, 90, 97, 98, 112, 124, 127,
  134, 147, 149, 155-6, 158, 164,
  167, 212n
Bern, 23, 156
Beskid Mountains, 188-9, 191
Bessarabia, 76, 140
Bethlen, Istvan, 155-6
Big Tatra Massif, 187-89, 191
Bîrlad, 103, 124-5, 131
Black Sea, 27, 40, 52, 76, 103, 107-
  8, 116, 193
Bohemia, 8, 148, 199, 222n
Braşov, 27, 58, 95, 131, 174
Braunschweig, 97, 224n
Brăila, 54-5, 118, 178
Breaza, 48, 90
Bucharest, 9, 10, 24, 26, 28, 37, 40,
  44-7, 52, 61, 64-6, 75, 80, 84-
  5, 88-9, 90, 92-6, 98-9, 117-8,
  125, 127, 142, 147, 151, 167,
  206n, 210n, 220n, 222n; Peace
  Conference (1918), 28, 243,
  220n
Bükk Massifs, 179, 181, 192
Bukovina, 41, 80, 93, 129
Budapest, 63, 79, 91, 108, 120,

230